Zabern 1913

Consensus Politics in Imperial Germany

Zabern 1913

Consensus Politics in Imperial Germany

DAVID SCHOENBAUM

London
GEORGE ALLEN & UNWIN
Boston   Sydney

George Allen & Unwin (Publishers) Ltd,
40 Museum Street, London WC1A 1LU, UK

George Allen & Unwin (Publishers) Ltd,
Park Lane, Hemel Hempstead, Herts HP2 4TE, UK

Allen & Unwin Inc.,
9 Winchester Terrace, Winchester, Mass 01890, USA

George Allen & Unwin Australia Pty Ltd,
8 Napier Street, North Sydney, NSW 2060, Australia

First published in 1982

Jacket illustration from *Simplicissimus*, January 1914

British Library Cataloguing in Publication Data

Schoenbaum, David
    Zabern 1913.
1. Germany – Heer – Officers
2. Saverne (France) – History – Third Republic,
1870 – 1940
I. Title
944'.38350813   DC611.R4/
ISBN 0–04–943025–4

Library of Congress Cataloging in Publication Data

Schoenbaum, David.
    Zabern 1913.
Bibliography: p.
Includes index.
1. Zabern Affair, 1913. I. Title.
DD228.5.S33   943.08'4   81–19136
ISBN 0–04–943025–4   AACR2

Set in 10 on 11 point Press Roman by
System 4 Associates Limited, Gerrards Cross
and printed in Great Britain by Billing and Sons Ltd,
Guildford, London and Worcester

Contents

For Michael and Miriam,
who have waited so long for this that they
can now read it

Introduction

It occurred to me some years ago that I would like to read a book about the Zabern affair. I was somehow aware that it had been an enormous sensation. There was also something tantalysing about those sentence- or at most paragraph-length references to the episode that inevitably appeared in any treatment of the period before the First World War. I used to wonder what had really happened. Was there really nothing more to say about it? Was it possible that even Wilhelmine Germans could be as malevolently silly as those references invariably implied?

Like any other hopeful reader I did the natural thing. I tried to persuade someone else to write the book I wanted to read. A graduate school contemporary with a fascination for Ludwig Frank, the Social Democrat from Baden, seemed to me an obvious candidate for authorship. Unfortunately I never managed to persuade her of it. Later I tried unsuccessfully to encourage one of my early doctoral students to consider Zabern as his Opus 2 after a brilliant dissertation on Alsatian resistance to imperial Germany.

I had no more luck at *Der Spiegel*, the Hamburg news magazine, while working on a book about the magazine's own 'affair' of the early 1960s. Unlike *Time* and *Newsweek*, *Der Spiegel* not only reviewed but produced contemporary history and took an intense and serious interest in defence policy and civil—military relations. In those days it even devoted a lot of space to the renewed discussion on the origins of the First World War, a subject its editor, Rudolf Augstein, clearly believed to be of more than antiquarian interest. The magazine's interest in historic German scandals seemed to me a given. One day I cheerfully suggested to Hans Detlev Becker, the managing editor, that they might like to take some interest in Zabern. He vaguely remembered the episode. 'Wasn't that the one where the kids followed the lieutenant down the street shouting *"Bettschisser!"*?' he asked me. At the time, that particular detail was new to me, though I nodded enouragingly. But nothing came of this initiative either.

Meanwhile my own curiosity about the episode continued to grow. The issue of continuity in German history, not to mention the immensely productive rediscovery of imperial Germany by younger German and foreign scholars that was going on at the time, was bound to have a catalytic impact on any historian of Central Europe. How did I explain, a German colleague asked me one day as I emerged from the archives to report to his class, that people who reacted with such vigour and volume to the overnight arrest of two dozen adolescents in 1913 could learn in another generation to tolerate mass murder as public policy? Save for an expansive general reference to the watershed experience of the First World War I was at a loss for an answer. But I still find it a remarkably interesting question.

There was also the interesting process of provincial rediscovery currently going on in various corners of Europe, Alsace included. I remember being scandalised in the early 1960s by a wise and thoughtful friend, herself a native Silesian. 'The Alsatians aren't French', she remarked one day matter-of-factly. 'They're not Germans either', she added. It was some years later before I saw the point of her remark.

At least as important to any American historian of my generation was what was going on at home. The country was dramatically different from the America of before the First World War or immediately after the Second, where it was no problem to regard Zabern, and the place where it happened, as funny, foreign and aberrant.

The gulf between Germany and 'the West' had been axiomatic in the history of both sides since my college days and long before. It certainly left its marks on those paragraphs and sentences about Zabern, and also on generations of German historians, including my contemporaries. But what impressed me, the closer I got to Zabern, was the relativity rather than the uniqueness of imperial German experience. Actually, even the traditional sentences and paragraphs, with their frequent allusion to 'the German Dreyfus affair', acknowledged a degree of relativity in a scene otherwise conventionally dominated by spiked helmets, blood and iron. But apart from its minimal merits as a guide to what was really involved, the cliché never came close to the ambiguities and complexities that make Zabern so interesting, and imperial Germany so unexpectedly familiar.

I recall with wry affection a lunch conversation with one of my German contemporaries, by any standard one of the young stars of his generation. I had only begun to dig into the Zabern documents. Both he and I were astonished by what I found. It was, of course, true, as the sentences and paragraphs had always testified, that a young Prussian officer had made himself ridiculous in an Alsatian village, that his asininity had been publicly defended as a matter of constitutional principle, that snickering civilians had been arbitrarily and illegally arrested, and that the offending officers had — at least *pro forma* — gone unpunished.

But what impressed me was both obvious to contemporaries and somehow lost from view. This was not so much that the arrests in Zabern had led to a spectacular public clamour and a dramatic parliamentary debate. These, too, appeared in the sentences and paragraphs, though with the implication that they had been ineffectual. But ineffectual, it turned out, was just what they were not. In fact there had been disciplinary measures against the immediate offenders. What was more important was that while both government and army responded reluctantly and defensively, they none the less confirmed that public clamour and parliamentary debate could be remarkably effective even in imperial Germany. For anybody inclined to look behind them no amount of fig leaves could conceal the subsequent transfer of officers, the metamorphosis of archaic military regulations or, perhaps more interesting, the army's obvious hesitation to take its chances before a civil court.

Like generations before him, my friend was reluctant to look. If imperial Germany had been as flexible, responsible, even liberal as this implied, he ruminated between mouthfuls, there was no way to account for the coming of Hitler twenty years later. Then what, I asked him, did he make of the demonstrable facts of the case? Well, he said cautiously, they showed that people were wrong to invoke Zabern, as they traditionally did, as imperial Germany's typical case.

My own impression is, on the contrary, that Zabern represents what the sentences and paragraphs always said it did, that is, a practical demonstration of imperial German reality. The demonstration shows, however, how complex and unspecific the reality could be. In all its fatuousness, the Dreyfus analogy at least confirms that civil—military confrontation was not a German specialty in the years before the First World War. Neither were accident-prone governments. Remarkably, Germans then and since seem never to have noticed the curious goings-on in Ireland in the spring of 1914, when senior British officers, supported by the parliamentary opposition, engaged in what could only be described as a kind of cold mutiny against the presumed orders of their civilian superiors, and Irish nationalists would have welcomed the home rule Alsatians enjoyed before, let alone after, 1911.

In a rather different historical perspective, the 'Germanisation' of the Western democracies, but particularly the USA, seems to me as interesting as the convergence with 'the West' of a new and democratic Germany. The counter-flow of bureaucracy, peacetime military investment and global foreign policy has been especially dramatic in the USA because Americans, with luck and persistence, had managed for so long to avoid such things. In many ways, Imperial Germany is a distant and distorted mirror to hold up to the nature of postwar Western society or contemporary America. But I found it virtually impossible to write about Zabern without being mindful of the impact of big-time foreign policy on democratic politics, and without thinking of Vietnam, Kent State or Watergate. Imperial Germany did not necessarily suffer by the comparison.

As interesting as the conceptualisation of Zabern was the problem of documenting it. What impressed me in general was how much material has actually survived, especially for those lucky enough to see the inside of an East German archive. What impressed me, in particular, was what

I never found. The Prussian army documents, for example, vanished like the army itself in the spring of 1945, and there were wistful moments when I wished that Baron von Forstner, the infantry lieutenant who made Zabern possible, had been a naval ensign, commemorated in surviving documents of spectacular richness. Various materials on Forstner, including court records, vanished long before, and have never reappeared, in Strasbourg where French officials — one can only guess who and why — had borrowed them at the end of the First World War. What has survived is a remarkably revealing collection of documents — more revealing, in fact, than their source or editor seem to have been aware — published in Strasbourg in 1934 after what can only have been a deliberate French leak. The obvious purpose was to call attention not only to the twentieth anniversary of Zabern but to current events on the other side of the Rhine, just in case Alsatians had forgotten what Germans were like. The implication is that the originals remained in France until at least 1940, conceivably longer. But neither the French nor the German archivists I consulted could account for their whereabouts or even their 1934 publication. I remind and console myself that my classicist and medievalist colleagues perform prodigies with far less material than I have.

In any case, my thanks are due to the archives and archivists, the libraries and librarians who made my work possible, and sometimes even pleasurable: the East German central archives in Potsdam and Merseburg, the West German federal archive and military archive, the Austrian house, court and state archives and military archive, the Public Record Office and *The Times* in London, the Saxon, Bavarian and Württemberg state archives and the Württemberg and Bavarian military archives, the state archive in West Berlin, the Departmental Archives of the Department of the Lower Rhine, the university libraries in Iowa City, Freiburg and Strasbourg.

More thanks are due to the German Fulbright Commission, the Guggenheim Foundation and the universities of Iowa and Freiburg which kept me afloat and in spirits during the long march through the archives and libraries.

Still more thanks go to my colleagues, firm of principle and of pencil, who read what I wrote and did what they could with it: John Lewis Gaddis, James Joll, Linda K. Kerber, J. K. McDonald, T. W. Mason, David Morgan, Peter Pulzer, Malcolm Rohrbough and Heinrich August Winkler; to Klaus Schwabe for deciphering what seemed to me an undecipherable but rewarding page of gothic squiggle; and the late Fritz Epstein, who I wish had lived to read this too.

And, of course, my wife for her patience and loyalty during innumerable hours over a hot microfilm reader, and before, and after; and my children, who coped.

David Schoenbaum
Iowa City

1 *The Best of Times, the Worst of Times*

I do not know whether there is more misery in Germany, but there are certainly more exclamation points. Where you used to see merely!, you now see !!! (G. C. Lichtenberg)

Life is full of surprises, among them that the citizens of a major Western democracy, the USA included, might find it harder than their grandparents to look back at imperial Germany without a certain shock of recognition.

For reasons as much of circumstance as conscious design, Germany had advanced in two generations from a provincialism some found lovable, and others hickish, to the status of world power. Its army was the most formidable in Europe, its navy second only to the British fleet. The impact of German goods and technology was seen and felt on every continent. German ideas on music, science, philosophy, industrial production, public administration, inspired an odd combination of ambivalence and respect.

Even 'German Empire', a designation conceived in 1870 as calculated homage to a romanticised past, had achieved an unexpected degree of contemporary reality. It embraced an expansive assortment of overseas territories in Africa and the Pacific. It extended to an economic hegemony in south-eastern Europe that promised to spill over into the Middle East. French businessmen and governments reacted to the challenge rather as their grandsons later reacted to the USA: with tariffs, monetary pressure and legislative dams against further German investment in key sectors of industry.[1]

Germany's industrial growth was exceeded only by the USA. By 1913 German coal production had nearly overtaken Britain's, the traditional European leader. German mills produced over two and a half times as much steel as the mills of Britain. Germans dominated the growth industries of the era: chemicals, electricity and machines.

Growth and power had undeniably paid off. Perhaps half to two-thirds of society were almost uncritically dedicated to the existing order. But the remainder were also among its beneficiaries. Sectarians on both the right and left talked revolution — or counter-revolution. But for most dissidents the issue was a more equitable share of the growing pie. Between 1871 and 1910 life expectancy had increased from about 36 years to 47. Between 1877 and 1912 the work year had declined from 3,300 hours to 2,970, only a little more than the British average which was unchanged over the same period. Measured against the back- and spirit-bending twelve-hour work day of the 1870s, the decline represented the equivalent of a work day less per week.[2]

If wages still lagged by comparison with Britain, France, Sweden and the USA, their progress was undeniable, even dramatic. Miners, a bell-wether group in the economy of the period, enjoyed a wage increase of almost 200 per cent in the quarter century after 1888. Insurance con-tributions included, they outearned their British counterparts by 1912.[3] In 1913, a recession year in the view of contemporary observers, the bank rate rose to 6 per cent. But Prussian bonds at 4 per cent were still selling at par, and unemployment was about 1 per cent. By the eve of the First World War, emigration, a traditional index of discontent, had declined to almost nothing.[4]

Familiarly enough, government grew too. While the population grew by about 50 per cent, both the empire and Prussia, its largest constituent state, tripled their number of employees. Before the First World War public employment at federal, state and local levels represented over 12 per cent of the labour force, not including the military. Modest enough by the standards of our day, this was unmatched and even inconceivable at the time in any other country. Between 1872 and 1913 federal budgets increased by a factor of 10 to something approaching the contemporary equivalent of $1 billion, compared to the $750 million Congress budgeted for fiscal 1914.[5] As early as 1901 naval building was explicitly prescribed as a corrective for unemployment. Counter-recessionary arguments for supplementary naval appropriations in 1907–8 and again in 1912 have a distinctly modern ring.[6] Fuelled by the imperatives of foreign policy and economic stability alike, government, too, had become a big business.

Large, strong, productive and increasingly rich, as millionaire spokes-men and foreign observers regularly noted, Germany was also divided, uncertain and curiously immobile. A well-developed state coexisted with a vigorous, but centrifugal, society, variously divided by class, region and religion. The state–society distinction was itself a German invention. Dubiously applicable elsewhere, it was ideally suited to the German scene.[7]

The parties to the imperial social contract coexisted vertically as well as hierarchically. The characteristic *verzuiling* – the 'pillarisation' – discovered by observers of modern Holland was a fact of life in imperial Germany.[8] Like the columns of the new Reichstag building, Catholics, Protestants, an urban bourgeoisie and a pre-industrial gentry, even a Social Democratic working class, supported a common entablature with minimal contact with one another. Clubbish, even clannish, they sheltered and sustained their members through all the ages of man. Particularism added another level of fragmentation. One could go through life, through school, even through the army without meeting — let alone voting for — people whose experience or accent were significantly different from one's own. On the eve of the First World War, 'How to reduce class conflict' was the theme of an essay contest sponsored by an organisation that named itself after Germany's greatest poet.[9]

Reflecting its origins in the agrarian oligarchy of East Elbian Prussia, the imperial élite tended to be Prussian, Protestant, rural or near-rural. They were well-born but hardly aristocratic in the traditional sense of a rural gentry. They, too, were 'state' not 'society', almost unimaginably remote from 'tout Paris' or the interlocking circuits that connected London with the great universities and country houses, the City, the Church of England and the major charitable foundations.

A self-contained and self-recruiting 'pillar' of officers, civil servants and operators of large landed estates, they were consistently remote from the realities of a modern economy and almost grotesquely insensitive to the realities of a modern culture. Of 278 von Bülow males over 20 responding to a questionnaire in 1913, 153 were in public employment or running the family estates. In other families the proportions were still higher; 93 of 108 von Kleists, 108 of 128 von Wedels. General Paul von Schmidt, an extreme but not atypical representative of his class in its classic form, regarded Bizet's *Carmen* as the story of 'a slatternly broad',[10] and worried that his junior officers might develop a taste for reading newspapers.

While the majority of his peers is likely to have found Schmidt's views a little quaint, even in 1892 when they first appeared in his memoirs, their coexistence with their times remained ambivalent and uneasy. Arthur Balfour, Britain's Conservative Prime Minister, attended the première of Shaw's *Major Barbara* in 1905.[11] His German counterparts regarded Gerhard Hauptmann, a Central European counterpart of Shaw, as a public nuisance if not an outright scandal. To imagine William II at Strauss's *Elektra* or the latest piece by Wedekind or Sternheim is to imagine Richard Nixon at *Deep Throat*.

Technology, which was at least superficially among the emperor's favourite enterprises, was a more obvious link between the people and the times, the old and the new élites. 'Quite remarkable this passionate interest in technology among aristocratic kids — Waldi [Varnbüler], Claus Bismarck, Bill's son, Felix Bethmann and the others dream of it day and night the way other generations dreamed of hunting, dogs and horses', the Countess Spitzemberg, an unusually perceptive conservative observer, noted late in 1913.

'The spirit of the times is irresistible, but it is contrary to the old aristocratic traditions', she added revealingly, 'and for the likes of us it has about it something unmanly, ungentlemanly, above all something cosmopolitan that could be a real problem in case of war.'[12]

But the characteristic synthesis was found less in the creation or development of a squirearchy in mufti than the eagerness of the bourgeoisie, or its sons, to look to the squires for cues. Such data as exist suggest a considerable degree of upward mobility, though it followed conventional channels: preparatory school, with a large dose of classical languages, law study, clerkship, political affiliation — or at least sympathy — respectably to the right of centre, and a job in the bureaucracy.[13] The prevailing distinction between the establishmentarian *Korporation*, that is, the aristocratic student club and the *Burschenschaft*, that is, the middle-class fraternity, declined to insignificance well before the end of the nineteenth century. The reserve commission in a professional officer corps, a manifestation of citizen soldiery in the USA, merged with the doctorate in Germany as the definitive outward sign of civil respectability.[14] Jews and Socialists were specifically excluded from reserve commissions.

But élite values were increasingly challenged by some, ignored by others, in a social system whose very dynamism created ever newer differentiations in a population increasingly remote from the relative simplicities of the farm. The urbanisation and industrialisation of German society intensified class-consciousness, Emil Lederer noted. But they also complicated the process of political compromise and equilibration that class conflict made necessary.[15] Press and theatre were almost startlingly irreverent. There would probably have been fewer official interdictions of subversive reading in the barracks had there been less of it actually going on. Both the beer-swilling, heel-clicking sycophant and the success of his caricature, the title figure of Heinrich Mann's novel *Der Untertan*, typify the realities of imperial Germany.

Ritual professions of national unity testified less to reality than to malaise. Contemporary apprehensions and even assertions notwithstanding, there was little likelihood of imminent, or any, revolution. Government itself was too diffuse, opposition too centrifugal, loyalties and interests too ambivalent for revolutionary politics in any traditional sense.[16] But the ambiguities themselves precluded the traditional sense of place and orientation among both rulers and ruled. Looking back on what were latterly remembered as good old days, and even a golden age, one is struck rather less by self-assurance than by undertones of pessimism and even panic.[17] Germans liked to ascribe to themselves a certain gravity and profundity that distinguished them favourably from the presumed frivolity and superficiality of their neighbours to the west, the most perceptive of contemporary American observers wrote. 'But nothing can be more profoundly and meticulously deliberate', he reflected, 'than the measured footsteps of the man who no longer knows where he is going, though he is on his way.'[18]

In prose of undeniable quaintness, the editor of a widely noted yearbook complained of undeniably modern symptoms:

> The times in which we live are among the most invigorating and exciting ever. Overripe with cultural values – and appallingly poor in cultural achievements, as the facts of political, social and individual life only too often and too painfully reveal.
>
> Unceasing catastrophes in nature and human life on the one hand – and on the other: new worlds of brilliant achievements in science and technology, one after another. Mass insensitivity and superficiality increasingly follow after this development! Where do we find a deeper resonance today that survives the hour and bears any relationship to the historical significance and perceptible effect of these experiences?
>
> Today's sensation is pushed aside by banalities tomorrow, and then forgotten. Eternal values give way to daily sensation, and epoch-making things become ephemeral.[19]

There was a certain consensus about some of the causes. There was less agreement about the indicated treatment. 'The author of these lines has often asked old people how they looked at the future in 1913, what they wanted and expected', Golo Mann has written. 'But he never got a definite answer.'[20]

A fundamentally conservative administration was under fire from the right. A literally imperial executive was congenitally divided and increasingly irresponsible in the sense that it was hard to tell who made decisions, or whether they were made at all. In a parliamentary election more interesting than any in decades, a third or more of the electorate had sent a message of fundamental disaffection to Berlin in 1912. But there was no consensus in the new Parliament either. In this sense and others it was considerably more representative than has often been believed. As in the USA a half-century before, states rights were an intractable issue, in many ways a fig leaf for the 'peculiar institutions' of incompatible social orders.

Some of the younger generation turned from politics, and even from conventional social life. Guitars, folksongs, open shirts, camp fires and nature found much favour. Though no one was exactly sure why, it was widely agreed that a large youth rally on a romantic mountain top, a kind of prototypical Woodstock, had been a very important event.[21] The style of life, public and private, was fundamentally authoritarian, reflecting a tradition of social deference deeply rooted in a feudal order still tangible in certain parts of the country. But authority was increasingly uncertain.

In Germany as elsewhere in Europe, the arts and press were free, the labour movement active — and restive. There were hysterical reactions in 1912 to a coal strike in the Ruhr area, but also considerable apprehensions about the moral consequences of dancing the tango.[22]

Notwithstanding a century of general European peace, there was a chronic sense of international threat, intimately connected with a dull fear of impending domestic chaos. There were Germans who favoured domestic reform over an active diplomacy, and the military appropriations that went with it. They were a minority, though by no means an inconsiderable one. A second group, probably larger and certainly more influential, gave the priority to national defence. But they understood it as defence of a status quo in which Germany's economic and military power grew consistently in ways that worried its neighbours. A third group, largely interesting as a curiosity, argued that the national defence was connected with domestic reform and even that the former was contingent on the latter. Among them were a few of the brightest people in German life. But they showed no great aptitude for electoral politics.

The malaise took idiosyncratic forms, as might be expected of a country whose problems were neither simple nor of recent duration. There was even a certain irony in 1913 in the heat generated by the year's anniversaries. The quarter-centenary of William II's ascent of the throne was relatively simple. People were enthusiastic or indifferent.

But the centenary of the victory over Napoleon at Leipzig, the 'battle of the nations', was less simple. Celebrated by conservatives as the victory of legitimacy, order and piety over the forces of revolutionary France, it was celebrated by their opponents as the victory of an oppressed people in arms over a despotic invader. The government of the day, tacking uneasily between the Scylla of military inadequacy, as diagnosed by the generals, and the Charybdis of fiscal calamity, as diagnosed by its financial experts, sought to contain the patriotic enthusiasm of both groups. It submitted the largest military appropriations Bill yet, then followed with proposals for a drastic tax reform. The backing and filling necessary to achieve both consumed the first half of the year.

A few months later there was another intimation of modernity in the form of public scandal. It was judiciously leaked to one of the most oppositional of opposition deputies in the Reichstag that the Krupp Company of Essen, the country's biggest military-industrial contractor, had been bribing officers in the War Ministry to keep it informed about the competition. An official investigation confirmed the worst: that the liaison had gone on for over six years and a lot of money had changed hands. At the trial in October the officers were discharged and jailed for six months, the Krupp agent in Berlin was jailed for four, and the head of Krupp's department of war materials sales was fined 1,200 marks, about the equivalent of the average German's annual income.

As so often after official investigations, there was a certain odour of whitewash in the aftermath, and a good deal of defensiveness in official places. 'It is not the case that I favour private industry', the War Minister told the Reichstag. 'But we are dependent on it. In critical times we have great masses of materials immediately ready. This cannot be secured in a state factory. On the other hand, we cannot give the private firms enough orders to keep them solvent in peacetime. Hence they are dependent on foreign orders. Who gets the advantage of that? Unquestionably the class that they support.' The transcript indicates laughter.[23]

The Krupp trial was followed, near the very summit, by a curious mini-campaign for revolutionary *conservative* change, involving the crown prince as messenger boy and a coup d'état as its goal. A murky episode, it was significant both for what happened and what did not.

In itself there was nothing very new about German ultra-nationalism. It went back at least to the 1890s. Three of its strongest institutional supports, the Pan-German League, the Agrarian League and the League of Commercial Employees, had been founded in the same year, 1893, three years after the dismissal of Bismarck, the empire's founding father. In presumed contrast to Bismarck, the new Chancellor, Caprivi, was suspected of softness on liberalism in a variety of forms. Subsequent chancellors were notably cautious about repeating his errors, appeasement of England and reduction of farm price supports among them.

There was also nothing very new about the Gordian knot solution as a theoretical answer to the nation's problems. It was speculation on a coup to unmake the imperial constitution that led to Bismarck's dismissal, and anxious German statesmen were fending off similar initiatives from various sources, including the military, for some years afterwards.

By the turn of the century much of this domestic bellicosity had been successfully diverted to an activist diplomacy. Its centre-piece was a programme of naval construction and a kind of parodistic Clausewitzian view of commerce that regarded trade like war, as the extension of policy by other means. This, too, had engendered counter-vailing forces, both abroad and at home. The 1912 election testified to their vigour. The various frustrations encountered *en route* to the supple-mental military appropriations of 1913 showed how, and where, these forces worked. Forgotten schemes woke to new life in the warmth of nationalist indignation.

What was startling about the new campaign was that it was the first to make a direct approach to the head of state. During the spring and summer of 1913, Baron Konstantin von Gebsattel, a retired cavalry general, had conferred with Heinrich Class, the president of the Pan-German League, on a new initiative. In September he submitted an extensive memo for the emperor's oldest son, the Crown Prince William. Class, whose connections with Germany's political and academic establishment suggest an influence far greater than might be inferred from the relatively modest membership of his organisation, forwarded the memo to the crown prince. Now 31, but still in the full flower of adolescent rebellion, the crown prince passed on the memo in November to his father and the Imperial Chancellor, Theobald von Bethmann-Hollweg.

The memo proposed strong measures — prorogation of the Reichstag, followed by the imposition of martial law, and abrogation of the nominal one man, one vote principle by which the Reichstag was constitutionally elected. There was then to be a full-scale purge of the opposition press and extensive proscription of German Jews — a policy currently favoured by embattled small businessmen.

Nothing demonstrable came of Gebsattel's *démarche* save a degree of embarrassment for the crown prince. Both Bethmann and the emperor were appalled. They expressed their consternation at length, and virtually by return mail.

Bethmann, a loyal royalist already almost overwhelmed by the problem of saving the monarchy from its supporters, tactfully avoided arguments of abstract moral principle. The major, and incontrovertible, argument against Gebsattel's proposed coup, he replied, was that it had no chance of success. It would only provoke war at home and, in all likelihood, abroad. War itself, he added significantly, was justified only by foreign attack or by interests unattainable by other means. Neither condition obtained.

The emperor, uninhibited by tact, expressed his dismay in unequivocal moral indignation. 'Coups d'état might be part of the statesman's art in South and Central American Republics', he wrote. 'In Germany, thank God, this has not been the usual case, nor must it be allowed to become one, neither from above nor from below. Even consideration of such methods is bound to disturb the fast bond of confidence that still unites the sovereign, thank God, with the broadest majority of the nation.'

Warming to the subject, he even found an unexpected good word for freedom of the press. With all its limitations, he declared, 'it performs both a useful and irreplaceable function in the modern state as a safety valve for all kinds of complaints and disaffections that would otherwise be aired in more dangerous ways'.[24]

His views are ironic, but by no means irrelevant, in the perspective of what followed only days afterward as the Zabern episode suddenly erupted. It continued to dominate German political life through the spring. But even after the strong emotions had ebbed, people continued to return to it as though fingering a scar.

As remarkable as anything was the triviality of its origins. Civil—military confrontation was also nothing new in Germany. It was almost inevitable in Prussian Germany where, if anywhere, the army was virtually the central institution of the state. But elsewhere, at least, there was a certain minimal dignity in the issues at stake.

More or less domesticated in their respective constitutional environments, the major European armies still reflected their origins in a pre-industrial, even a pre-constitutional, society. This was even true of the army of the USA. To a point all were sanctuaries for the casualties of a revolutionary era, fugitives from modern politics who found in the armies the discipline, the hierarchy, the authority, and even the horses, that vanished little by irreversible little from civilian life.

In general civil—military coexistence was successful, save as it impinged on those basic pre-industrial issues — order, loyalty, honour. Whatever their differences, these were the common denominators of the famous civil—military clashes of the prewar era, the Dreyfus affair, which shook Frenchmen for the better part of a decade beginning in 1894, the Curragh barracks incident, which shook Britons and Irishmen in the tumultuous spring and early summer of 1914, and the Zabern episode, which preoccupied the Germans.

But the Dreyfus case originated in something approximating seriousness: the army's efforts, however inept, to defend itself against a real spy. It could be argued that the issue at the Curragh was whether, and to what extent, professional soldiers could be called upon to take arms against friends, relatives and a northern Irish population determined to maintain its existing link with the country the soldiers were sworn to defend.

Zabern by contrast was trivial, even funny. The issue at stake was little more than the right of a 20-year-old lieutenant to make an ass of himself in public. Even the military was disinclined to defend this to the last ditch. What they resented, and resisted, was the right of civilians, particularly the citizens of an obscure garrison town in Alsace, to set the limits of permissible military behaviour. And determined as they were to prove themselves in earnest, they arrested civilians who laughed. The result was a major constitutional crisis. An incredulous world concluded, as the crisis progressed and reached its anticlimactic resolution, that it was somehow watching real life imitate the satirical art of a cartoon in *Simplicissimus*.

References

1 See Raymond Poidevin, *Les Rélations Économiques et financières entre la France et l'Allemagne de 1898 à 1914*, (Paris, 1969), pp. 809ff.

2 Statistics can be found in Michael Balfour, *The Kaiser and his Times* (Boston, Mass., 1964), pp. 437ff., and H. -U. Wehler, *Das deutsche Kaiserreich* (Göttingen, 1973), pp. 48ff.

3 See Fritz Fischer, *Krieg der Illusionen* (Düsseldorf, 1969), pp. 516ff; Peter Christian Witt, *Die Finanzpolitik des deutschen Reiches* (Hamburg, 1970),

pp. 384–6; Wehler, op. cit., pp. 48ff.; Frederic C. Howe, *Socialized Germany* (New York, 1916), pp. 77.

4   See Gustav Stolper, Kurt Häuser and Knut Borchard, *The German Economy* (New York, 1967), pp. 22.

5   See Eberhard Pikart, 'Die Rolle der Parteien im deutschen konstitutionellen System', *Zeitschrift für Politik* (1962), p. 13; *Statesman's Year Book* (London, 1914), pp. 409, 900.

6   See Volker Berghahn, *Rüstung und Machtpolitik* (Düsseldorf, 1973), pp. 49ff.

7   See Pikart, op. cit., pp. 28–9.

8   On 'verzuiling' see Johan Goudsblom, *Dutch Society* (New York, 1967), p. 32–3.

9   See Ralf Dahrendorf, *Gesellschaft und Demokratie in Deutschland* (Munich, 1965), pp. 245ff.; Ernst Arnold, *Mars regiert die Stunde* (Basle, 1914), p. 3.

10   Cited in Otto Graf zu Stolberg-Wernigerode, *Die unentschiedene Generation* (Munich, 1968), pp. 198, 336.

11   Barbara W. Tuchman, *The Proud Tower* (New York, 1967), p. 419.

12   Entry of 19 December 1913, Hildegard Baronin von Spitzemberg, *Tagebuch* (Göttingen, 1961), p. 565.

13   See Wolfgang Zapf, *Wandlungen der deutschen Elite* (Munich, 1965), pp. 42–6.

14   See Eckart Kehr, 'Zur Genesis des königlich preussischen Reserve-offiziers', *Der Primat der Innenpolitik* (Berlin, 1965), pp. 53ff.; Werner T. Angress, 'Prussia's army and the Jewish reserve officer controversy', *Year Book XVII* (London: Leo Baeck Institute, 1972).

15   Emil Lederer, 'Die wirtschaftlichen Organisationen', in D. Sarason (ed.), *Das Jahr 1913* (Berlin and Leipzig, 1914,), p. 138.

16   See Pikart, op. cit., p. 32.

17   See Fritz Stern, *The Politics of Cultural Despair* (Berkeley, Calif., 1961); Jost Hermand, *Von Mainz nach Weimar* (Stuttgart, 1969).

18   Thorstein Veblen, *Imperial Germany and the Industrial Revolution* (Ann Arbor, Mich., 1966), p. 240.

19   Sarason, op. cit., p. v. See also Walter Lippmann, writing a year later: 'We are unsettled to the very roots of our being. There isn't a human relation, whether of parent and child, husband and wife, worker and employer, that doesn't move in a strange situation. We are not used to a complicated civilization, we don't know how to behave when personal contact and eternal authority have disappeared. There are no precedents to guide us, no wisdom that wasn't made for a simpler age. We have changed our environment more quickly than we know how to change ourselves. And so we are literally an eccentric people, our emotional life is disorganized, our passions are out of kilter. Those who call themselves radical float helplessly upon a stream amidst the wreckage of old creeds and abortive new ones, and they are inclined to mistake the motion which carries them for their own will. Those who make no pretentions to much theory are twisted about by the fashions, "crazes", at the mercy of milliners and dressmakers, theatrical producers, advertising campaigns, and the premeditated gossip of the newspapers (quoted in the *New York Times*, 26 May 1967).

20   Golo Mann, *Deutsche Geschichte des XX. Jahrhunderts* (Frankfurt, 1958), p. 67.

21   See Walter Laqueur, *Young Germany* (New York, 1962).

22   Holger Herwig, *The German Naval Officer Corps* (Oxford, 1973), p. 33.

23   Cited in William Manchester, *The Arms of Krupp* (Boston, Mass.: 1968), p. 280.

24   An analysis of the entire episode, including the replies of Bethmann and the

kaiser, can be found in Hartmut Pogge von Strandmann, 'Staatsstreichpläne, Alldeutsche und Bethmann-Hollweg', in Pogge von Strandmann and Immanuel Geiss, *Die Erforderlichkeit des Unmöglichen* (Frankfurt, 1965). For an apologetic view of the crown prince see Paul Herre, *Kronprinz Wilhelm* (Munich, 1954), pp. 34ff. For a surprisingly sympathetic view of the crown prince see Alastair Horne, *The Price of Glory* (Harmondsworth, 1964), pp. 218–22.

2 *En route to Zabern: the Constitution*

Something is rotten in the state of Denmark. How enormous is Denmark! (Stanislaw Jerzy Lec)

Like other great powers, before and afterwards, Germany scared its neighbours by indirection as well as design. Their apprehension, in turn, spilled back over into the domestic polity. It was symptomatic of something deeper than the gloomy intimations of an old man that August Bebel, who died in 1913, had been in contact with the British Foreign Office since 1901. The old Social Democrat, leader of his country's major party whose 1912 election victory had been hailed at home and abroad as a secular event, was inalterably convinced that his country was a menace. A man whose political memory extended back to the aborted democratic revolution of 1848, his parliamentary career had begun with the very birth of the empire. He warned the British to keep their powder dry.[1]

The German malaise was compounded of three major elements. It was largely, but not entirely, self-made. As so often, it also testified not only to earlier failures and omissions, but to the unassimilated, even unwanted, by-products and after-effects of success.

The first element, an obvious function of geography, was foreign policy. The second was a delayed but dramatic industrial development. The third was a set of political institutions arguably adequate to the nineteenth century, but increasingly inadequate to the realities of the twentieth.

In 1913 Germany had been a major continental power for nearly half a century. But it looked back on a history of impotence, whose various humiliations were never far from the minds of policy-makers and private citizens alike. Germany had been Europe's battlefield since the Reformation. The Thirty Years War, when foreign armies and the German allies had crossed and recrossed the land in endless, murderous swarms, was a lasting trauma. The Treaty of Westphalia that brought it to an end was seen as a a contractual perpetuation of German impotence. As late as 1940 Josef Goebbels, Nazi Germany's Minister of Propaganda, was to celebrate the victory over France with unquestionable sincerity as the revenge for Cardinal Richelieu.[2]

The response to the trauma had catalysed and shaped the transformation of the Electorate of Brandenburg, a conspicuously vulnerable principality, into the subsequent Kingdom of Prussia, a state whose every action was governed by the contingencies of military self-preservation until it had itself become a major, if precarious, power of European rank.

Successive Prussian leaders played for high stakes, domestic and foreign, laboriously hauling their feudal polity through the rigours of purposeful absolutism. As elsewhere in the world of the *ancien régime*, military necessity set off complicated trains of social change. Arms required money, money required economic development, economic development — and tax collecting — required increasing bureaucratic sophistication, bureaucratic sophistication required educated people.

But Prussia was in a class by itself. Paradoxically this was less for reasons of Prussian peculiarity than because of the absence of any. Tied neither to culture, territory, language, cuisine, religion or any transcendent sense of mission, Prussia existed for its own sake like a kind of patriarchal corporation or a company town. Unencumbered by the ties and centrifugal interest of empire, nation, region or Third Estate, it was state pure and — with its anaemic infrastructure, limited resources and provincial society — simple.

Under the circumstances, what was good for the Crown was considered good for the country — at least for those who owned shares, or held jobs in the management. Brutal and enlightened, enterprising and cautious, innovative and relentlessly conservative in turn, Prussia seemed made for the heady competition of dynastic warfare, aggrandising itself at the expense of Poles, Swedes and its Austrian neighbours until it had become Germany's second state.

The experience left two lessons. The first was that success required allies. Like George Washington, Prussian statesmen might well have warned their countrymen against 'entangling alliances'. But there was no equivalent sense that entanglement and alliance were interchangeable. The point was rather that alliances were expedients to be used when advantageous, and dropped and changed when not.

The other lesson was a corollary of the first. Coalitions without Prussia were a threat. To a degree unfamiliar to other peoples, Prussia's history was coloured by its shocks and even disasters. There had been the near-miss calamity of the Seven Years War when only the convenient death of Catherine the Great saved an isolated Prussia from a tight squeeze between Russia and Austria. There was the military débâcle of Jena in 1806, when a superannuated Prussian army was routed by the French under Napoleon as no German army had ever been routed by the French under the Bourbons. There were the humiliations of 1848 when domestic civilians had inflicted a symbolic defeat on the Prussian army like none since the defeat by French armies, and new invasions or interventions by Russia, France and even Britain seemed at least a possibility.

It was at such points that foreign policy tended to impinge on domestic society and politics. A dynastic state on the make in an era of mercantilism, Prussia had to import a good deal of its entrepreneurial talent. French names, evidence of the cost to France of repealing the Edict of Nantes, figure prominently in Prussian history. The dogged loyalty of German Jews, further beneficiaries of Prussian toleration – Bleichröder, Rathenau, Warburg, Ballin – was itself to become a diplomatic asset.

The relatively easy mobility of the seventeenth century gave way to the aristocratic oligarchy of the eighteenth. Effective social integration of the new bureaucratic élite with the indigenous squirearchy, and of both with the dynastic interests of the Crown, was the Frederician idea of more perfect union.

But military defeat and the Napoleonic challenge set off a round of that characteristic revolution from above that was Prussia's particular specialty. Typically the principal initiators were also foreigners, at least in the contemporary sense: they were non-Prussian Germans.

Their response to the hazards of new coalitions was a new alliance. It tied the Prussian Crown not to other princes, but to its own people, understood both socially and nationally. Over ferocious resistance, conservative and chauvinist alike, the reformers dragged their employer kicking and screaming into the nineteenth century. Feudal prerogatives were liquidated. In effect both the agrarian and the urban economies were made safe for capitalism. A degree of self-government was introduced at the municipal level. The educational system was overhauled in the interests of pure, that is, free, research: middle-class soldiers, the presumptive graduates and beneficiaries of the new schools and the new economy, were recruited for a non-professional army that was intended to drive a foreign invader not merely from the estates of the Prussian state but from the fatherland of a rediscovered German nation.

With the French revolutionary threat behind, the reformers were out of business. Their work was variously aborted, dismantled or indefinitely deferred. Prussia was now part of a new, and very conservative, alliance of princes, not peoples. But their work lived on. In part it was a mystique that still warmed the hearts of middle-class Germans a century later. In part it was the basis of a system of technocratic public administration that came to be admired by foreigners only a little less than by Germans themselves.

The latter was a matter of particular importance if Prussia were to continue tooting its horn in the emerging European concert. The peacemakers had seen fit, in their plans for the containment of France, to transfer that proverbial 'watch on the Rhine' that was also to figure in the patriotic repertory a century later.

Austria withdrew from the lower Rhine to be replaced by Prussian forces. Prussian acquisition of the coal fields that were to nourish Europe's most powerful industrial concentration was an unintended side-effect. The Spartan East Elbian principality suddenly doubled its population. It now extended clear across Germany, from the French border on the Rhine to the Russian border far up the Baltic coast. It had also acquired substantial numbers of such traditionally un-Prussian types as independent peasant proprietors, aspiring entrepreneurs and large numbers of Catholics.

In principle the issue remained what it had been before: stability, and even marginal advantage, in what was ultimately viewed as a vale of tears if not a world of wolves. But foreign policy was also no longer what it had been before. The peace conference left southern Germany largely as the French had reconstructed it. Constitutionality was introduced shortly thereafter. The remaining absolute sovereigns of Central Europe, sworn to the twin principles of legitimacy and mutual non-intervention, found it impossible to stop it. The peace conference had also made its concessions, limited as they were, to the renascent sense of German nationhood. Frankfurt, a traditional seat of that rococo anachronism the Holy Roman Empire, now entertained a German federation, where representatives of the respective German governments variously coaxed and dampened a sense of common identity.

It was symptomatic that the Protestant King of Prussia should assume the patronage of a campaign to complete the gothic Catholic cathedral of Cologne, where construction had stopped some 300 years before. Its view resolutely turned to the past, Prussia almost unwillingly marched into the future.

The recipe was to become increasingly familiar. Theoretically there were three options. Prussia could undertake a systematic restoration of the status quo, cost what it might — which would obviously be plenty. It could undertake systematic liberalisation, if not overt democratisation. In effect it could anticipate the British reforms of 1832 without the intervening stages of civil war and Glorious Revolution. But neither was a real choice. Instead, in the tradition of their predecessors, Prussian kings opted for economic development as the best hope of domestic conservatism.

Economic development took two forms. One was an approximation of *laissez-faire*, Prussian style, as big agriculture grew and flourished in East Elbia. The reforms made land accessible to money. British industrial growth made it profitable. Like the American South, East Elbia grew relatively rich as a satellite of Lancashire and Manchester. Even the established gentry discovered unsuspected liberal yearnings, at least to the extent that liberalism meant free trade. Previously entailed estates changed hands with startling velocity. By mid-century only a little more than half the registered estates of 1,250 acres and up were still in the hands of the indigenous squires, the recently knighted included.[3] Between 1815 and 1865 the estate owners acquired 2½ million acres at the expense of small holders. Between 1835 and 1865 11,800 estates had changed hands 23,600 times, an average of nearly twice each in a generation. Only a third of the transfers were by inheritance. The rest were by sale, and there had been 1,300 foreclosures.[4]

The other form of economic development consisted of familiarly technocratic, state-supported ventures in vocational education, railway building and industrial protection, but also in *de facto* commercial annexation of northern Germany. To what extent this was intentional is another question. Later Prussian historians, raised in the Hegelian tradition and pleased with what they saw around them, discovered their own version of manifest destiny. Personified Reason may or may not have been sitting in the Prussian Ministry of Finance, but they found it hard to believe that Providence had not at least sharpened the pencils.

In actual fact, at least in their initial phases, the Prussian tariff and the North German Customs Union seem to have originated, like the *biedermeier* culture around them, in a yearning for practical comfort. What motivated them were mutual convenience among the partners, maximal integration of the considerably different economies of Old Prussia and the new western provinces, and a level of *ad valorem* duties high enough to protect German enterprise, while low enough to channel entrepreneurial ambitions away from smuggling and into other lines of work. Revenue was also a consideration, though Prussia's neighbours understandably suspected coercive intent. As so often in Prussian administrative history, arguments of a grander kind came from outside, for example, from Friedrich List, a re-immigrant from the USA, where he had been powerfully impressed with the internal development schemes of Henry Clay.

Irrespective of motive, Prussia was doing what came naturally. It was growing incrementally by administrative initiative, feeding on the little fish, swimming among the big ones. Nominally things remained the same. Prussia was an amalgam of bureaucracy and conscripted military manpower, coexisting with a patriarchal gentry, similar in kind if smaller in scale than comparable social groups in England, Hungary or the southern USA.

But there were also important differences. Almost inadvertently, prophylactically, Prussia was on the way to becoming a modern country. Its birthrate soared, its traditional social structures crumbled both in the countryside and − such as there were of them − in the towns. Its metallurgy and chemistry impressed a qualified English visitor as significantly better than anything at home.[5] In London people referred to the Danzig grain quotation as they were later to refer to the Chicago Board of Trade. In the 1820s, when the ratio of children in school to adult population was 1:16 in England 1:30 in France and 1:700 in Russia, it stood in Prussia at 1:8.[6] By mid-century Prussian universities, particularly Humboldt's Berlin foundation of 1810, were a standard for the rest of the world.

It was still unclear to Prussia's leaders whether, and to what extent, they wanted their affairs mixed up with those of an amorphous, but increasingly clamorous 'Germany' of lawyers, teachers, journalists and businessmen in search of a state to accommodate them. But however ambivalently, 'Germany' looked to Prussia.

Powerful, efficient, relatively unencumbered by non-German nationalities and German across a 700-mile territorial axis, Prussia was openly, even proudly, reactionary in the most literal sense. Where possible, it had not only repealed Napoleonic reforms, it had cancelled its own. What liberalism there was had characteristically turned peasants, hitherto sheltered by feudal convention, into sharecroppers and hired labour. The press, the theatres, the universities were enveloped in the oppressive stagnation of official conservatism. Constitutional promises, issued in the heady atmosphere of the anti-Napoleonic crusade of 1813—15, were discreetly forgotten or reduced to the lowest common denominator of provincial diets. Rather like Louis XVI, Frederick William IV convened a United Diet only on the eve of revolution.

But the revolution, when it came in 1848, was ambiguous too. Both its achievements, which were more considerable than has been generally appreciated, and its failures, which soon became legendary, dominated German life for decades afterward. Chickens cast aloft in 1848 were unmistakably among those that came to roost in 1913.

In 1848 German liberalism, the beneficiary of a generation of structural change, materialised on a scale unknown before or after. It was determined to claim the political dividends hitherto undistributed, and to reconstruct Germany in its own image as a kind of Central European common market. Institutionalised in the Frankfurt Parliament, it was full of plans, some of them distinctly hard on their neighbours, for doing things done elsewhere over decades or centuries. It was rather as though the Continental Congress of the War of Independence and the Constitutional Convention of twelve years later were meeting concurrently, with the Mexican War and even an invasion of Canada also on their agenda.

The casualties of the preceding generation materialised too. There were small farmers embittered by the residues of feudal restrictions. There were the handicraftsmen of a pre-industrial economy, anxious to regain the lost paradise of status and security lost to occupational overcrowding and factory competition. There were journeymen panicked by the foreclosure of traditional vocational tracks and desperate to avoid the humiliation of proletarian wage labour. There was the underemployed workforce of an embryonic industrial economy. All suffered alike from a contemporary European recession and the structural inadequacies of an economy unable to employ a booming population, driven from the land by the de facto land reform of capitalist agriculture.

The old order seemed the first to capitulate. The Prussian army was ordered out of Berlin. The king appeared publicly, without his hat, at the behest of the revolutionaries. The 330 delegates to the Frankfurt Parliament entered St Paul's Church in triumph. The altar was covered with a large allegorical picture of Germania. Journalists came from far and wide. It was reported that there was also a substantial audience of ladies in the gallery, and that they preferred to sit on the left. Even the wives and daughters of conservative members preferred standing on the left to sitting in the box on the right arranged for them by the Austrian Prince Lichnowsky.[7]

But inside and outside St Paul's the revolutionaries were far from united on the path ahead. With neither money nor arms at their disposal, there was little they could do even if they were. The revolution was both at the mercy of princes and of popular discontent. It was further threatened by the intervention of neighbouring powers, disposed, if necessary, to meet the threat of German revolution by forward defence. The spectre of an Anglo-French—Russian entente, aligned in 1913—14 against a German threat to the European balance, was not without its precedents. Conventional wisdom was to ascribe the defensive entente of 1914 to the inevitable aggressiveness of a conservative, Prussian-dominated Germany. But the hawks of 1848 were on the left, where they called themselves democrats, radicals and even communists. Belief in the reciprocity of popular war and social revolution was the one thing that united the King of Prussia with Karl Marx, a sectarian revolutionary journalist and one-time student of the University of Berlin, then age 30.

The revolutionary coalition disintegrated accordingly. The pieces were retrieved by the embattled princes. Once they had appreciated that the sky would not fall down, they found it relatively simple to deal with the contending parties. The opposition was variously bought and shot. What was to be known as the 'Greater German' solution, a supra-Germany including Austria, ceased to be an alternative with the recovery of the old regime in Vienna. With skill and resolution it managed to buy off its dissident peasants and shoot down its dissident Czechs, Hungarians and Italians, not to mention its students. A 'Lesser German' solution vanished over the horizon with the refusal of a Prussian king to accept the sovereignty over a federal Germany from a delegation of Frankfurt parliamentarians. He, too, had successively bought and fought off the revolution, liquidating the last remnants of feudal obligations and paralysing Prussian liberals with a constitution conferred on his terms, not theirs.

Meanwhile Prussia restored order. In the process it demolished the remaining possibility — national unification on the basis of the constitution laboriously worked out in Frankfurt. In May 1849 Prussia declared war on the Grand Duchy of Baden, where the constitution had been ratified, and duly routed the surviving revolutionaries. By this time nobody, least of all the proverbial workers and peasants, was prepared to come to their support.

Liberals concluded from the experience that their side had lost. The 'Glorious Fourth', the 'Glorious Revolution', the 'jour de gloire', of other times and places was recalled by Germans as 'the crazy year'. Conservatives assumed that they had won. The reconstituted German Federation liquidated the surviving achievements of the Frankfurt convention. Its fleet, built to defend German commerce against the Danes, and itself a symbol of Liberal German nationalism, was sold at public auction.[8]

The Prussian constitution itself was fixed to buffer the supposed excesses of liberal passion. It was to remain fixed until all of Germany, Prussia naturally included, lost the First World War. The suffrage for the Lower House of the legislature remained universal, but public and unequal. The electorate was divided into classes according to their local tax assessment. The plutocratic potential of the new suffrage awaited the development of a real plutocracy. But whoever the beneficiaries, the premise of the system was robust inequality: 5 per cent, 15 per cent and 80 per cent of the electorate each elected a third of the lower house. And the initiative remained, in any case, with the Crown and an hereditary House of Lords. A population politicised in the grand manner in 1848 subsided again into abstinent indifference. Between 1849 and 1863 an average of 27.3 per cent of the eligible electorate actually voted. Even among the first class half stayed home. It was the Polish scare of 1861 that produced benchmark voting in Posen on the extreme eastern frontier. In the west, where both literacy and industrial development were relatively advanced, voter turnout was relatively low.[9]

There were lessons for everybody, though not only the obvious ones. Change as things might, nobody was to forget them again for many decades. Deny it as they tried, Prussian kings had acknowledged that even they no longer governed by the will of God — or only by the will of God. Fudge it as they might, Prussian liberals had acknowledged that the Crown was not merely an obstacle to economic rationality and national self-fulfilment, it was conceivably an instrument for the attainment of both. It was also their ultimate defence against the wrong-headedness and over-enthusiasm of fellow citizens, who failed to understand how the developing industrial economy, that threatened, impoverished and starved them, was actually in their best interest.

Prussia had found another ally. Liberalism had lost one. In other and happier places the revolutionary coalition also went separate ways —

Federalist and Republican, Girondin and Jacobin — but only after winning the crucial battles. In Germany the disintegration of the left came first: the symptomatic schism of right and leftwing liberals in the 1850s; of leftwing liberals and socialists, but also some Catholics, in the 1860s.

The characteristic high-mindedness of 1848, the natural expression of a generation trained to think of politics as the realisation of the third *Leonore* overture in public life, was also among the victims. In 1848 Germans learned about power. Neither good ideas nor good intentions were a satisfactory substitute. A decade later an anonymous Frankfurt pamphlet declared as a truth it held to be self-evident that

> Our nation of '40 million dreamers and idealists' has learned a good deal in the hard school of reality, and it has also fortunately forgotten some things. Above all it has become more practical. Romanticism and sentimentality, transcendental philosophy and supernaturalism, have not withdrawn from the public life of our people into private life. For realism and steam, machines and industrial exhibitions, the natural sciences and practical interests now fill the great marketplace of life and work at the humming loom of our time.[10]

Realism meant growth. What had grown before 1848 grew still more. Population was an obvious case. In 1815 there were about 25 million Germans, in 1870 about 40 million. Population had increased by 37 per cent between 1815 and 1845, by 17.6 per cent in the quarter-century that followed. Between 1815 and 1864 the Prussian population increased by 87 per cent, initially by annexation, thereafter by natural births. Increased longevity was a demographic factor only after the foundation of the empire in 1871. It was estimated that nearly half the Prussian population was under 20 in the 1850s and 1860s, only 13 per cent over 50.[11]

Population, as elsewhere, was a function of economic opportunity, though this was not always obvious to those affected. It was the rural poor who multiplied fastest. Emigration was their salvation: 727 of every 10,000 small farmers — seven and a half acres and down — left the Palatinate between 1848 and 1854. But many took their chances on the city. Berlin grew at 4 per cent per annum in mid-century. The bulk of the urban population consisted of young, displaced peasants.[12]

Despite the world's first experience of international recession in 1856–7, industrial production grew at a dramatic rate, increasing by 168 per cent between 1848 and 1857, by 74 per cent between 1860 and 1870. By 1857 German producers satisfied an estimated 66 per cent to 76 per cent of domestic demand for iron; by 1864, 93 per cent. The modern German economy materialised within contours still easily perceptible two generations later. Foreign trade tripled between 1850 and 1870. The valuation of imports increased nearly four and a half times. Between 1850 and 1870 mechanisation, as measured in horsepower, increased nearly tenfold, outstripping France and reaching 60 per cent of the capacity of Great Britain. Capital was, and remained, a problem. The value of Prussian bonds declined by 10 per cent between March and June 1866, and only a rapid victory in the summer war with Austria saved Prussia from fiscal disaster.[13]

For all this, people got richer. Per capita income rose by about 12 per cent betwen 1851 and 1870, though one hesitates to say how this might have affected those families in the Eifel, a kind of West German Appalachia, who saw meat only at church fairs and the most important holidays. Noon and evening, their normal diet consisted of potatoes with salt, and usually fat, supplemented by black bread — in contrast to the white bread long since institutionalised in the French diet on the other side of the border — and coffee with chicory.[14] Even if everyone did get richer, the rich got richer faster than the poor. The very rich, the new entrepreneurial class, got richest fastest, though there was a tangible payoff for those who helped. A Saar coalminer earned 386 marks a year in 1850 compared to a national mean of about 266. In 1869 he earned 729 marks, nearly two and a half times the national average.[15]

But whatever the shifting locus of economic power, political power remained unmoved. Or so it seemed. In fact, economic growth proved at least as incendiary as the economic dislocations of the 1840s. The eccentricities of the Prussian suffrage only reinforced it. In 1855 there had been 236 Conservatives in the Prussian Lower House and only 57 Liberals. In 1858 there were 210 Liberals and 57 Conservatives; in 1861, 256 Liberals and 15 Conservatives; in 1865, 285 Liberals and 11 Conservatives.

The issue was not, as it might have seemed in 1848, princes *v.* people. It was now a conflict between contending oligarchies, an old one of landed gentlemen and a new one of aspiring doctors, lawyers and locomotive manufacturers. Whatever their antagonists liked to believe, the new men were not trying to destroy the traditional clubbishness of politics. What they were after was membership, even executive office, in the club.

The issue they chose seems formalistic in the extreme: the relative merits of the three-year draft for army recruits as opposed to the prevailing two. The king favoured the three-year draft. The arguments were fiscal and practical, not really matters of principle. Temperamentally the legislature was hardly less sympathetic to the army than the king himself. But a principle was involved for both. The question was not whether there was to be a strong Prussian army. It was who was to determine its strength. The conflict escalated as the legislature refused to vote a military budget.[16]

The Prussian government fell. It was replaced by a new ministry under Otto von Bismarck, who was to change the face of Prussia, Germany and Europe in ways not even he anticipated on assuming office in 1862. He remained in office until his dismissal by a new and very different king twenty-eight years later. Theoretically the conflict between king and Parliament might have ended in civil war or abdication. There were active proponents of both.[17] Instead it ended in another of those eminently Prussian compromises. There was something for everybody, but less of it for the challengers and more for the traditional rulers.

Bismarck united Germany with three quick and brilliantly successful wars. This, if anything, was what its modernisers and liberalisers most wanted. He also saved the Prussian monarchy virtually intact, beat Austria out of its traditional place of honour at the German table, and transformed both domestic liberalism and conservatism. His achievement was ratified *post facto* by the European powers who refrained from intervention, and by the liberal parliamentarians, who eventually won the battle of the two-year draft, but lost the war for control of the army.

Later generations were to rewrite and vulgarise his achievements. It was blood and iron that would decide the great issues of the day, Bismarck told an audience of Prussian parliamentarians. People came to believe this is what really happened. There was evidence that he even came to believe it himself. In 1895, on the occasion of his 80th birthday, a delegation of ageing veterans turned up all the way from America to present him with an honorary membership in the German Veterans' Association of Chicago. German solidarity was now quite general, Bismarck noted with satisfaction, not at all the way it was before the wars of unification. 'With parliamentary speeches and the press, things wouldn't have worked out as they did with the war', he told them.[18]

This was true enough, but only part of the story. According to later versions there had been a kind of crusade. The terrible swift sword of the German hosts had avenged the accumulated humiliations of bygone centuries. The sentiment was preserved in masses of commemorative statuary, the aesthetic and functional equivalent of the Civil War cannon and statues that still grace nineteenth-century American courthouses.

There had, in fact, been a wave of patriotic feeling. Gymnastic societies were an idiosyncratic index. In a country where, as a Russian diplomat observed, people preached doctrine in bathing suits, they had increased from 100 to 2,000 between 1859 and 1864. At Easter 1864 an estimated 250,000 people had attended 269 rallies staged on behalf of the Germans under Danish rule in Schleswig-Holstein.[19]

If popular enthusiasm for the war with Austria two years later flagged perceptibly, mobilisation revived it. Even ageing radicals of 1848 joined in support. 'Wait till we've won', Bismarck told sceptical domestic liberals, 'and you'll have all the constitution you want.'[20] The war with France in 1870 engaged feelings to a point near religiosity. Lutheran hymns mingled with 'The Watch on the Rhine'. British observers were reminded of Cromwell's Ironsides.[21]

Bismarck and Moltke, the German commander, squabbled ferociously on the relative priority of political and military goals. Like William T. Sherman, Moltke took the view that 'we are not only fighting hostile armies, but a hostile people, and must make old and young, rich and poor, feel the hard hand of war, as well as the organised armies'.[22]

He also took the view that it was for the generals to decide how this was to be done. 'I believe', he informed the king, 'that it would be a good thing to settle my relationship with the Federal Chancellor definitively. Up till now I have assumed that, especially in time of war, the Chief of the General Staff and the Federal Chancellor are equally competent and mutually independent agencies under the direct command of Your Majesty.'[23] Bismarck won the day, but neither easily nor altogether completely.

The actual character of warfare was an obvious source of subsequent misperception. Bismarck's wars were mercifully short — the longest of them, the war with France, was over in six months — but hardly inconsiderable. They were fought with large, conscripted armies of the kind associated only half a century before with revolution, and implicit in 'the people's right to bear arms' of the US Constitution. Troops were equipped by something approaching mass production with weapons that testified to the new industrial technology. Things were moved by railways. In this sense all that distinguished the Franco-Prussian War from the American Civil War was that there were three and a half years less of it.

The outcome was also punitive in a way more typical of the people's wars of the twentieth century than the Cabinet wars of the eighteenth. War on civilians to wipe out the last reserves of resistance was followed by substantial reparations, at least by the standards of the time, and annexation of the losers' territory on the far side of the Rhine, including a good-sized piece of Lorraine and the entire province of Alsace. The independent states of south Germany, that had hitherto managed to avoid falling in behind the concentrated horsepower of the Prussian economy, fell in behind the concentrated firepower of the Prussian army. As in other great revolutionary struggles, their acclamation changed the map. On 18 January 1871, a new German Empire was proclaimed in Louis XIV's chateau at Versailles. As never before — or in all likelihood again — Germany was united from the Alps to the North Sea, from the Baltic to the Rhine.

But the appearances were deceptive. If not in means, Bismarck's wars were limited in ends. There was no serious intention of conquest, still less of revolutionary transformation of the opponent, let alone of Prussia itself. These limits, far from obvious to contemporaries or even later generations, can be observed to particular advantage by comparison with the American Civil War. In America the nature of society was the very heart of the conflict, unconditional surrender was a feasible goal, and the restraining influence of potential foreign intervention was out of the question.

Germans, and not only Germans, had reason enough to admire Bismarck's genius. Their calamity, like his own, was to misjudge it. The essence of Bismarck's achievement had been the appreciation, and exploitation, of constraints, some domestic, some foreign. The national revolutions that had failed in 1848, not only in Germany but in Italy and to a degree in Hungary, succeeded in the 1850s and 1860s. In part this was because those who had opposed them, Bismarck included, were now prepared to lead. But it was also because those who had led in 1848 were now prepared, however reluctantly, to follow. It was agreed that revolutionary nationalism was a menace, and liberal nationalism − the nationalism of professors, railways, manufacturers, uniform weights and measures − was a risky business. But conservative nationalism, something not previously considered, proved remarkably promising, not least because conservatives and liberals discovered their common interest in containing international socialism.

The essence of Bismarck's genius was the recognition not only of possibilities, but of impossibilities. In the Europe of the 1860s, there was no place for revolutionary war, and none at all for unconditional surrender. To the extent these limits were appreciated, the emerging Germany offered any number of other possibilities: free trade, civil marriage, even universal manhood suffrage. Bismarck, like Disraeli and Louis Napoleon, plausibly assumed the last would only reinforce domestic conservatism. In Germany, as in England, liberals took their chances. English Liberals co-opted working-class votes and rode to glory with them. Between 1868, the first exercise of the second Reform Bill, and the First World War, Liberals governed Britain for thirty of forty-six years. In Germany Liberals lost. At their peak in the 1860s, they were in decline a decade later.

The new equilibrium was codified in a new constitution as eclectic as the circumstances that produced it. Conceived in 1867, after the war with Austria, as the constitution of a North German Federation, it was transferred intact to the new empire four years later. Designed with an eye to the contingencies of diplomacy and war, it was then subverted and finally destroyed by war a half-century later, when the constraints that had previously governed diplomacy and war no longer operated.

The blessings of liberty were not conspicuous among its goals. It was the only major constitutional document of the period to appear without a Bill of Rights.[24] Aspirations to a more perfect union, common defence, domestic tranquillity and prosperity were more apparent. But as it proved, these were not only goals. They were essential conditions. That none of these was as self-evident as it had seemed in 1871 was among the reasons for the malaise of 1913.

German constitutionality had never been a simple matter. It could hardly be avoided that the new constitution both addressed and reflected problems of some antiquity. The dilemma of traditional German constitutionality had been the failure to reconcile the centrifugal tendencies of a highly diverse people and a proliferation of regional sovereignties with that minimum of central authority necessary to keep order within, and defend against enemies from without. Samuel von Pufendorf, a qualified seventeenth-century observer, had regarded it with despair. Neither a monarchy like Spain or France, nor an aristocracy like Poland, Germany was certainly no democracy like the ancient city-states, but also not a federation of states like Switzerland. It was, he concluded, 'an irregular and almost monstrous constitutional construction'.[25]

For better or for worse, the same could be said of the new constitution. The juridical consummation of national statehood, it defined an entity that excluded Swiss and Austrian Germans, while including the Poles of Silesia and Prussia's eastern provinces, a Danish minority in Schleswig, and a French-speaking population in various parts of the conquered territory of Lorraine. The annexed Alsatians, a case *sui generis*, were overwhelmingly German-speaking. Whether they regarded, or would ever regard, themselves as German after 200 years of French statehood was another question.

The new empire was a confederation of existing sovereignties, disparate in size, constitutional development, religion, social structure, economy and historical origin. It included four kingdoms, six grand duchies, five duchies, seven principalities, and three city republics. The conquered territories on the Upper Rhine, amalgamated as the province of 'Alsace-Lorraine', were, revealingly, the only common national jurisdiction. Students of British history might recognise a certain similarity to Ireland. Americans might see a certain remote similarity to the District of Columbia or even Guam. The territories were administered by a variety of German bureaucrats, occupied by a variety of German troops, and governed from Berlin.

Legislative authority was vested in two autonomous and deliberately asymmetrical houses. The first, the Bundesrat, was composed of instructed delegations from the empire's member states, that is, it did not consist of peers or senators but of civil servants. Prussia, which was incomparably the largest state with nearly two-thirds of the empire's area and population, naturally sent the largest delegation, and claimed the presidency. Prussia's seventeen seats in a total of fifty-eight were far less than it might have claimed relative to population. But fourteen sufficed to veto constitutional amendments. There was never a serious question about which of the represented sovereignties was most equal.

The other house, the Reichstag, was a popular assembly of 397 deputies, about one per 100,000 population, elected from single-member constituencies. It had legislative initiative, and still more importantly the budgetary prerogative. One of the startling innovations of the constitutional design — direct, equal and universal manhood suffrage for citizens over 25 — was theoretically reinforced by constituencies of equal size: one man, one vote. But there was, in fact, no subsequent reapportionment despite dramatic shifts in population. The representativeness of the Reichstag was further vitiated by the stipulation that the deputies should not be paid. Its effectiveness was deliberately checked by fiscal undernourishment. The empire was indirectly financed: excise taxes and subsidies from the states were to be its principal sources of income.

The prerogatives of the Reichstag, particularly the budgetary one, were none the less considerable, and generally appreciated as such. At least in its early days, liberals regarded the Reichstag as separate from, but equal to, the executive. Given their apprehensions about universal suffrage, they also regarded this as desirable. Notwithstanding traditional liberal Anglophilia, parliamentary government on the British model was not an issue.[26]

The executive was lodged in the emperor, inevitably the King of Prussia, and his delegated representative, the chancellor. The chancellor served at the emperor's discretion, and only the emperor's discretion, but exercised autonomous responsibility during his term of office. Although the nature of this responsibility was almost metaphysically vague, it was obvious, that the chancellor was something more than the emperor's lieutenant. Considering that Bismarck had designed the office for himself, this is not surprising. The chancellor, in turn, named secretaries of state, not ministers, to the respective federal offices, not ministries. They served at his discretion as he served at the emperor's. There was, quite explicitly, no collective responsibility, not even a government in any determinate corporate sense.

The military led a constitutional life of its own, save as it was constrained by the distinctly limited budgetary prerogatives of a Reichstag whose military appropriations were largely pre-empted by state governments. A plausible corollary of the confederal design, the army itself was conceived as confederal, though the navy was specifically German. Since the events of 1848 and 1870 alike had confirmed to the empire's founding fathers that command was among the essential conditions of kingship, command remained, at least *pro forma*, with the emperor's constituent monarchs, the kings of Prussia, Saxony, Bavaria and Württemberg. The facts of military life being what they were, the constitution anticipated that there would be a subsequent integration on the basis of Prussian law and practice. But the envisaged legislation never materialised, an omission that had some practical consequences forty-odd years later in Zabern.

The national economy was a rather different case. There was no mistaking that economic convenience, even necessity, had been among the prime movers of German unification. The constitution bore permanent witness to it. Tariffs, insurance, weights and measures, various monetary matters, large areas of civil law, citizenship and internal migration were all among the prerogatives of the central government.

But in theory, at least, the empire remained confederal to a startling degree. Bavaria retained its railway, Bavaria and Württemberg their post offices. Notwithstanding the creation of a national citizenship, concurrent state citizenship continued to exist, and even a degree of diplomatic autonomy. Representatives to the Bundesrat enjoyed diplomatic status. The states not only delegated representatives to Berlin. They exchanged them with one another, and even with foreign governments, for example, a Prussian minister in Karlsruhe, the capital of Baden, a Bavarian minister in Vienna, the capital of Austria. States conferred titles, decoration, commissions. Bavaria concluded a concordat with the Vatican.

None of this, of course, was as straightforward as it seemed. Posterity might wonder to what extent the constitution's founding fathers envisaged that *novus ordo seculorum* that moved other constitutional gestations before and afterwards and that is still commemorated on the dollar bill. But there was no question that they had a keen eye for the realities of the world around them, where all men were distinctly not created equal, where nominal confederation in fact confirmed Prussian hegemony, and where the business of the nation — as distinct from the state — was increasingly business.

It was somehow characteristic of the very inception that no one, including the presumptive emperor, was entirely happy about the new empire. Hours before its proclamation, he burst into tears as he contemplated the imminent farewell to the 'old Prussia' the new constitution seemed to require of him. The passing of the old order was even reflected in the new imperial title, 'German Emperor' — though this was less comprehensive than 'Emperor of Germany', the title he would have preferred.[27]

As is often the case, his reservations were more than nostalgia. The 'old Prussia' had undeniable virtues. They were now submerged in the eclectic combination of horsepower, bureaucracy, countervailing instances and popular politics that made up the new empire. But the 'old Prussia' was irrecoverable anyway. The new constitution was the effect, not the cause, of its loss. Its creators, Bismarck above all, saw the present, and it worked. Closer inspection revealed how much 'old Prussia' he had actually managed to preserve, and how much of it the citizens of the new empire carried along, willingly or unwillingly, in their knapsacks.

For population, industrial capacity, military capacity and sheer size made it inevitable that Prussia would set the pace of industrial development, establish the standards of military effectiveness and define the goals and issues of war and peace. At the same time Prussia itself remained the 'old Prussia'. At least in form, it was still the interlocking directorate of bureaucrats, soldiers and squires incorporated a century and a half before, and reconstituted in 1850 at gunpoint as the self-appointed policeman of both domestic and international order.

None of this was so remote from American experience as Americans, then and since, have generally imagined. The southern committee chairman, himself a product of single-party politics, congenial rules, systematic voter exclusion, and artfully drawn constituencies, had played a similar role in American legislative politics since Reconstruction.

What distinguished the German case was the influence on, even domination of, the executive branch and the judiciary as well by such solid southerners — or, in the German case, solid easterners. To understand it, one might try to imagine the Civil War with the roles reversed: a secessionist North annexed by the superior weight of southern numbers, wealth and arms, and the political genius of an incomparably superior Jefferson Davis.

Both creature and creator of the new empire, Prussia was also linchpin, gear box, motor and brakes. Wheels turned, or stopped, on Prussian initiative, and meshed in the duality of executive office. Beginning with Bismarck, the Federal Chancellor was variously Prussia's Prime Minister, presiding officer of the Bundesrat, and master of ad hoc majorities in the Reichstag, whose term of office effectively depended on his goodwill.

The very stability of the empire presupposed a consensus between Germany and Prussia, a capacity for coexistence between Germans and the 'old Prussia'. So far as the juridical imagination could contrive it, 'old Prussia' retained a veto where it saw its interests in jeopardy. 'A parliamentarily be-figleafed, feudally-reinforced, bourgeois-influenced, bureaucratically-constructed, police-tended military despotism', Marx called it in one of those virtuoso cascades of participles that are among the glories of the German language. (' ... ein mit parlamentarischen Formen verbrämter, mit feudalem Einsatz vermischter, schon von der Bourgeoisie beeinflusster, bürokratisch gezimmerter, polizeilich gehüteter Militärdespotismus.')[28] As might be imagined, there were many people who found this at least exaggerated. Still others agreed. But, in contrast to Marx, this was the very reason they liked it.

Later observers were of two drastically different minds about the new state. Critics inclined to regard it as a transitional phase, even a holding action, between an autocratic past and the 'normal' parliamentary democratic future of a country whose economy, legal institutions, social structure and even intellectual traditions increasingly resembled those of

West European neighbours. Admirers found it sufficient unto itself. It was a distinctly German contribution to constitutional experience, different but not inferior to any other.

Both arguments have their merits. The constitutional status quo was under fire almost from its inception, not only from radical critics, but from thoroughly establishmentarian legislators, who were almost desperately anxious for a piece of the executive power so artfully and tenaciously withheld from them. Bismarck himself came close to fundamental reconsideration late in 1877, when he considered the appointment of Rudolf von Bennigsen, the leader of the majority party and speaker of the Prussian Diet, to a Prussian Cabinet position. The king was outraged. But this was not ordinarily an insuperable obstacle, nor do his objections seem to have addressed Bennigsen's qualifications, or disqualifications, as a parliamentary politician. The issue was Bennigsen's liberalism. Imaginably he would have accepted a Conservative politician. But the case is theoretical. There was no reason for Bismarck to propose one. Given the logic of the Conservative position, which tended, if anything, to be more royalist than the king's, one can even imagine that a Conservative would have turned the position down. In any case Bennigsen complicated the issues. He raised the stakes by requesting the appointment of two colleagues to ministerial office as well. Bismarck changed parliamentary horses a few months later. The Liberals were left behind, the Conservatives off and running. The experiment was never repeated, at least in Prussia.[29]

But this had little enough to do with constitutional issues as such, notwithstanding frequent and high-principled trumpetings to the contrary. To take a distant but by no means unreasonable analogy, little stands in the way of a US President, like President Carter, disposed to appoint a member of Congress, like Senator Muskie, to Cabinet rank.

But there were also precedents enough at home, at least by the first decade of the new century. In fact if not in form, the Grand Duke of Baden appointed ministers acceptable to a Liberal parliamentary majority in 1904. The King of Württemberg did the same in 1907. Confronted in early 1912 with the stonewall intransigence of a Catholic majority, the Bavarian regent conceded his preference for Liberal ministers and installed a Prime Minister from the Catholic Party.[30] Neither direct nor indirect parliamentarisation was constitutionally incompatible with German monarchy (nor Dutch, nor Scandinavian), nor was co-optation of parliamentarians or appointment of governments contingent on parliamentary majorities.

The incompatibility was with German, above all with Prussian, politics. Its intricate and increasingly anachronistic dynamics required Conservative governments long after German electorates, and even an elaborately manipulated Prussian one, had ceased to return any semblance of a

Conservative majority. With a single exception, Germany's chancellors between 1871 and 1917 were Prussian and Conservative. But Conservative strength had declined from almost 24 per cent of the Reichstag on Bismarck's departure in 1890 to less than 15 per cent in 1912, even with the help of gerrymandered constituencies. Conservatives, who had shared, and even dominated, the quasi-governmental majorities on which successive chancellors relied, steadily advanced towards parliamentary isolation.[31] The Reichstag voted 'no confidence' in Bismarck symbolically and *post facto*, rejecting a congratulatory 80th birthday greeting 163 votes to 146.

Again in fact, if not in form, it had been a coalition of Conservatives and Liberals that ratified the empire, and that maintained it intermittently thereafter. The normal alternative was a coalition of Conservatives and Catholics, incorporated in the Centre Party, that proved marvellously effective, as the need arose, at keeping the Liberals in their place. But between 1907 and 1912 both alternatives had suddenly run out, and a coalition of the centre-left materialised as a practical possibility for the first time in over half a century.

It had actually been known from early on that constitutional monarchy, German style, was a compromise and a fragile equilibrium. Bismarck himself conceded as much in private correspondence in 1877, shortly before the abortive invitation to Bennigsen. He wrote

> The task of being both an obedient servant of the king and a con-
> stitutional minister in need of a parliamentary majority is basically
> impossible. Good manners has preserved the tradition of absolute
> obedience to the king; the fiction of absolute obedience can only
> be maintained if the monarch observes it with moderation — the
> minister otherwise finds himself in a Procrustean position between
> king and country.[32]

The very hegemony of Conservatives in executive position and the persistent deference to their parliamentary representatives, especially in Prussia, testified to parliamentarisation of a sort. 'What does von Heydebrand say about this?' was invariably asked in the Prussian Cabinet whenever a question of domestic policy arose, Reinhold von Sydow, a former minister, recalled in his memoirs. Heydebrand was the Conservative floor leader in the Prussian Lower House.[33] It was the kind of question American administrations have asked about such larger-than-life Congressional committee chairmen as Russell Long, Mendel Rivers and Wilbur Mills.

But this was hardly parliamentarisation in the classical sense. What complicated and obscured the discussion was that political objectives, as so often, were decked out in constitutional clothes. These, in turn, testified to their Liberal, Radical and eventually Socialist owners' predilection for London tailors and Paris couture. The result was a persistent case of mistaken identity.[34] It was compounded in part by fundamental misunderstandings of foreign institutions, in part of fundamental, even wilful, misunderstandings of the genuine eccentricities of German politics. When left of centre critics said British or French institutions, what they really wanted was British or French political life.

But the empire, at the moment of its constitution, was genuinely different. Its constitution testified to real forces, not only including the force of Prussian arms. It also bore witness to the non-existence, or at least underdevelopment, of other forces. Among them were those that most fundamentally distinguished French and British from German experience. In Germany there was no comparable sense of political nationhood. There was no political class disposed and accustomed to the wheeling and dealing of parliamentary government.[35] Save for the Conservatives, there was no electorate prepared not only to see its interests represented, but to see them amalgamated and transformed into the political tender of jobs and offices.

In their place were viable state governments, some of awesome antiquity like Bavaria, with a continuous history going back over a thousand years. There was fundamental religious division going back to the Reformation. Perhaps most importantly, there was a bureaucratic tradition that was among the wonders of the world. Much of the difference between Germany and Britain can be traced to the development of British parliamentary institutions in the seventeenth and eighteenth centuries, of a modern civil service early in the nineteenth. In Germany the sequence was exactly reversed. However they might claim to derive their mandate from the fountainhead of absolute monarchy, German civil servants saw themselves − but were also seen by others − as the real executors of the public interest. From the wars of unification on, the army shared by extension in the general esteem. 'Their army' in 1848 and for some years later, it became and remained 'our army', for better or for worse. It was a genuinely popular institution.[36]

The congruence of the imperial constitution with these realities and the extraordinary virtuosity of Bismarck in exploiting them, made the new system work. They even made it a system. Existing interests were contained within a new majority, 'the friends of the empire' in Bismarck's perspective. Themselves divided among nationalists and particularists, agrarians and industrialists, liberals, technocrats and scarcely reconstructed supporters of absolute monarchy, all had something to gain.

Their initial differences were worked out in a new status quo in 1878. It was perhaps the empire's real watershed year, a kind of 1787 to its 1776. The complaints of agrarians and industrialists were accommodated in a system of tariff protection. A year later they were subsumed in an alliance with Austria that advanced the interests of Conservatives and Liberals alike. Both the tariffs and the alliance were to prove permanent, quasi-constitutional fixtures of the empire.

Those left out of the new majority were ignored or proscribed. The integration achieved by the war on foreign enemies was maintained by a campaign against ostensible domestic enemies. Until 1878 the enemy was the Catholics. Thereafter it was the new Social Democratic Party, the party of industrial labour. Between 1878 and 1890, proscription of the Social Democrats, the only party to claim complete alienation from the existing order, was almost, though never quite, total.

The campaign left its monuments. Each was a testimonial to the empire's premises, its methods and the relativity of its success. Among them were programmes of social insurance, beginning in the 1880s, that were matched in Britain only a generation later and in France and the USA only after half a century. Another was a Catholic party that became, ironically, virtually indispensable to the survival of constitutional government. A third was a Socialist party that seemed positively to thrive on proscription. By the beginning of the twentieth century it had become the biggest party in Germany, and the largest Socialist party in the world.

Each campaign ended somewhere short of negotiated peace, but somewhere short of total victory, as though domestic politics was a single long armistice in an undeclared war. Sometimes sequentially, sometimes concurrently, the empire proscribed, harassed, bribed and ultimately accommodated Catholics, Liberals and Socialists in turn. With differential success and consistency, Catholics, Liberals and Socialists resisted and accepted the constitutional norms. Contending forces were neither joined nor beaten. Even radical democrats developed a taste for imperialism and government contracts. Catholics exhibited their patriotism. Socialists, the most consistent of oppositions, seemingly surrendered a claim on whole loaves for half-loaves, slices and even crumbs, as they yielded to the superior battalions on extra-parliamentary action, colonial expansion, reform of the unequal Prussian suffrage, religion in the schools, and supplementary military spending.[37]

'The cornerstone of Germany's modern development is the policy inaugurated by Bismarck in 1878', a Conservative spokesman declared in 1913. 'We still live on the political ideas and political achievements of that time.' In effect, he noted with satisfaction, the Conservatives had won: national unification, tariff protection, an active public sector, social legislation, nationalised railways, colonial expansion, resettlement of German peasants on Polish homesteads on the eastern frontier — all bore witness to the dimensions of the victory.[38]

But much of this was in the eye of the beholder. Conservatives also paid a price. The more things remained the same, the more they also changed in ways both eccentric and illuminating. The Social Democrats of contemporary caricature inevitably appear in cloth caps. But middle-class hats are ubiquitous in a widely reprinted photograph of a 1912 election rally in a Berlin park. In their correspondence party leaders addressed one another with the conventional-respectable *Sie* rather than the fraternal-conspiratorial *Du* of the party's origins. Without exception, a 1908 class portrait from the party's training academy shows both faculty and student functionaries in ties and collars, and a blouse in the case of Rosa Luxemburg.[39]

By the same token, Conservatives discovered as early as the 1890s an unsuspected talent for mass organisation, management and expensive propaganda that was to transform them, too, into a plausible facsimile of a popular party. If Count Posadowsky, a retired Prussian minister, made his 1912 Reichstag candidacy contingent on the anachronistic verities of gentlemanly independence – no campaign, no party affiliation – it could hardly be overlooked that gentlemen were no longer in fashion. By the beginning of the twentieth century even Conservatives had their small businessmen and dirt farmers on the parliamentary ticket.[40] The defence perimeter of both rye and the traditional social order was systematically extended to the henhouse and pigpen of the small family farmer. Tariff-supported grain prices in 1910–13 remained at the 1870–9 level. Meat, milk and egg prices, also tariff-supported, were consistently, even dramatically, higher.[41] Seen through German glasses, the populist Democrat, William Jennings Bryan could be taken for a Conservative. President McKinley, a business-oriented Republican, was a Liberal.

The convergence of its extremes testified both to the flexibility of the imperial constitution and its rigidities. The convergence was incomplete, ambiguous and, in certain ways, illusory. Born of nicely balanced incompatibilities, it also perpetuated them: Prussia *v.* Germany, federalism *v.* centralism, authoritarian legitimacy *v.* liberalism, plebiscitary dynamism *v.* parliamentary control.

The considerable difficulties of constitutional amendment are themselves both illuminating and slightly misleading. Prussia exercised a double veto. Not only did fourteen votes in the Bundesrat suffice to stop constitutional change, but opposition from any affected state sufficed to block amendment of any specifically stipulated state's right, any 'peculiar institution' like the military hegemony of the Prussian king.

The constitution was none the less formally amended at least ten times between 1871 and 1918. Sometimes it was rather trivial, as with reapportionment of administrative expenses incurred in collecting brewery taxes or certain stipulations limiting the emigration of draft-eligible males. But amendments could also be significant like provisions to extend Reichstag sessions, pay deputies, and issue railway passes for travel between Berlin and their constituencies. Once, at least, with the provision for a considerable degree of home rule in Alsace-Lorraine and Alsatian votes in the Bundesrat in 1911, amendment reached matters of real substance in a debate that generated as much incidental heat as the concurrent British and American debates on the income tax and the House of Lords. 'Yet it does move', some constitutional Galileo might have said.

Even more revealing was the volume of de facto constitutional amendment by legislation, administrative order, parliamentary procedure or just usage. Shortly before the First World War Paul Laband, one of the constitutional authorities of the era, itemised whole areas of constitutional change effected without any formal amendment at all: accession of territory, reapportionment of federal and imperial jurisdictions, permanent Bundesrat sessions, deputation of imperial authority via the appointment of a vice chancellor and an imperial governor (*Statthalter*) in Alsace-Lorraine, creation of a Bavarian section of the imperial court of military appeals, introduction of direct imperial taxation, amendment of the criminal code in supersession of previous constitutional provisions.[42]

At yet another level, constitutional change was a matter of practice. Though extra-constitutional, the parties existed as an unchallenged and self-evident fact of constitutional life. If only to get deputies out of adjacent cafés, the Reichstag from the beginning put rooms at their disposal and looked after their mail.[43] The rare deputy who resisted party affiliation led a hermit's life.[44] From the Chancellor down, the executive branch increasingly acknowledged the parties' power, not to mention their existence. The appointment of mixed commissions of parliamentarians and civil servants before 1914 testified at least to the complementarity of the governmental functions. Irrespective of the constitutional stipulations securing the supreme military command, war ministers found it expedient to answer parliamentary questions just as military empire builders found it expedient to organise parliamentary support. Trident beard aside, Admiral Tirpitz can be imagined without great difficulty in the Pentagon, Georgetown or on the Capitol Hill of a few generations later. By 1913 major policy-makers testified before deputies in executive session in ways not significantly different from the way American colleagues testified generations later before the Senate Foreign Relations or Armed Services Committees,[45] notwithstanding the prodigies of propaganda and systematic bad manners still invested in maintaining that it was none of Parliament's business.

It was true that there were no handshakes for Gustav Noske, the Social Democratic defence expert, when he toured a navy yard in 1913. Count Westarp, a prominent Conservative, assured Ernst Bassermann, the leader of the National Liberals, that he would not have attended a meeting had he known that Philipp Scheidemann, a leading Social Democrat, would be there too.[46] Asked about his wife's health by Bethmann in the Reichstag corridor shortly before his own death in 1913, Bebel remarked to an acquaintance in passing that it was the first time in a parliamentary career going back to 1870 that he had ever been addressed unofficially by a member of the government.[47] A year later, when war threatened, it was understandable that Social Democrats, durably traumatised by proscription in the 1880s, looked to the security of their party treasury and their persons.

But nothing really happened. On the contrary, a thoroughly, if shrewdly, conservative government, already persuaded of the imminence of war on two fronts abroad, went to some lengths to avoid a third front at home. Impervious to fire-eating injunctions from the Prussian right, Bethmann manipulated events in ways that would find favour with the Social Democrats. Comparison with the US Senate's Bay of Tonkin resolution, a kind of blank cheque for executive conduct of the war in Vietnam, is by no means farfetched. If Germany could not be governed with, or by, the nation's largest party, it was also clear in an hour of real national emergency that it could not be governed without or against it. Without Social Democrats there could be no credits, no mobilisation of conscripts, no industrial peace, that is, no war.[48]

But there was no real change of heart, nor even a more or less graceful capitulation to the facts of life. Usage was ambiguous. What was given with one hand could theoretically be taken back with the other. Intransigence grew with successive concessions. If constitutional space grew to accommodate changing structures, it was also true that the structures accommodated themselves to the peculiar limits of the constitutional space.

The behaviour and development of the parliamentary parties was a good example. Divided by the eccentric dynamics of national unification, divided again by the eccentricities of Central European religious and social history, they were divided again by their ambiguous relationship to the executive branch, and yet again by their ambiguous relationship to one another. With good reason, traditional critics have charged the parties both with excesses of ideological principle and with orgies of pragmatic accommodation. Party programmes had a hortatory consistency about them rather different from the quadrennial manifestoes of American political life. They spilled over into campaign oratory and parliamentary debate alike, turning politicians into an odd combination of chaplain and cheerleader, endlessly warning the faithful against the perils and seductions of other people's views.

Anchored to the need for preserving party identity, and buffered only by formal procedure, parliamentary debate took on the stylised rigour of the classical ballet. Prepared text followed prepared text, solemnly proclaiming elaborately negotiated positions to the cheers of the faithful and the heckling of the unbelievers.

Accommodation took place elsewhere. It went on in the quiet – and not so quiet — negotiations between parties and their increasingly well-organised extra-parliamentary clients. It went on in the elaborate negotiations required to produce the constitutionally required absolute majority from a multi-party system in a single-member constituency. Finally it went on in the committees of the Reichstag themselves.

But accommodation was tactical and conditional, an almost unavoidable consequence of a system fundamentally deficient in rewards. In principle there were few reasons for long-term accommodation between parties. There were any number of plausible arguments against it. These, in turn, tended to be both circular and self-fulfilling. The system precluded the only possible goal commensurate with the sacrifice of identity, that is, power. On the other hand, it could be made to produce favours and adjust to the pressures of specific domestic constituencies. The 'government' parties that played ball, and even the Centre Party that threatened to sit on the ball, enjoyed both the benefits of the status quo and a relative advantage over the other parties.

With the stagnation of the Centre and the massive growth of the Social Democratic vote, the only electorate formally committed to major constitutional change, the advantages of the status quo became all the more obvious to the traditional beneficiaries. The weaker the party, the more obvious, in fact, was the advantage. So long as the Social Democrats were to be kept out, even the weakest of parties was useful, even necessary, to the parliamentary majority that stayed in.

None of this precluded a keen and growing awareness of the weaknesses of the constitutional system. By 1908 the system was in trouble across the board. The emperor's famous interview with the London *Daily Telegraph*, a triumph of windy indiscretion, managed at a blow to antagonise every party from left to right. It catalysed disaffections going back to Bismarck. In 1909 the victorious electoral coalition of 1908 collapsed over the modalities and extent of taxation. It was the last approximation of stable parliamentary support any government was to know before the war. To a degree unknown since the 1880s, parliamentarians were hostile to the government, and by extension to the status quo. 'Constitutional regime is just a nice way of saying government by a bureaucracy which refuses to permit the development of an effective parliament', wrote Matthias Erzberger, one of the most active Catholic deputies, in 1914.[49]

Arguments were none the less found for the status quo, if only as a lesser evil: the imperatives of foreign and military policy, an atavistic fear of government by special interests or 'the mob', appreciation of the genuine difficulties of reconciling and co-ordinating agencies of central government with their unreconstructed Prussian counterparts, apprehension that parliamentary government might somehow end in a Cabinet dictatorship with a de facto loss of power by the remainder of Parliament, even a subliminal fear of being publicly identified as 'chancellor killers', that is, a threat to established order.[50]

But the crucial argument was that parliamentarisation threatened a net loss to the non-socialist parties. They were the principle beneficiaries of the status quo, and they represented the majority of the electorate. Assumption of executive power was therefore opposed by a majority of parliamentarians. 'The complicated structure of a federal state and its organs of government is quite incompatible with that basic premise of unity and resolution without which parliamentary government is impossible', Otto Hintze, one of the shrewdest contemporary observers, noted in a famous essay in 1911.[51] And so it was.

But while demonstrably different from the familiar systems of western Europe, the German system was no less remote from the troglodytic absolutism of Imperial Russia and only distantly akin to the pleasurably aggressive caricatures of foreign and domestic critics who were disposed to take William II at his invariably bombastic authoritarian word. Foreigners and left-of-centre Germans, who measured German institutions by romanticised examples of Britain and France, and German history by what they called 'western' standards, understandably took a dark view. With some reason they assumed that a system so obviously stacked to favour the forces of domestic conservatism was necessarily stacked against the forces of domestic change.

But political participation was only a marginal goal of the political system, just as it was only a partial goal of an American political system that was in many ways so different. In fact, the convergences only increased as Americans struggled to accommodate their constitutional practice to the challenges and seductions of foreign policy that had dominated German experience from the start.

Apparent eccentricities of German constitutional practice — the emperor's supreme command of the armed forces, the hegemony of the executive in foreign affairs, the proliferation not only of a ministerial bureaucracy but of an inner circle of imperial advisers — had, or were to find, their analogues in American life. Of this, it should be added, Germans were both contemptuous and almost wonderfully ignorant. 'Near as it is to us, our official circles already regard America as "terra incognita", and the United States, tomorrow's superpower, as a 'quantité négligeable', Bernstorff, the German Minister in Washington, complained in a personal letter in late 1913.[52]

The odd Prussian-German complexity of war minister, chief of staff and supreme commander was eventually recapitulated in the ambiguous relationships of defence secretaries, joint chiefs and President.[53] Even the peculiar relationship of Emperor and Chancellor was not entirely different from the formidable junction of Secretary of State and National

Security Adviser of a later day, with the latter serving autonomously at the President's discretion.

The Supreme Court's Curtiss & Wright decision of 1936, reaffirming the virtual sovereignty of the President in the practically extra-constitutional realm of foreign policy, would hardly have surprised Bismarck. Louis Henkin's description of the foreign policy role of Congress as 'rear wheels, indispensable and usually obliged to follow, but not without substantial braking power', would probably not have surprised observers of the Reichstag on the eve of the First World War.[54] Woodrow Wilson's assertion of the President's 'control, which is very absolute, of the foreign relations of the nation' would have seemed self-evident to a succession of emperors and chancellors.[55] The 'imperial presidency' of recent American experience was a fact of German life. So, with disastrous consequences, was the metamorphosis of the commander-in-chief from a technical-functional figure to one with overtones of the mystical and sacramental.[56]

'The Constitution could not easily sustain the weight of indiscriminate globalism ... It was hard to reconcile the separation of powers with a foreign policy animated by an indignant ideology and marked by a readiness to intervene speedily and unilaterally in the affairs of other states ...'[57] The speaker is Arthur Schlesinger Jr, referring to America after the Second World War. But it could as well be a reflective German on the eve of the First.

'The movement of the United States into the forefront of balance-of-power realpolitik in international matters has been accomplished at the cost of the internal balance of power painstakingly established by the Constitution.'[58] The speaker is Senator Ervin of North Carolina, the chairman of the Senate's Watergate investigating committee. But it could as plausibly be a Reichstag deputy of the centre-left, or even an unreconstructed Prussian conservative.

'If only this country could really be isolated for a few years – in the sense I mean of having no foreign foes for use at home', J. E. N. MacKenzie, *The Times* correspondent in Berlin, wrote to his editor in late 1913.[59] It sounds like Senator Fulbright, the long-time chairman of the Senate Foreign Relations Committee, though it also recalls de Tocqueville, the first great student of the tortuous relationship between foreign policy and popular politics.

But the analogies are again imperfect and incomplete. Contemporary observers and historical commentators have inclined to the view that the imperial constitution favoured executive autonomy, even the emperor's 'personal regime'.[60] The contrary can be argued as plausibly. The system's crucial weakness was not really a failure of balances. It was an incapacity to deal with a proliferation of checks, both domestic and foreign.[61]

Increasingly vulnerable to the vetoes of domestic constituencies and intransigent legislators, increasingly sensitive to the threat and challenge of foreign powers and unreliable allies, the imperial executive was further hampered by its internal divisions. Conservative diehards, apprehensive technocrats, a hawkish military and a universally unpopular Chancellor hauled and tugged without direction beneath the blanket of imperial authority.

Viewed by its neighbours as purposeful and aggressive, a model of armoured autocracy, imperial Germany in 1913 seems on closer inspection to have been significantly different. It was a country where decision-making was increasingly difficult and policy increasingly irresponsible, governed by fearful — and dangerously fearful — men.[62]

But this is only half the story. The history of the prewar years confirms that things were difficult. It does not prove that they were impossible.

References

1   R. J. Crampton, 'August Bebel and the British Foreign Office', *History* (June 1973), pp. 218ff.
2   Willi A. Boelcke, *Kriegspropaganda 1939–41* (Stuttgart, 1966), p. 396.
3   Hans Rosenberg, *Probleme der deutschen Sozialgeschichte* (Frankfurt, 1969), p. 17.
4   Theodore S. Hamerow, *The Social Foundations of German Unification* (Princeton, NJ, 1969), pp. 36ff.
5   J. H. Clapham, *The Economic Development of France and Germany* (Cambridge, 1961), pp. 102–3.
6   Hamerow, *Social Foundations*, p. 279.
7   Priscilla Robertson, *Revolutions of 1848* (New York and Evanston, Ill., 1960), p. 153.
8   Theodore S. Hamerow, *Restoration, Revolution, Reaction* (Princeton, NJ, 1966), p. 204.
9   Hamerow, *Social Foundations*, p. 302.
10 ibid., p. 3.
11 ibid., p. 44.
12 ibid.
13 ibid., pp. 12ff.
14 ibid., p. 85.
15 ibid., pp. 59–60.
16 Michael Howard, 'William I and the reform of the Prussian army', in Martin Gilbert (ed.), *A Century of Conflict: Essays for A. J. P. Taylor* (New York, 1967), pp. 89ff.
17 See Gordon Craig, 'Portrait of a political general', in his *War, Politics and Diplomacy* (New York and Washington, DC, 1966), pp. 91ff.
18 Quoted in Arthur Mennell and Bruno Gerlepp, *Bismarck, Denkmal für das deutsche Volk* (Akron, Chicago, Berlin, London and Paris, 1895), p. 154.
19 ibid.
20 Otto Pflanze, *Bismarck and the Development of Germany* (Princeton, NJ, 1963), p. 320.
21 Michael Howard, *The Franco-Prussian War* (London, 1961), p. 59.
22 Russell F. Weigley, *The American Way of War* (New York, 1973), p. 149.
23 Craig, op. cit., p. 123.

24   See Pflanze, op. cit., pp. 337ff., on the genesis of the constitution; a graphic representation can be found in Hermann Kinder and Werner Hilgemann, *dtv Atlas zur Weltgeschichte* (Cologne, 1966), p. 411.

25   Quoted by Wolfgang Sauer, 'Das Problem des deutschen Nationalstaates', in H.-U. Wehler (ed.), *Moderne deutsche Sozialgeschichte* (Cologne, 1966), p. 411.

26   Rudolf Vierhaus, 'Kaiser und Reichstag zur Zeit Wilhelms II', *Festschrift für Hermann Heimpel* (Göttingen, 1971), pp. 257ff.

27   See Pflanze, op. cit., p. 497; Golo Mann, *Deutsche Geschichte des XX. Jahrhunderts* (Frankfurt, 1958), p. 377.

28   Quoted by Mann, op. cit., p. 404.

29   See A. J. P. Taylor, *Bismarck* (London, 1965), pp. 160–1; Erich Eyck, *Bismarck and the German Empire* (New York, 1964), pp. 229ff.

30   Beverly Heckart, *From Bassermann to Bebel* (New Haven, Conn. and London 1974), pp. 90ff., 197.

31   See E. R. Huber, *Deutsche Verfassungsgeschichte* (Stuttgart, Berlin, Cologne and Mainz, 1969), Vol. 4, pp. 32–7, 279.

32   Quoted by Werner Frauendienst, 'Demokratisierung des deutschen Konstitutionalismus', *Zeitschrift für die gesamte Staatswissenschaft* (1957), p. 725.

33   ibid., p. 730.

34   See Ernst Fraenkel, 'Belastungen der parlamentarischen Demokratie in Deutschland', in his *Deutschland und die westlichen Demokratien* (Stuttgart, 1964), pp. 11–69.

35   See ibid; Max Weber, *Gesammelte Politische Schriften* (Tübingen, 1958), pp. 233ff.

36   See Gerhard Ritter, *Staatskunst und Kriegshandwerk* (Munich, 1960), Vol. 2, pp. 117ff.

37   See Heckart, op. cit., pp. 70ff., 161ff.

38   G. von Below, 'Politik vom Konservativen Standpunkte', in D. Sarason (ed.), *Das Jahr 1913* (Berlin and Leipzig, 1914), pp. 1–2.

39   Rosa Luxemburg, *Ausgewählte Reden und Schriften* (East Berlin, 1955), facing p. 624.

40   James J. Sheehan, 'Leadership in the German Reichstag 1871–1918), *American Historical Review* (December 1968), pp. 521–4; see Huber, op. cit., pp. 9–10.

41   James C. Hunt, 'Peasants, grain tariffs and meat quotas', *Central European History* (December 1974), pp. 313ff.; see Hans-Jürgen Puhle, *Agrarische Interessenpolitik und preussischer Konservatismus* (Hanover, 1966), *passim*.

42   Edwin H. Zeydel, *Constitution of the German Empire and German States* (Washington, DC, 1919), pp. 6–7.

43   Eberhard Pikart, 'Die Rolle der Partein im deutschen Konstitutionellen System', *Zeitschrift für Politik* (1962), p. 19; Huber, op. cit., pp. 3–9.

44   Helmut von Gerlach, *Das Parlament* (Frankfurt, 1907), pp. 1ff.

45   See Jonathan Steinberg, *Yesterday's Deterrent* (London, 1965); Heinrich Hasenbein, 'Die parlamentarische Kontrolle des militärischen Oberbefehls im deutschen Reich von 1871 bis 1918' (unpublished dissertation, Göttingen University, 1968), *passim*; M10, Bd. 41, 'Aufzeichnungen der Vertrauenskommission des Reichstags über die militärische und politische Lage Deutschlands am 24. April 1913', HStA Stuttgart.

46   Heckart, op. cit., p. 241.

47   ibid., p. 85.

48   Egmont Zechlin, 'Bethmann-Hollweg und die SPD', *Der Monat* (January 1966), pp. 17ff.

49   Quoted by Dieter Grosser, *Vom monarchischen Konstitutionalismus zur parlamentarischen Demokratie* (The Hague, 1970), p. 77.

50   ibid., pp. 12–15.
51   Pikart, op. cit., p. 26.
52   Egmont Zechlin, *Die deutsche Politik und die Juden im ersten Weltkrieg* (Göttingen), 1969, pp. 457–8.
53   See Samuel P. Huntington, *The Soldier and the State* (New York, 1964), pp. 315ff.
54   Louis Henkin, *Foreign Affairs and the Constitution* (Mineola, NY, 1972), p. 123.
55   Quoted in Arthur M. Schlesinger, *The Imperial Presidency* (Boston, Mass., 1973), p. 91.
56   ibid., p. 188.
57   ibid., pp. 168–9.
58   ibid., p. 207.
59   Letter to D. D. Braham, 11 December 1913, *The Times* archive, London.
60   Erich Eyck, *Das persönliche Regiment Wilhelms II* (Erlenbach and Zurich, 1948), *passim*.
61   See Huber, op. cit., pp. 840ff.
62   See Fritz Stern, 'Bethmann Hollweg and the war', in *The Failure of Illiberalism* (New York, 1972), pp. 77ff.

3 En route to Zabern: the Army and the Reichstag

'How's it going?' a blind man said to a lame man.
'As you see', answered the lame man. (G. C. Lichtenberg)

Both difficulties and possibilities can be seen to advantage in the development and interaction of two of the empire's most characteristic institutions, the army and the Reichstag.

The army was unquestionably the senior service with a continuous history going back to the middle of the seventeenth century. Its status as a 'peculiar institution' is arguable. The formidable and rather complicated mystique of the Prussian military notwithstanding,[1] there was rather less to its peculiarity than has conventionally met the foreign, and even the domestic, eye. The odd brew of feudal loyalty, nationalist élan and aggressive technocracy that brought a warm flush to German cheeks had a similar effect elsewhere. Even Anglo-Americans, relatively abstinent in this respect as they were in others, shared a taste for it. Wilhelm Groener was probably on the mark in assuming a substantial degree of similarity between German officers and their French and British colleagues.[2]

The eccentricities of the institution were internal. They were a product of those peculiar circumstances common to most western countries that made their armies both an alternative to civil society and its fairly accurate reflection. Living testimonials to the age of the sword and the horse, career officers everywhere shared a nostalgia for the knightly canon of loyalty, honour and hierarchy and a genial indifference to politics. There was also an increasing streak of cultural pessimism as they brooded over the depredations wreaked by the terrible twins of liberalism, votes and money.

'During my time at the War College, I read a lot of newspapers and was annoyed by the endless squabbling in the Reichstag', Groener recalled in his memoirs. 'Not so much for reasons of inner urging, but just for the sake of having been there, I visited the Reichstag without taking away any lasting impression. I found domestic politics unpleasant.'[3]

'It is a self-evident proposition that a democracy based on the will of millions of people, expressed through devious and changing channels, cannot be as skillful or efficient in the conduct of military affairs as a monarchy headed by a wise and powerful chief', a contemporary declared with the evident approbation of his peers and superiors. As Groener suggests, the speaker could as plausibly have been German, French or British. He was, in fact, a junior officer in the US army, writing in a professional journal in 1906.[4]

The views were generic, specific rather to an occupational group than a corps of uniformed gentlemen. But gentlemen admittedly set the tone. It was Germany's misfortune that it boasted a military class before developing a political one. But the military class, as such, differed only marginally from its European, and even American, peers.

While only Germans gloried whole-heartedly in the cult of the reserve officer, the *bourgeois gentilhomme* as officer and gentleman was a fixture of foreign as well as military life from Potsdam to Fort Riley.[5] The militia idea, anachronistically commemorated in the minute-man and variously celebrated between the French Revolution and 1848, survived only in the shadows − or in Switzerland − until its renaissance in the socialist programmes of the early twentieth century. In real life, the colonel and Mr O'Grady, like their ladies, were siblings under the skin. But the family similarity was even closer where O'Grady, now Grady perhaps and a paid-up member of the Episcopal Church, was also gorgeously uniformed as a member of the New England Guards or the Honourable Artillery Company.[6]

Commentators have rightly noted the continued aristocratic bias that manifested itself in almost every imaginable way in a corps of 29,000 active and 91,000 reserve officers. In 1913, 51 of 108 male von Kleists, 61 of 128 von Wedels, 71 of 278 von Bülows were career army officers.[7] Over half the army's colonels and generals were, in effect, Kleists, Bülows and Wedels − though this was down, it should be added, from three-fifths in 1900. In 1909, 151 of 190 infantry generals were aristocrats. But among majors the ratio was about 50:50, that is, the frequency of aristocrats increased with rank. The regimental system inevitably reinforced clubbishness. In 1913 aristocratic officers held parity or better with middle-class officers in over 60 per cent of Prussia's regiments. In 16 of about 100, presumably the very classiest of cavalry and Guards regiments, there were no non-aristocratic officers at all despite official pressure, beginning in the 1890s, for recruitment of 'the token Smith' (*der Kompromissschulze*) in response to political pressure from outside.

From 1908 to 1913 the number of bourgeois Guards officers increased from 4 to 59. In 1906, 60 per cent of the General Staff, the army's most prestigious unit, were aristocrats. So, in 1909, were 80 per cent of its new accessions despite coded qualification exams.[8] If anything, according to one commentator, coded entries positively favoured the aristocratic candidate. He was more likely to be familiar with the 'particular nature of military thinking' the exam was looking for.[9]

Overall it was estimated that more than 85 per cent of the active officer corps were sons of officers, civil servants, clergymen, lawyers and successful businessmen, 62½ per cent sons of officers, civil servants and university-trained professionals. In part this was a matter of philosophical preference, a practical expression of those characteristics of 'physical health, freedom from debt, single status and reliability of family origin, education and character', specified by regulation. In part it was also a matter of practicality. Over a nine-year period, admission to a military academy could cost a cadet's family 90 to 800 marks a year, assessed according to merit and need. By comparison, three and a half years training as a naval officer cost some 8,000 marks compared to an estimated annual industrial wage of about 1,300. For the empire's aspiring officers, money was one of the outward signs of 'family origin, education and character'.[10]

In a formal sense 70 per cent of the officers, and 75 per cent of the lieutenants, were bourgeois by 1914.[11] The aristocratic contingent among the estate-owners of Prussia's six eastern provinces had declined meanwhile to a third of the total. Deliberate recruitment of bourgeois qualified by 'love of king and fatherland, and Christian character' began in 1890. It was a concession to changing times – and also to a shortage of infantry and field artillery officers. In effect, Wilhelm Deist has argued, the military recapitulated what had happened in civilian life a generation earlier.[12]

But status, comfort and good billets declined demonstrably with distance from Berlin and such unaristocratic specialties as artillery. In Metz, at the greatest possible physical and cultural distance from the East Elbian heartland, only 2 of 30 officers of the 70th infantry regiment were aristocrats. There were no aristocrats at all in the 18th foot artillery. By comparison the aristocratic/bourgeois ratio in Spandau, a comfortable middle-class suburb of Berlin, was 10:37.[13]

Like the proximal sectors of civilian life, the style of military life remained intransigently unreconstructed. Fairly or unfairly, the regimental junior officer, like his student counterpart, was known for a characteristic combination of arrogance and dissipated rakishness, with an element of atavistic anti-intellectualism thrown into the package.

Officially a decent secondary education was considered desirable. This might even include the *Abitur*, the college-entrance certificate. It was a reflection of the professionalisation that was overtaking traditional career patterns everywhere, even in the army. The navy made the equivalent of high-school graduation a general requirement. Between 1880 and 1912 the number of officers with the *Abitur* actually increased from 33 per cent to 65 per cent. But at least in the field grades, 'character' retained its traditional priority over education. Even the navy was uncharacteristically liberal with exemptions from its official requirements.[14]

The philosophical dispute led to practical, and instructive, conflict after 1911. The General Staff, genuinely anxious about the outcome of the Second Moroccan Crisis, began submitting requests with increasing urgency for substantial reinforcements in the army. It met tenacious opposition not only from the Treasury, but from the Prussian Ministry of War, whose anxiety about the national defence was exceeded by its anxiety about the traditional standards of the officer corps. The ministry found itself at a loss to solve the problem 'without tapping the reservoir of social groups inadequately qualified for the officer corps and that, apart from other hazards, would be susceptible to democratization'. Without lowering standards, the ministry concluded, it would be imposs-ible to meet such drastically increased requirements from the recruitment pool available for 1913 and 1914.[15]

In practice, standards had their objective measure. A systematic — though non-racist — anti-Semitism was one. Religious conversion evidently constituted acceptable evidence of 'character'. Rich Jewish girls were also permissible marriage partners and even the Jewish reserve officer was not absolutely unknown. But there were no Jewish line officers in the Prussian army in 1910, though numbers of Jewish officers were discernible in Austria-Hungary, France and Italy.[16] By comparison there were measurable numbers of Jews in the higher German civil service grades. According to official statistics, Jews constituted about 1 per cent of the population, but nearly 2 per cent of the senior civil service, academic ranks not included.[17]

'Courts of honour', whose *ultima ratio* was the duel, were another evidence of social exclusiveness. In the last years before the war, voluble public criticism had at least reduced the frequency of duels — with pen-sions in the event of casualties. While such gentlemanly scuffles tended increasingly to be adjudicated by peers, occasional duelling none the less continued among reserve officers. The courts of honour were also used from time to time to harass critical reservists and even retired officers.[18] Honour, predictably, was what the peer group said it was. The standards so imposed were accepted not only in the military but by acquiescent civilians. Civil-servant reserve officers were called up without regard to their schedules, and even docked for holidays. Prostitutes, in the company of officers, went unprosecuted. After protests from the local garrison, plans for a monument to Carl Schurz, the student revolutionary of 1848 and subsequent US Senator from Missouri, were suspended in Rastatt near the Swiss border.[19]

As might be imagined, the enlisted man's life was both the complement and the antithesis of his officers. It was an extension of the class society of civil life circumscribed by legal norms that undeniably made him a second-class citizen, but a citizen none the less. The officer in trouble got house arrest with normal meals. NCOs got 'mild arrest' in a three-by-six-pace cell with a wooden bunk, sometimes a table and chair, normal meals, a straw mattress and bed clothes at night. But lower-ranking NCOs and enlisted men got 'middle arrest': a cell with bread and water, one blanket on summer nights and two in winter. For longer terms they got normal meals and a straw mattress on the fourth, eighth and twelfth day, then every third day thereafter. 'Severe arrest' was reserved for enlisted men only: a darkened cell with water and dry bread, and blankets and light on 'good' days.[20] (A French equivalent was 'W. C. pour MM. les officiers, Cabinets pour les sous-officiers, Latrines pour la troupe'.)[21]

The conscription system itself, while theoretically universal, demonstrably favoured those groups most accustomed to deference. Of a pool of nearly 1,300,000 in 1911 and 1912, fewer than half were actually inducted. But of these nearly two-thirds were from the country, though only about 40 per cent of the population still lived there.[22]

Like the endemic high-living in cavalry regiments, mistreatment of recruits drew parliamentary fire. The debates were evidence not only of a real, though not peculiarly German, problem but also of the discovery that appeal to elected representatives could be very effective. From 1900 on the subject was debated annually. In 1913 statistics on military discipline were even submitted in the Reichstag budget debate.[23] Specific cases were often debated in some detail. Social Democratic deputies were particularly, if not exclusively, active. They also had some effect. This, of course, was a two-way traffic. The military hounded the merest traces of Social Democratic activism in its ranks with positive ferocity, though with little enough co-operation from the police. Both consumer co-ops and Social Democratic saloons were declared off limits wherever possible. Unsurprisingly the president of the subsidised Anti-Social Democratic League was a retired general. But as military budgets and Social Democratic election gains increased, even the army backed down. It conceded the obvious, that Social Democratic troops were as loyal and efficient as any other and tacitly acknowledged that the whole effort was incomparably more expensive and time-consuming than it was worth.[24] In its place, the army introduced a pilot programme in historical and agricultural instruction as part of basic training. It even tried songs and direct political indoctrination.[25] None of the new programmes seem to have had much success.

Local colour excepted, little seems to have distinguished the realities of German military life from those of any other contemporary, or even most subsequent, peacetime armies. Recalled and rehearsed in a stream of memoirs, popular novels and daily journalism generally similar to French counterparts,[26] the enlisted man's life seems to have been a series of generally minor harassments, buffered by a degree of institutional paternalism, the qualified adventure of a tour away from home, and an afterglow of camaraderie.

Sadism, while not unknown, seems hardly to have been the normal experience. It was certainly not a peculiarly German one. 'We all understood in those days that this was how people were, that they were children of a system we call "militarism" for short', a reflective NCO later recalled. 'It was just not so that what happened could only happen in Germany. What happened was also possible in France and every other country with a large army.'[27] It was estimated in 1890–5 that suicides numbered about 200 a year in an army of about half a million.[28] But Falkenhayn, the Prussian Minister of War, also reported credibly in the Reichstag's 1914 army debate that the rate of military suicides was actually slightly lower than it was overall in the comparable civilian age groups.

The officer's life was undeniably warmed by the prestige of the uniform. In the more popular garrison towns it was even invested with a degree of extra-curricular glamour. But honorific tedium seems to have been the common denominator. The career was also distinctly underpaid, though at least convertible into credit at local shops, whose owners figured to get their money back by the time the Herr Leutnant had made captain or major. But promotion was distinctly slow. In 1910–11 it was estimated that the average age of first lieutenants was 35 to 36, captains 38, majors, who were the normal retirement grade, 46 to 47.[29]

The qualified exception to the tedium was the General Staff. It was the institutional manifestation of German military life that perhaps more than any other inspired the flattery of imitation. According to the folklore of the prewar European establishment, there were five perfect institutions in the world: the British Parliament, the French Académie, the Roman curia, the Russian ballet, and the German General Staff.[30]

At least a by-product of that early-nineteenth-century intellectual revolution that had also transformed the German university into an institution of international importance, the General Staff theoretically represented that combination of general and technical military education that was officially believed to constitute the basic difference between the Germans and other armies, and was the heritage of military philosophers from Clausewitz to Moltke. Again like the university, the General Staff came to symbolise the highest standard of professionalism, but also that tunnel-visioned expertise that modern Germans refer to so eloquently as *Fachidiotie*.

'Indeed', the venerable Lorenz von Stein declared in 1872, 'how deep and significant is the difference between that which our times demand of the professional soldier and that which sufficed fifty years ago! How rich is the military establishment of our century in words and ideas!'[31] Over half a century later, Groener, one of the General Staff's most brilliant products, approvingly quoted a Russian colleague: it was science – or scholarship, or system, since the German *Wissenschaft* in fact subsumed them all – that constituted the source of Prussian-German military success.[32]

Whether, and to what extent, this was true was to be a matter of endless debate from 1918 on, after *Wissenschaft* had so palpably failed — or, as was also argued, after it had been so inadequately practised. There was evidence enough for German technical backwardness.[33] There was at least as much for a kind of institutional bias favouring anachronism in an army that resolutely gave 'character' — understood as snotty young cavalry lieutenants with the inevitable 'von' before their names — priority over the mathematically literate lieutenant of artillery.

But arrogant or not, aristocratic or not, with the characteristic red stripe on their trousers as the visible badge of their exclusiveness, there was no question that General Staffers were bright and serious. If the evidence of their War College yearbooks can be believed, they could even be consciously funny.[34] Germany could survive a bad chancellor, Bernhard von Bülow observed — perhaps with particular authority. The army could survive a bad minister of war. But the very question of victory or defeat was contingent on the choice of the best possible chief of staff.[35] There were 239 General Staff officers in 1888, 625 of them in 1914, with 350,000 marks incidentally budgeted for espionage. Without exception they were survivors of one of Germany's toughest examinations, the rigours of the War College, and the relentlessness of the professional routine with its unending round of staff rides, war games and systematic newspaper clipping. It was customary, one recalled, that a messenger from the venerated Schlieffen appeared at the door on Christmas Eve with a tactical problem as a present. The solution was expected by the next evening.[36]

Systematically dosed in history, as befit a generation and a nation that believed in history, War College graduates were ignorant, and even proudly ignorant, of economics and contemporary politics. Groener read Treitschke, he recalled. 'But even senior officers were unpolitical types, and not only those who came from military academies.'[37] There was no close equivalent of the polytechnical education French officers had known since Napoleon. A military-technical institution on the French, or even American, model was founded only just before the First World War.

The great virtues of the General Staff, like its equally proverbial weaknesses, met in the Schlieffen Plan. Assuming that the Franco-Russian Alliance inevitably confronted them with the hazard of two-front war and the rigours of a long war with Russia, German planners prepared to meet the contingency by a massive pre-emptive campaign in France, initiated by an invasion through Belgium that was almost certain to provoke Britain. Combining strategic vision, historical extrapolation, technical virtuosity, powerful deductive imagination and disastrous political naïveté, the Schlieffen Plan could be regarded as their ultimate product. It was certainly a characteristic one. For the sake of the definitive 'Cannae', a crushing battlefield victory, pre-emption of the bad case, meaning war on two fronts, was achieved at the price of the worst case, meaning the war on three. Even the choice of historical example was revealing. Hannibal, the victor of the original Cannae, had, after all, eventually lost the war.

Wrong-headed and eventually calamitous as the Schlieffen Plan was, there was nothing really mysterious about it. The military logic, if limited, was plausible – at least to other professionals. Generals elsewhere argued from similar premises, though without the consistency and astigmatism that made German generals both better and worse than their foreign colleagues by a matter of degrees. The arguments were also familiar to civilians, not only ministers and parliamentarians, but even the interested newspaper reader.

They were rehearsed with startling candour before a committee of prominent deputies in the course of the military budget debate in late April 1913. The top military leaders were joined by the Chancellor and Jagow, the Secretary of State for Foreign Affairs, at first for a private briefing, but later for an open session.

According to Falkenhayn, Germany's situation, with the inevitability of war on two fronts, left no alternative but a purposeful offensive. It would only be carried out against France. Bethmann's arguments, considerably more circumspect in form, differ rather less in substance. French chauvinism and Russian enmity were facts of life, he said. Belgium would stay out if possible. 'But this will not be possible', he added.

Under fire from Bebel, and the Progressive spokesman Müller-Meiningen, who immediately probed the touchy question of Belgian neutrality and relations with England, Falkenhayn was uncompromising. 'The military position must be separated from the political', he announced. 'The job of the military was to prepare things for every eventuality.'

Military affairs were a different thing from politics, Falkenhayn repeated a few days later. What would happen if the Socialist assumptions about the peaceful disposition of Germany's neighbours were wrong? 'The French themselves assume that the Belgians will be on their side', he said. They had three cavalry divisions on the Belgian frontier. 'What matters to us is a speedy offensive in order to succeed against France', he declared. 'War breaks out when a people's basic interests are in jeopardy, and then treaties are no help.'

Falkenhayn was supported by Bassermann, the leader of the National Liberals, and even by Erzberger of the Centre. Accepting Bebel's argument that the next war would be a world war, Erzberger saw this as just another reason to approve Falkenhayn's requests.

Conservatives understandably took Falkenhayn's side, too. They questioned his premises only to the extent of registering some anxiety about the security of East Prussia in the event of Russian attack. They were reassured. So was Bassermann of Mannheim who was concerned about a French strike across Belgium against Aachen, or across the Upper Rhine in Alsace against his native Baden. The then Lieutenant-Colonel Groener's detailed discussion of comparative logistics, with its premises of relative French advantage in mobilisation, was accepted almost without resistance. The issue of Belgian neutrality, repeatedly raised by Social Democrats, was as repeatedly dodged by official spokesmen, both military, like Falkenhayn, and civilian, like Jagow. Assurance of Belgian neutrality could only be granted in confidence, Jagow insisted in open testimony. 'We can't tell the French where they should be waiting for us.' Falkenhayn was immediately at his side. 'A public declaration that we should respect the Belgian frontier before the French have violated it would only cause diplomatic complications', he said.[38]

The underlying assumptions were spelt out for the general reader by the assiduous General Friedrich von Bernhardi, the acknowledged guru of respectable civilian opinion. Future war, Bernhardi wrote, would be dominated by the secular innovations of the preceding century, mass conscription and technology, requiring extensive rail transport, support services and sophisticated communications, large operational areas, and severe discipline if retreats were not to end in chaos.

He anticipated that increased firepower would mean the end of closed formations and cause great difficulty for the infantry. Mobility would be reduced by the dependence on artillery as an offensive weapon, and the problems of maintaining its ammunition supply, he said. While he foresaw that rail transport, motor vehicles, aircraft and both wire and wireless communications might be countervailing forces, he doubted that they sufficed to counter the forces of immobility. And so, he concluded, the offensive had an initial advantage – naturally providing that the attacker got a headstart on the defending side. The lesson of modern warfare, according to Bernhardi, was the necessity of concentrating offensive power.[39]

The question is not so much how German generals had come to hold such views, and transform them into active policy. Staff officers everywhere are paid to anticipate worst cases. The folklore, even the reality, of Blimpishness notwithstanding, soldiers everywhere had some sense of social and technological developments in the half-century since Moltke, and their impact on the conduct of the war.[40] Worst-case anticipations can be self-fulfilling. Perhaps, after decades of largely uninterrupted European peace, this was less obvious than it later became. In any case, the blindspot was again a common one. As for the mystique of the offensive, French theorists like Grandmaison carried it beyond anything that might have occurred to Bernhardi, and evidently startled British observers fresh from their own instructive experience in South Africa.[41]

Even reduced to the nuts and bolts of practical logistics, the option for the three-year law in 1913, that is, of increasing the French conscript pool by 50 per cent, was an option for a forward strategy.[42] Unspecified as it was in its ultimate objective, Plan XVII was France's answer to the Schlieffen Plan and unequivocally offensive. While avoiding any pre-emptive violation of Belgian neutrality, if only out of deference to potential British allies, French strategists put their forces where the nation's hawkish mouth was. Be it by way of Metz in the lost province of Lorraine, be it by way of Mulhouse in the lost province of Alsace, they were ready for the great thrust to the Rhine.[43]

The interesting question is why responsible civilians were prepared to cover, support, even endorse such plans – and be covered, supported, even endorsed by parliamentarians and public opinion. The answer has to do in part with the way people perceived their neighbours and them-selves. But it also had to do with the way they perceived their armies, and the complicated system of law, institutions and usage they had de-veloped for dealing with them.

It was here that the significant differences lay. Soldiers, whatever their differences half a century before, had attained a degree of roughly interchangeable professionalism by the First World War, arguably com-parable with scientists, lawyers or professors. But while the differences were probably less radical than has generally been assumed, the civil–military relationship varied appreciably, and even significantly, between the European states.

The army's special relationship to the empire was among the facts of German constitutional life. The existence of the empire itself testified to a victorious army – just as the existence of the Third Republic, with its rather different civil–military relationship, testified to a defeated one. Holstein was fond of quoting Bismarck on the subject: 'The branch on which we sit is the army, and whoever lays a saw on this branch is my enemy.'[44]

One subtlety in the metaphor is entirely consistent with Bismarck's own difficult, but generally masterful, relationship to the army: the sitter, after all, is the active party to the relationship, compared at least with the branch. But the image also contains a more basic nuance. The branch is only part of the tree. Under normal circumstances it coexists with other branches. Like all organic growth, it also draws sustenance from its environment.

Bismarck himself acknowledged that the environment had not entirely exhausted its liberal fertility in the early 1880s by introducing a constraint on the military that was neither self-evident nor generally appreciated elsewhere. It was a normal principle of liberal jurisprudence that even the actions of the state are judicable. The German Empire itself later created a court system (*Verwaltungsgerichte*) where such claims could be decided. Though understandably concerned with limiting liability, Bismarck ex-tended the principle to the army. A consistent extension of the

Rechtsstaat, that peculiar combination of civil liberties and positive legality of which German liberals were so proud, it meant in practice that German civilians could sue the German army for damages.[45]

With his inexhaustible curiosity about the workings of government combined with his luminous confidence in their ultimate rationality, Lorenz von Stein sought manfully and even helpfully to systematise the civil–military relationship that existed at the empire's birth.[46] A pioneer work, it was to become definitive almost by default. Contingent on intellectual taste and political disposition, academic contemporaries were prepared to join, finance, admire and reminisce about their armies, to expose, deplore and ignore them. What they were not prepared to do, save for an occasional historian, was to study them. Stein's closing words are not only instructive but, even now, surprisingly modern. 'The next task, to which we felt ourselves inadequate, is to introduce the study of military organizations with positive data and comparative material into the academic curriculum and the popular consciousness', he wrote. 'May this great objective soon be realized by more competent people.'[47]

Stein's problem, like Germany's, was a fundamental ambiguity, even inconsistency. Sociologically and constitutionally the army was a body apart with a special, even a pre-constitutional, relationship to its sovereign and supreme commander. 'Like every part of the executive, the army is subordinate to the constitution and its body of laws,' Stein noted. 'But there is still a quality of the military that has always been outside the constitution and will remain there. The constitution can create and administer the army, but there is one thing the constitution cannot do: it cannot command the army.'[48]

'The military establishment is subordinate to the law, the army to the command structure', Stein continued. 'Both have always met in the sovereign as commander in chief, in all times and in all states. The objective of the law is to establish the army's requirements. The objective of command is the application of these requirements.'[49]

To the extent that the command function was itself subsumed within the constitutional structure, the problem was theoretically solved. But this, in fact, is only where it began — and not only for the irenic Stein.

'It is one of the most significant demonstrations of our century's morality that the old Roman proverb "law stops where military service begins" no longer applies even to soldiers on active duty', Stein observed,[48] with that same serene confidence in the beneficence of the *Zeitgeist* that led him some years later to propose the internationalisation of Europe's railways.[50]

Like the authors of the Second Amendment to the US Constitution, he regarded the citizens's right to bear arms as axiomatic, even equating conscription with citizenship. It was virtually his starting premise that universal service had transformed 'an armed population' into a 'people in arms' and had made military affairs a matter for the whole people.[51] 'The more intimately universal service welds army and people, the greater the unity between the army's spirit and the spirit of a people in arms', he declared with unmistakable, if slightly tautological, enthusiasm.[52] He was convinced that the proximity of social order and army, a principle in France, was reality in Germany.[53]

Yet he was on the mark when it came to the distance, both structural and institutional, that separated his philosophical position from military reality. 'We speak with good reason of "the hour of the military"', he noted, 'but of course this applies to the commanders, not the enlisted men.'[54] Whatever his theoretical premises, his empirical observations made it clear that he perceived the German army of his time as something more than a corps of minute-men.

'As a rule, the upper classes either make excellent soldiers, or altogether mediocre ones', Stein reported. 'The middle class make first-class militiamen, but only rarely professional soldiers.'

The working class produced the least useful of soldiers, Stein continued. They might be the most numerous. They were also the least valuable, deficient in physique and education. They became professional soldiers only out of desperation.

The best military material, predictably, were the yeoman farmers. 'The peasant's son has been the best soldier as long as there have been armies', Stein declared. He might be unresponsive to big ideas. But he was very loyal.[55]

That the army was an organ of the state comparable to the civil service and the diplomatic corps was another of Stein's first premises.[56] But this left room for doubt about a service in many ways distinctly separate, and in others rather more equal. It was also less equal to the extent that service imposed certain statutory limits on immigration, marriage and suffrage.[57] In time the inequalities changed in both directions, and in ways that might have provoked second thoughts even from Stein. But no one, whether of the left or right, argued seriously that there had been any quantum jump, any discontinuity in the army's position. It was doing what it had done from the beginning, perhaps only more so. By 1914 well-subsidised paramilitary fan clubs, youth groups and veterans' organisations enrolled hundreds of thousands. Cross-contacts extended even to the Boy Scouts, though the pitch was more conventionally aimed at the sons of small tradesmen and farmers.[58] 'At least it was something to try to establish contacts with the majority of the country's youth', one commentator observes a little self-consciously.[59]

The post-retirement problem was itself illuminating of the army's differences and difficulties. What other public agency so regularly, and with so little reciprocity, solved its problems by passing them on to others? In 1900 the post office employed about 38 per cent of the year's retiring NCOs, in 1914 about 42 per cent of a total that had itself doubled in the intervening years.[60] There were still an estimated 16,000 retired NCOs in need every year by 1914. There was also a solidly organised pressure group working on their behalf, despite its members' characteristic reservation about being mistaken for a union. Other government employees were understandably exasperated about a policy that made public jobs a substitute for adequate pensions.[61]

Officers, by comparison, could make it into the diplomatic service with relatively little difficulty, an adequate private income permitting. It was estimated that a year of diplomatic service cost up to 15,000 marks, in St Petersburg up to 18,000 marks of personal income, compared with the 5,000 mark pension a captain looked forward to after twenty-five years service.[62]

Retired officers were otherwise hard to employ for reasons having more to do with themselves than with the economy. Despite speculations about a prototypical military-industrial complex,[63] officers were basically disinclined to go into business after retirement. Given the social squeamishness of contemporary society, there was an understandable reluctance to take jobs where they might have to work under a retired NCO. As might be imagined, a number of retired officers found jobs with the burgeoning veterans' and 'patriotic' organisations.[64] The proposal by a liberal pamphleteer in 1914 that officers be treated like the general class of civil servants with improved educational standards and normal civil rights, for example, the right to vote and read what they wish, was defensible enough in the logic of 'a people in arms'.[65] But it was also emphatically not among those proverbial great ideas whose time had come.

The distance between soldiers and civil life, as Stein himself acknowledged uneasily, was manifest in the perpetuation of military law as a distinct category administered by military courts. Granted, he wrote, that military law had approximated the civil, criminal and public law of the empire. There remained an inconsistency. 'The task of our time is to promote not only an appropriate development of the respective statutes', Stein said, 'but a general understanding of the unity of the legal system.' This need not be difficult, he added with his characteristic optimism, providing people learned to regard the military establishment as an organic part of public life.[66]

But this was not so easy. Even the military oath of office, a pledge of loyalty not to the constitution but to the emperor, implied at least a degree of ambiguity, though Stein was largely unconcerned about it. To the extent that the army was an institution of public life subordinate to the constitutional process, he argued, there was no more need for the soldier to swear loyalty to the constitution than for the individual citizen or civil servant. The whole question, in his view, was anachronistic.[67]

But, as he himself implied, this only led to other difficulties. States and their armies had been groping towards a constitutional relationship since the end of the Thirty Years War, when military free enterprise gave way almost everywhere to that socialised and domesticated entity, the standing army. The conflict between command and administrative sovereignty had been resolved by a constitutional master-stroke: assumption of command by the sovereign himself, for example, Frederick the Great. The subordination of the Minister of War, that is, of the army's administrative chief, was a consequence and was then regularised by constitutional law.

'The essence of constitutionality consists of the people making laws and the executive agencies assuming responsibility for the faithful execution of these laws.' This was what the Minister of War was for. Unfortunately, as Stein himself had to admit, there was nothing very clear about the extent of the minister's responsibility.[68]

The untidiness, of course, was not peculiar to Germany. Even where the supreme command was established in law, there were problems enough – Americans have variously discovered and rediscovered them since at least the Civil War. The distinction between command and administrative responsibility, like all such distinctions, has never been without a degree of wishful arbitrariness. Third Republican France was an instructive case. The military débâcle of 1870–1 had at least led to the unchallenged principle of civilian control, with theoretical parliamentary sovereignty over military affairs and a Minister of War who was responsible, like any other minister, to Parliament. Germans believed this was how things in France actually worked. They were even vindicated to a point by the revolving door at the Ministry of War. Between 1871 and 1900, twenty-six ministers in thirty-two governments had already passed through it.[69]

For all that, French and German practice were considerably closer than might be imagined. Institutions are rarely sovereign merely because someone says they are. The French Assembly appreciated its incapacity for running the army early on. Despite distinguished exceptions, French ministers of war were ordinarily soldiers, the non-partisan professionals Stein regarded as essential,[70] and they usually got their way.

'An increasingly large sector of military affairs came to be handled by executive decrees', David Ralston writes. 'If it was necessary to enact a law pertaining to the army or to amend already existing law, it was generally done in the most perfunctory fashion. The Minister of War would introduce the measure and announce that it was needed. After a minimum of discussion, the vote would then take place.'[71]

Though budgeting was annual, it proved a frail reed for the practice of parliamentary control. Already filtered through the ministerial bureaucracy, the budget reached the Assembly floor practically ready for ratification. The intervening stage of committee discussion had to await the invention of standing committees in 1902. 'Because parliament was unable to compel the military to heed its abjurations and the soldiers were determined to manage their own affairs with only minimal governmental interference, the budget was an ineffective instrument of civilian control', Ralston concludes. French parliamentarians, like others then and since, tended to be proud of their record as co-operative military appropriators. The occasional sceptical voice proves the rule. If only French parliamentarians were as conscientious in debating requests as their counterparts in the Reichstag, an embittered French deputy mused in 1897, that is, in the middle of the Dreyfus affair.[72]

But the very conscientiousness of German debate, which was a fact, can be seen, paradoxically, as a symptom of something wrong. The relative casualness of the French Assembly reflected not only a basic consensus about the relationship of Frenchmen to their army, and vice versa, but a fundamental consensus about the sovereignty of the Assembly itself, that was to survive two world wars and the demise of the Third Republic.

The Reichstag had it harder. Conceived at best as one of a plurality of powers, its relationship to the army and the executive branch was at times defensive, at times co-operative, but almost always a relationship of adversaries. The competence of the executive, which French parliamentarians accepted *de facto*, was integral to the very theory of the German system. To the extent that the command function transcended administration and lodged in the emperor as commander-in-chief, the army was not only beyond parliamentary control, it was beyond the reach of the civil government.

Considerable ingenuity was in fact invested in assuring the military the greatest possible autonomy. But unreconstructed absolutism had come to an end, even in Prussia. The revised constitution of 1850, though in many ways the proverbial step back after at least two steps forward, required ministerial counter-signature of all sovereign acts, military decisions included. Like all Prussian ministers, the minister of war was henceforth answerable − if not directly accountable − to Parliament. Theoretically the distinction between command and administration obtained here too. But since the minister of war enjoyed uninterrupted royal support, the question never arose.

A second distinction, introduced in 1861 and subsequently maintained and even elaborated, distinguished 'acts of government', that is, budgetary and administrative decisions, from 'service regulations', that is, provisions having to do with the internal administration of such military matters as duels, discipline, recruitment and promotion. Never seriously challenged, its effect was to remove a fundamental sphere of military affairs not only from parliamentary review, but from civilian control. But under the Prussian, and the subsequent imperial, constitution the legitimacy of the distinction was dubious. Both specified counter-signature by the head of government, the prime minister and/or chancellor, not only for 'acts of government' in the sense of formal legislation, but also in the sense of 'decrees and dispositions' (*Anordnungen und Verfügungen*), a blue-blooded iconoclast, Baron Marschall von Biberstein, observed in 1911 in a study of the constitutional limits of the commander-in-chief.

But even Marschall concluded that the traditional practice was binding on grounds that the soldier, as such, was precluded from challenging the orders of his commander-in-chief. 'In its command authority, the crown retained a bit of absolutism until the end of the monarchy', a modern student of the imperial civil—military observes.[73]

Not only before, but after the end of the monarchy, at least one standard constitutional authority, Otto Mayer, regarded command of the military as a fourth branch of government.[74] Like the Bundesrat, the Reichstag, even the princes of the federated states, the chancellor was excluded from the line of command. It extended instead from the emperor to the various organs of command, the twenty-five corps commanders and even a proliferation of adjutants, for which William II had a particular weakness. In the full flower of the Wilhelmine system, some forty individuals and military agencies reported directly to the emperor.[75] His prerogatives included mobilisation, declaration of martial law, declaration of war, and conclusion of peace — though a declaration of war formally required Bundesrat ratification where no immediate attack of German territory was involved. While his authority was notably circumscribed, requiring the chancellor's counter-signature and positive evidence of invasion or public disorder within a specified area, the emperor could even subordinate all civil agencies to the military.[76]

Whatever the theory, practical reality was messy just as its underlying premises were arbitrary. Though there was no military equivalent of the chancellor, Bismarck exploited his budgetary responsibility to score a qualified victory over the army. He transformed the Prussian minister of war *de facto* into an imperial under-secretary, who had to appear at appropriate intervals to face the Reichstag.[77] On taking office in 1913 Falkenhayn was briefed by War Ministry officials who told him that the emperor's decisions on military administration fell under the chancellor's jurisdiction, and that therefore the war minister was responsible to the chancellor.[78]

Since Bismarck, parliamentary resistance had served as an excuse for systematic devaluation of the office of war minister. There was a corresponding inflation of the General Staff and the Military Cabinet, an odd creation of doubtful constitutionality, formally responsible for postings and promotions.[79] This had unfortunate consequences for the unity of command that had also been one of the particular glories of the reformed Prussian military. It should be added in fairness that the French had similar problems.[80] The creation of a distinct Imperial Headquarters in

1889 by an emperor who loved to play soldier (though he liked playing sailor even better) added another dimension of confusion.[81] The emperor saw the Prussian minister of war once a week, the chief of the Military Cabinet three times a week, the chiefs of the army and navy general staffs and the chief of the Naval Cabinet once a week, compared to a single weekly meeting with the chancellor and two with the chief of his Civil Cabinet.[82] The often-noted accessibility of the emperor to his military advisers reflects the place and weight of the military in the imperial German scheme of things. But it also reflects a fragmentation of real authority bordering on the chaotic, if not the irresponsible.

The emperor's dislike for domestic politics, his disdain for the Reichstag in particular and parliamentarians in general, achieved a kind of constitutional status of their own. They also inspired the emulation of millions of Germans, who looked to their sovereign for cues. Parliamentarians are conspicuously absent from the horsey goings-on so lovingly described in a typical contemporary weekly like the *Berliner Illustrierte Zeitung* with its voluminous reports of hunts, balls, garden parties and hotel ads. If His Majesty's ministers saw him only irregularly, the parliamentary leadership saw him rarely, and in most cases not at all. The most loyal of the loyal, Ernst Bassermann, the veteran National Liberal chairman, complained during the First World War that he had been received and interviewed at length by the King of Bulgaria. But never in his entire parliamentary career had he been received by the emperor he returned to serve in 1914 as a 60-year-old reserve major on active duty.[83]

This only meant that the emperor's lieutenants were left to tread the minefields of domestic politics without his support and guidance — or even sympathy as the risks increased and the rewards declined. The stakes and hazards of domestic politics grew apace with industrial productivity, trade volume and social diversity. Flooding the traditional channels of social deference and political manipulability, they inevitably overflowed the anachronistic riparian frontage presumed to separate domestic affairs from the classic preserves of foreign and military policy.

Like so many parliamentarians and Parliament watchers before and after, Max Weber, writing towards the end of the First World War, was gloomily convinced that the Reichstag's golden age was far behind it, that it had reached its peak of talent and influence in the years immediately after unification.[84] Helmut von Gerlach, himself a critical deputy of considerable sophistication, expressed both admiration for the Reichstag's increasing efficiency and strong reservations about its effectiveness in an instructive brochure published in 1907.

By formal standards, Gerlach's Parliament undeniably compared well with its institutional peers. Unlike Congress its members could be depended on to maintain a respectable degree of internal discipline. Compared with the House of Commons and the French Chamber, its committee system was well developed and its members relatively expert and conscientious. To a point, he conceded, they were all but compelled to responsibility by the expertise of the executive branch that confronted them and the unavailability of legislative staff to do their dirty work.

The introduction of parliamentary salaries in 1906 itself constituted a significant professional breakthrough. Though comparatively modest — Gerlach and his colleagues earned 3,000 marks and a rail pass between Berlin and their district compared to the US Representative's 20,000 marks ($5,000) or the French deputy's 12,000 (Ff 15,000) — they constituted an adequate reward for the Reichstag's official four-month session. Even the limitations on the session were arguably lined with silver though Gerlach, understandably, failed to see it that way. There were eight months a year in which the deputy could earn such supplementary income as was necessary to sustain his political career. The occupational make-up of the Reichstag, as Gerlach described it, was indirect evidence of accessibility. Whatever it was, Gerlach noted, the Reichstag was not an Academy of Who's Who Entries (*Akademie der nationalen Berühmtheiten*). Membership extended from trade unionists to country gentlemen. As Gerlach himself demonstrated, there was a sprinkling of 'vons' — though admittedly disproportionate — all the way across the House. On the other hand, businessmen, the nation's income leaders, and professors, who were among its status leaders, were under-represented.[85]

Despite credible evidence to the contrary, Gerlach was none the less convinced of the Reichstag's impotence. But he was also aware that its failings lay not in its stars but in itself. Later critics have been slow to grasp the hint. From the beginning, Gerlach noted, the House rules had permitted a systematic critique of the emperor's annual programme. But the rule had not been invoked for decades. Unlike the British question period, which could be called with relative ease, interpellation of an imperial minister required thirty signatures. Initiation of a subject for debate from the floor required fifty. The chancellor could also refuse to answer questions while ministers could theoretically attend Reichstag sessions at their discretion. Legislative initiative, predictably, was with the government. Gerlach estimated that the Reichstag devoted five of every six hours to government Bills. In a presumably typical period between February and May 1907 it had devoted no hours at all to consideration of its own Bills, though 100 of them had actually been submitted. But this, he sighed, was the whole sad story of the Reichstag. 'Its lack of influence is not so much the fault of the Constitution as of its own lack of energy', he said. 'It weaves and bobs where it could stand erect if it only wanted to.'[86]

In fact, it periodically did. It did so increasingly as successive governments lost their parliamentary support, or found it necessary to pay

through the procedural, and even the substantive, nose in order to keep
it. Colonial conditions in general, and an unpopular war against Southwest
African insurgents, had led in 1906 to a respectable parliamentary investigation and a government defeat. By a slim majority the Reichstag rejected
an interim budget to carry on the war. At least indirectly, it even shot
down His Majesty's Colonial Secretary.

In the backlash campaign that followed in 1907, Liberals of every hue
wrapped themselves ostentatiously in the imperial red, white and black to
win a famous, if short-lived, victory for conventional patriotism. But they
exacted a liberal price from Bülow, the incumbent Chancellor. There was a
significant liberalisation in the law of assembly and the definition of *lèse-
majesté*. A year later there was near rebellion in the entire House after the
emperor's interview with the *Daily Telegraph*. In its complicated aftermath, the emperor withdrew visibly, if not absolutely irreversibly, from his
problematic role as solo performer, and Bülow fell, *de facto* if not *de jure*,
for lack of a parliamentary majority. In 1909 he was replaced by Theobald
von Bethmann-Hollweg, the first chancellor to have made his career and
reputation as a reformer, though hardly a fire-eater, in domestic politics.[87]

But even as it tended to confirm Gerlach's suspicions, the Reichstag
managed to frustrate Bethmann's cautious hopes. Neither capable of, nor
disposed to, leadership, the Reichstag made it equally clear that it was
disinclined to fall in and follow. Though frustrated in tax reform and electoral reform by intransigence from right and left alike, Bethmann produced
a qualified success in 1911 with the new constitution for Alsace-Lorraine.
It was the first significant change in the status of the conquered provinces
since their annexation forty years before. But contemporary observers
could hardly overlook how Bethmann and the Reichstag both assumed the
roles described in the familiar French anecdote about the leader in hot
pursuit of his followers.

Previous chancellors as recent as Bülow had taken up electoral arms
against a sea of troubles. Premature dissolution of the House enhanced the
effect. The 1907 Reichstag was wisely allowed to run out its normal life.
When the electorate finally went to the polls in 1912, it still registered
the most dramatic dissatisfaction with the status quo since the founding
of the empire. Like its predecessors, the new House was ill-prepared for
national leadership. But it was uniquely well-prepared to make things hard
for the government. The extraordinary manoeuvring involved in electing
new leaders was a preview of things to come. At least partially commensurate with their role as the Reichstag's biggest party with 27.7 per cent of
the seats (and 34.8 per cent of the nation's votes), Social Democrats were
elected to deputy speakerships for the first time ever, though cold feet
eventually prevailed and the elections were reversed. In the end two
Progressives, that is left-of-centre Liberals, and a National, that is, right-of-
centre, Liberal, were elected to preside while Social Democrats accepted

co-chairmanships of the committee on the budget, the Reichstag's most powerful one, and of that on naval appropriations.[88] Since the navy, unlike the army, was financed entirely by the central government, and since it had been for nearly two decades the country's biggest consumer of military spending, the symbolic significance of the second chairmanship was hardly less than the first.

In its entire existence, the Reichstag had never been further left, the government so drastically outnumbered or the Conservatives so isolated. Over Conservative protests, the new majority proceeded to amend the standing rules to permit formal censure of the chancellor. In late January 1913 it put the rule to use, resoundingly rejecting the government's policy of expropriating Polish landowners in order to settle German peasants on eastern homesteads.[89]

The army understandably was also among the new Reichstag's major concerns. Again contrary to the general wisdom, parliamentary interest was not entirely new. For reasons of constitutional mandate, political sense or recollections of their high school Latin, there had always been deputies who took the position 'I am German, and nothing German is alien to me'. Constitutional limitations and administrative obstacles aside, the Reichstag could hardly ignore what was, in many ways, the most German of institutions, whether as a major item in their budget or a major factor in the life of their voters.

The internal organisation of the army, as well as its overall size, had figured repeatedly in Reichstag debates from 1874 on. The Minister of War himself had been compelled to testify in detail on the matter in 1896 before the budget committee was prepared to accept a compromise on the status of the cavalry. The cavalry again figured in the budget debates of 1905 and 1913 without attempts by the government to declare the subject constitutionally off-limits.[90] The budgetary function, it was tacitly conceded, inevitably included the cost of horses.

It was on the plausible grounds that colonial affairs were an internal matter and the indigenous Hereros in some sense German citizens that the Reichstag intervened in the Southwest African War in 1906.[91] Uniforms, another dimension of the budgetary role, were a recurring topic of consideration. Before the beginning of the century it was their pretentiousness that attracted legislative attention. Thereafter it was their visibility. At least indirectly, it was Reichstag concern that led to the introduction of field grey in place of the traditional Prussian blue in 1910.[92]

Between 1895 and 1900, at the height of the Dreyfus affair,[93] the Reichstag engineered a significant advance in military justice as part of a general reform of the criminal procedure. It brought general German usage into line with foreign and, as it happened, Bavarian practice by making courts martial public, and adding a military court of appeals.[94] Military discipline was a recurring topic in the budget debates of 1911–14. The budgetary requests for 1913 included comprehensive statistics on arrests and disciplinary actions.[95]

A number of factors favoured the Reichstag's expanding role and influence. Some followed from the nature of the representative function itself. This was a matter of practical interest to all parties, not only the Social Democrats. Like all armies, the German army was a factor in domestic politics, and business too. From the 1880s on, deputies regularly expressed interest in the location and supply of garrisons, for example, in their own districts. By the beginning of the century, even Conservatives had discovered this as a good thing. Mindful of the economic stagnation endemic in their East Elbian districts, they pleaded for small town garrisons, preferably in the Prussian east, where the environment was congenial to horses and uncongenial to Social Democrats.[96] In 1912 a kind of rustic popular front mobilised behind a Conservative request for extended furloughs for rural draftees to make them available for the harvest. It passed unanimously.[97] Concern for constituents played a role in a variety of related causes: discrimination against medical and engineering officers, preferential treatment for Guards regiments, mistreatment of recruits.

Three other considerations amplified the normal considerations of domestic politics. One was the rising standard of professionalisation. The long-term impact of universal conscription itself spilled over into the Reichstag. A sizeable number of deputies in every party had personal experience with military affairs. The larger parties, at least, had specialists. A second factor was implicit in acceptance of the empire, whether it was stoical or enthusiastic. Virtually no one denied any more that the empire was a fact. It made meaningful debate possible. The great debates of the nineteenth century had not so much been debates about the army as debates about the nature and future of the state. By the eve of the First World War army debates tended to be about the army. There were still radical differences of opinion. But not even Social Democrats denied the army's legitimacy. Like the empire itself, it was something they wanted to reform, not revolutionise, and it was the reformers who won the 1912 election. South German democrats and bread-and-butter trade unionists were conspicuous among the 110 Social Democratic deputies in the new Reichstag. Representatives of the traditionally 'radical' Prussian party were distinctly under-represented.[98]

The third consideration had to do with the nation's complicated military and diplomatic situation, of which the army was at least an indirect beneficiary. By 1911 it was generally appreciated that the empire's expensive romance with naval power had led to a dead end, diplomatically and domestically. The Treasury was on the edge of chaos, domestic support was in steep decline, surviving allies like Austria and Italy were showing signs of wear and potential unreliability, and foreign adversaries were closing in on three sides in unanticipated fraternity.[99]

As long as the army's size was fixed to population, and in relative decline *vis-à-vis* an ascendant Tirpitz, the Reichstag could be contained – at least to a point. But a government that brought in supplemental military budgets in 1911, 1912 and 1913 knew, or soon learned, what side its appropriations were buttered on. (The requests also included funds for the special infantry units needed to solve the tricky technical problems posed by the Belgian fort of Liege.)[100] The Krupp scandals hardly made the government's situation any easier.

In May, Bethmann traded off direct taxation of estates and incomes, an unprecedented concession to the left, for more troops. In the course of the debate he also heard incidental complaints about duels, non-recruitment of Jewish officers, the proliferation of adjutants, the size of horses' rations, military intervention in business rivalries, the use of Hussars at a royal wedding, violation of budgetary prerogatives in the unauthorised military acquisition of a piece of Berlin real estate, the anachronism of maintaining a German personal adjutant to the Tsar of Russia, and the inadequacies of the code of military justice.[101]

In November the government acquiesced in a joint weapons procurement committee, composed of civil servants, Reichstag deputies and representatives of the public. The British military attaché reported that the presumptive chairman of the committee had opposed it in May on constitutional grounds. But after all parties but the Conservatives had unanimously authorised the committee – and placed its formation and calendar entirely in the government's hands – the government had obviously reconsidered.[102]

On the last day of the year, the Saxon military attaché in Berlin reported an impending visit to Saxon facilities by Matthias Erzberger, the Centre's military budget expert. He warned his superiors that Erzberger wanted to see all relevant documents and plans having to do with accommodation of the army's newly authorised reinforcements. What to do? 'In order to make this self-important man cooperative', the attaché concluded, 'I recommend that all material he wishes to see be made available by his arrival on January 5.'[103] The more things remained the same, a commentator with an aphoristic turn of mind might have said, the more they were apparently changing.

References

1   See Michael Howard, 'Lord Haldane and the territorial army', *Studies in War and Peace* (New York, 1972), p. 92.
2   Wilhelm Groener, *Lebenserinnerungen* (Göttingen, 1957), pp. 59–60.
3   ibid.
4   Quoted in Russell Weigley, *History of the United States Army* (London, 1968), p. 281.

5   See Corelli Barnett, *Britain and her Army 1509–1970* (Harmondsworth, 1974), pp. 313–14; David Ralston, *The Army of the Republic* (Cambridge, Mass. and London, 1967), pp. 203ff.; Morris Janowitz, *The Professional Soldier* (New York, 1960), pp. 79ff.

6   See Marcus Cunliffe, *Soldiers and Civlians* (Boston, Mass. and Toronto, 1968), p. 220; Howard, *Studies in War and Peace*, p. 87.

7   Otto Graf zu Stolberg-Wernigerode, *Die unentschiedene Generation* (Munich, 1968), p. 198.

8   Martin Kitchen, *The German Officer Corps 1890–1914* (Oxford, 1968), p. 24.

9   Stolberg-Wernigerode, op. cit., p. 313.

10 Report by the Austrian military attaché in Berlin, 15 April 1914, Gstb. 25½, HHStA and Kriegsarchiv Vienna; Holger Herwig, *The German Naval Officer Corps* (Oxford, 1973), pp. 37ff.

11 Gordon Craig, *The Politics of the Prussian Army* (New York, 1964), p. 235.

12 Wilhelm Deist, 'Die Armee in Staat und Gesellschaft', in Michael Stürmer (ed.), *Das kaiserliche Deutschland* (Düsseldorf, 1970), p. 321.

13 Kitchen, op. cit., p. 24.

14 See Stolberg-Wernigerode, op. cit., p. 310; Herwig, op. cit., pp. 37ff.; Kitchen, op. cit., pp. 26–30.

15 Hans Herzfeld, *Die deutsche Rüstungspolitik vor dem Weltkriege* (Bonn and Leipzig, 1923), pp. 62ff.

16 Kitchen, op. cit., pp. 40ff.

17 Egmont Zechlin, *Die deutsche Politik und die Juden im ersten Weltkrieg* (Göttingen, 1969), p. 50.

18 Kitchen, op. cit., pp. 59–63.

19 ibid., pp. 115ff.

20 Wilhelm Höflich, *Affaire Zabern* (Berlin, 1931), p. 190.

21 Alastair Horne, *The Price of Glory* (Harmondsworth, 1964), p. 71.

22 Report from the British military attaché in Berlin, 13 November 1913, FO 371–1653, PRO London; and Kitchen, op. cit., p. 148.

23 Heinrich Hasenbein, 'Die parlamentarische Kontrolle des militärischen Oberbefehls im deutschen Reich von 1871 bis 1918', (unpublished dissertation, Göttingen University, 1968), pp. 65ff., 124.

24 Kitchen, op. cit., pp. 148ff.

25 ibid., p. 170.

26 See Ralston, op. cit., pp. 258ff.

27 Höflich, op. cit., p. 190.

28 Kitchen, op. cit., p. 182.

29 Stolberg-Wernigerode, op. cit., pp. 322–3.

30 Quoted by Adolf Gasser, 'Deutschlands Entschluss zum Präventivkrieg 1913–14', in Marc Sieber (ed.), *Discordia Concors, Festgabe für Edgar Bonjour* (Basle, 1968), fn. p. 179.

31 Lorenz von Stein, *Die Lehre vom Heerwesen* (Stuttgart, 1872), p. 191.

32 Groener, op. cit., pp. 59–60.

33 See Stolberg-Wernigerode, op. cit., p. 321.

34 Examples can be seen in the library of the Bundesarchiv/Militärarchiv, Freiburg.

35 Stolberg-Wernigerode, op. cit., p. 307.

36 ibid., p. 314.

37 Groener, op. cit., pp. 59–60.

38 M10, Bd. 41, 'Aufzeichnungen der Vertrauenskommission des Reichstags über die militärische und politische Lage Deutschlands am 24 April 1913', HStA Stuttgart.

39 Friedrich von Bernhardi, 'Das Heer', in D. Sarason (ed.), *Das Jahr 1913* (Berlin and Leipzig), 1914, pp. 63ff.
40 See William McElwee, *The Art of War* (Bloomington, Ind. and London, 1974), pp. 298ff.
41 Horne, op. cit., pp. 18–21.
42 Ralston, op. cit., pp. 319ff.
43 See D. W. Brogan, *The Development of Modern France* (New York, 1966), pp. 466–7; Barbara Tuchman, *The Guns of August* (New York, 1963), pp. 58–61; B. H. Liddell Hart, *Reputations* (London, 1928), pp. 23ff.
44 Karl Buchheim, *Das deutsche Kaiserreich* (Munich, 1969), p. 173.
45 Bundesrath, Session von 1880/1, Nr. 25, 'Entwurf eines Gesetzes, betreffend die gerichtliche Verfolgung von Personen des Soldatenstandes wegen Diensthandlungen nebst Begründung', 4 February 1881; Session von 1881/2, Nr. 38, 'Bericht der vereinigten Ausschüsse für das Landheer und die Festungen, für Seewesen und Justizwesen über den Entwurf eines Gesetzes' usw., 23 March, 1882.
46 See Kaethe Mengelberg, 'Lorenz von Stein', in Lorenz von Stein, *The History of the Social Movement in France* (Totawa, NJ, 1964), pp. 3–39.
47 Stein, *Die Lehre*, p. 274.
48 ibid., p. 12.
49 ibid., p. 139.
50 See Herbert Lüthy, 'Das Ende einer Welt 1914', in his *In Gegenwart der Geschichte* (Cologne and Berlin, 1967), p. 304.
51 ibid., pp. 1–2.
52 ibid., pp. 30–1.
53 ibid., p. 156.
54 ibid., p. 64.
55 ibid., pp. 14ff.
56 ibid., pp. 5–6.
57 ibid., pp. 167ff.
58 Kitchen, op. cit., pp. 133–42.
59 Stolberg-Wernigerode, op. cit., pp. 337–8.
60 Deist, op. cit., p. 325.
61 Kitchen, op. cit., p. 121.
62 ibid., p. 128.
63 See Volker Berghahn, *Rüstung und Machtpolitik* (Düsseldorf, 1973).
64 Stolberg-Wernigerode, op. cit., p. 322.
65 Ernst Arnold, *Mars regiert die Stunde* (Basle, 1914), pp. 26–7.
66 Stein, *Die Lehre*, pp. 142ff.
67 ibid., pp. 166–7.
68 ibid., pp. 118–20.
69 Ralston, op. cit., pp. 138ff.
70 Stein, *Die Lehre*, p. 123.
71 Ralston, op. cit., p. 94.
72 ibid., p. 126.
73 Eckart Busch, *Der Oberbefehl* (Boppard, 1967), p. 17.
74 ibid., p. 18.
75 Deist, op. cit., p. 316; Ludwig Rüdt von Collenberg, *Die deutsche Armee von 1871 bis 1914* (Berlin, 1922), p. 115.
76 Busch, op. cit., pp. 30–2.
77 ibid., pp. 38–45.
78 E. R. Huber, *Deutsche Verfassungsgeschichte*, Vol. 4 (Stuttgart, Berlin, Cologne and Mainz, 1969), p. 530.

79   Kitchen, op. cit., pp. 7—9.
80   Ralston, pp. 138ff.
81   See Kitchen, op. cit., pp. 16ff.; Herwig, op. cit., pp. 16ff.
82   Craig, *The Politics*, p. 240.
83   Theodor Eschenburg, *Das Kaiserreich am Scheideweg* (Berlin, 1929), pp. x—xi, 31ff.
84   Max Weber, *Gesammelte Politische Schriften* (Tübingen, 1958), pp. 301ff.
85   Helmut von Gerlach, *Das Parlament* (Frankfurt, 1907), pp. 1ff.
86   ibid., pp. 85ff.
87   See Konrad H. Jarausch, *The Enigmatic Chancellor* (New Haven, Conn. and London, 1973), pp. 45ff.
88   See Beverly Heckart, *From Bassermann to Bebel* (New Haven, Conn. and London, 1974), pp. 197ff.
89   Huber, op. cit., p. 510.
90   Hasenbein, op. cit., pp. 9ff.
91   ibid., p. 152.
92   ibid., pp. 38ff.
93   See Ernst-Otto Czempiel, *Das deutsche Dreyfus-Geheimnis* (Munich, Berne and Vienna, 1966), pp. 77—8.
94   Deist, op. cit., pp. 313—14.
95   Hasenbein, op. cit., pp. 65ff.
96   ibid., p. 42.
97   ibid., p. 104.
98   Fritz Fischer, *Krieg der Illusionen* (Düsseldorf, 1969), p. 52.
99   See Berghahn, op. cit., pp. 83—4.
100 Herzfeld, op. cit., pp. 11ff.
101 ibid., pp. 106ff., 162.
102 Report from the British military attaché in Berlin, 17 November 1913, FO 371—1653/3676, PRO London.
103 Berichte des Militärbevollmächtigten 1913, 1434, StA Dresden.

4 *En route to Zabern: Alsace*

How terrible are the weaknesses of power!
(Stanislaw Jerzy Lec)

In Alsace, where army and Reichstag intersected hundreds of miles from Berlin, the speed, course and risks of change in imperial Germany could be observed to particular advantage.

The problems of Alsace were intrinsically interesting. They were also prominent among the empire's unfinished business, high on the priority lists of natives, foreigners and Germans alike. Perhaps still more interesting was what contemporaries almost universally regarded as the 'Problem of Alsace'. Endowed with transcendental significance, it enjoyed the symbolic importance, the mystical passion and patriotic archaeology that were invested elsewhere in the Eastern, the Irish, the Polish, the Jewish Question. Perhaps most interesting was the fact that so attractive, agreeable and well endowed a place should have become a problem at all.

Notwithstanding the salvoes of learned reference that accompanied it, the problem was in fact a relatively recent discovery. Other generations, before and after, took a different view. Geography and culture had combined to make Alsace a province. Considerably more than an administrative convention, it was rather less than a nation. Well into modern times the map of Europe had been conspicuous for such things. There were those who believed, and subsequently rediscovered, that they were among the Continent's peculiar glories.

In a dynastic Europe where provinces were rather the rule than the exception, Alsace had made a good thing of its provincialism. There were provinces where life was hard and the beauty of the landscape was a consolation for the hardship it required of people. Alsace was not one of them.

Its white wines were marginally tarter, its characteristic garnished sauerkraut and goose liver were marginally richer, its Alemannic dialect was marginally quainter, its culture was marginally more flavourful than those around it. In Alsace the bourgeois style and virtues, regarded elsewhere with ambivalence and even antipathy, were known, admired and savoured. 'Bourgeois' itself was commonly understood as a good thing to be.[1] 'As happy as God in France', Germans were known to say as they reflected on the favoured state of their western neighbours. The same goodness was also at home below the Vosges on that western bank of the Rhine, where Germany stopped, in most people's perception of things, but France had not begun.

Its very success, in a sense, was its undoing. A congenial home for the Catholic high culture of medieval western Europe, it subsequently played its part in that remarkable flowering of Rhenish humanism that extended from Rotterdam to Basle. It then lined up almost without resistance on the Lutheran side as the Reformation reached the Rhine. A Protestant haven for French reformers on the flank of a major Catholic power and an outpost of the old German empire on the flank of an increasingly potent and self-assertive national kingdom of France, Alsace became something of a European power in its own right. It then became a theatre of the religious and dynastic wars that crossed and recrossed the Rhine. Even the architecture shows the transformation in the militant geometry of Vauban's fortified town of Neuf-Breisach alongside the gothic spires of Strasbourg and Thann.

A turning-point came in 1681 with the annexation of the German city-republic of Strasbourg by the armies of Louis XIV. It was followed by the incremental annexation of the rest of the province in succeeding decades. The motives were strategic and economic. The intention was fundamentally defensive: liquidation of an imperial bridgehead on the French side of the Rhine. The *mission civilisatrice* so characteristic of subsequent French enterprise from Strasbourg to Tahiti followed only at a distance. On the contrary, French administrators were fundamentally respectful of the cultural, and even the political, status quo. If Alsace was governed by French viceroys, Alsatians continued to be governed in their daily lives by local oligarchs despite some French immigration and substantial reconversion to Catholicism. Though French culture arrived not only with the new immigrants, but as an affectation of the wealthy natives, most Alsatians continued to speak their German dialect at home and in public.

Paradoxically a province that had been both German and cosmopolitan became more, not less, provincial for the introduction of a second culture. The key to the paradox was the political reorientation. Alsace lost contact with German culture without becoming significantly French.[2] The French cultural institutions of Strasbourg – theatre, salons and the like – did well enough. They were supported both by the French colony and the local bourgeoisie. But they were fundamentally foreign, like the German theatres of Prague or the Georgian culture of Dublin. Germans from across the Rhine were both attracted and repelled by them. For the first time in decades the University of Strasbourg became rather popular as Germans of real talent settled ambivalently in the shadow of the cathedral, resolved both to resist French culture and enjoy it.

In the years before the French Revolution, Strasbourg was a home to Goethe, Herder and Lenz, and cradle of a literary movement called 'Storm and Stress' that affected Germans for decades afterwards. Indirectly at least, it even left its marks on the French. But Alsatians were unmoved, and probably mostly unaware of it. What moved them, relatively anyway, was German music. Unlike Parisians, Strasbourg audiences had the sense to admire Mozart on his way through the town in 1777.[3] While the decorative arts were demonstratively French, it was no accident that musical life, both sacred and secular, continued to be dominated by Germans of some distinction, including Franz Xavier Richter, himself a respectable minor composer, and Haydn's student Ignaz Pleyel.

What upset the fragile equilibrium of provincial life were two things. One was inevitably that universal shaker of European equilibria, the French Revolution. The other, at least a partial function of the first, was the discovery by successive generations of Europeans that people were not meant to live in provinces, but in national states.

Other west European provinces, endowed by their history and geography with luck and native virtuosity, adjusted to the circumstances by declaring themselves nation-states in their own right, and getting away with it. It came to be accepted without great difficulty that the French- and German-speaking populations between Geneva and Basle were Swiss. Despite some scepticism and resistance, it was later agreed that other French- and Dutch-speaking populations in Flanders and Brabant were Belgians. As late as 1907 Norway, by mutual agreement, ceased to be a part of Sweden.

But there was no serious chance of doing the same with Alsace, for all that anti-German particularism in the years before the First World War came to be known, revealingly, as Alsatian nationalism. In part the obstacle was the Alsatians themselves. Hitherto largely passive, they had learned something fundamentally important during the French Revolution and its Napoleonic aftermath. For the first time they genuinely liked being part of France.

Germans, who had come to startling new conclusions about their own national identity in the course of the Napoleonic experience, were surprised, even appalled. On reaching the Rhine in 1813 they found that the Alsatians were indifferent, even hostile, to what a new generation of German nationalists assumed was their liberation. 'What is the German's Fatherland?' Ernst Moritz Arndt had asked in innumerable stanzas en route from St Petersburg to Köningsberg with the advancing armies. 'Wherever German tongue is heard', was the answer. Generations of German fire-breathers, who fondly quoted him on every imaginable occasion, found the answer self-evident. But it was not, nor was it ever to become, self-evident to the Alsatians.

Cheerfully untouched by the French language despite a century and a quarter of contact, they had discovered great attractiveness in French revolutionary politics. The Place des Vosges, renamed in their honour in faraway Paris, bore witness to their enthusiasm. Despite its name, the 'Marseillaise', the revolutionary hymn itself, was composed in Strasbourg, and translated without difficulty into Alemannic.[4] In the years that followed, an impressive number of marshals' batons — Kellermann's, Schérer's, Rapp's, Kléber's — emerged from Alsatian knapsacks.

German appeals to the glories and parochial 'liberties' of the imperial past left Alsatians unmoved. It was the cautious perpetuation of just such anachronisms that had cost the *ancien régime* the loyalty of the great majority of Alsatians. It was their liquidation by the revolution that won Alsatians to the new regime of — as they saw it — *freiheit, gleichheit, brüderlichkeit*. As Franz Schnabel noted, the revolution meant freedom for the peasant and his property and a new legal system based on freedom of contract for the bourgeoisie. Alsatian trade and business flourished within a large, unitary market area. The heavy industry of neighbouring Lorraine owed its birth to Napoleon. The corporate restrictions of the German past gave way to the advantages of central administration and personal freedom still unknown in Germany.[5]

But even this would hardly have sufficed had Alsatian preferences not coincided with the rather different interests of the European powers. The Congress of Vienna was not sentimental about local self-determination. But after a quarter century of struggle with the demons of unleashed nationalism it was not exactly sympathetic to national enthusiasms either.

It was part of the irony of postwar Strasbourg that Josef Görres, the Rhenish-German patriot who had so passionately advocated German recovery of Alsace, soon afterwards sought asylum there from the conservative restoration on his own side of the Rhine. To the Strasbourg-educated Metternich and to Talleyrand it was clear that south German acquisition of Alsace, and the compensation of Prussia it would require could only mean trouble. On the other hand, perpetuation of the last great Bourbon conquest under the restored Bourbon Crown was considered a useful contribution to postwar stability.

And so the Alsatians remained an anomaly, generally respected by subsequent French regimes, whether royal, republican or imperial. They were German-speaking Frenchmen. Even accounting for a substantial French-speaking minority in the annexed part of Lorraine, nearly 80 per cent of the people of the province the Germans conquered in 1871 reported German as their native language.[6] As Jack Morrison has said, people were not anti-German because they spoke French. They spoke French — to the extent they did — because they were anti-German.[7]

The enmity, that was widely and a little simplistically understood to be one of the fixed points of European political life, had to do with the motives as well as the fact of German annexation. German motives in 1815 had been an odd mix of fervour and calculation. German motives in 1870 were the same, but somewhat more so, as though Germans had taken it into their heads to play Shakespeare's Henry V to an Alsatian Kate. 'It is possible dat I could love de enemy of Alsace?' Alsatians might have asked. 'In loving me', the Germans might have replied, 'you should love the friend of Alsace, for I love Alsace so well that I will not part with a village of it.'[8]

It was the reappearance of a Bonaparte on the French scene that had originally inspired Marx's famous observation about the repetition of historical events as tragedy and farce. His reappearance on the German scene as challenger and potential invader in 1870 implied a kind of repetition too. Only this time Marx, and others, might have argued that the sequence of tragedy and farce was reversed.

Alone among its countrymen, the central committee of the German Social Democratic Party deplored the annexation of Alsace-Lorraine. Their statement reads like Görres or Ernst Mortiz Arndt in reverse. 'In the common interest of France and Germany, in the interest of peace and freedom, in the interest of western civilization against oriental barbarism, German workers will never patiently accept the annexation of Alsace-Lorraine.'[9] One irony of the story is that August Bebel, one of the signatories, lived to represent a Strasbourg constituency in the Reichstag. As enlightened conservatives in the Berlin and Strasbourg governments duly noted, it was another irony that the SPD itself became one of the few German institutions the Alsatians voluntarily accepted.[10] 'Alsatians cease to be Alsatians', said Jules Guesde, the pope of French Marxism, 'when they become Socialists.'[11]

Other Germans regarded the annexation as divine justice. It was not only God's judgement on Bonapartes, but on a congenitally aggressive French nation. With little difficulty military arguments were found − or actually lightly dusted − to justify perpetuation of the German presence as an elementary consideration of national security. More ironical still, similar arguments were found within two generations for the restoration of a French bridgehead on the Rhine. For at least another generation, the assumption of congenital German aggressiveness was part of the common currency of European politics.

It was widely believed that Bismarck himself had opposed the annexation, but capitulated to the raucous demands of domestic hawks. But the source seems to have been Bismarck himself. Particulars, for example, the fortress of Metz, were momentarily negotiable. Alternatives were actually proposed, including Luxembourg, money or a mutually acceptable French possession like, of all places, Saigon.[12] But there were far too many German interests at stake to buy them off. The Prussian army wanted the bridgehead and the fortresses of Strasbourg and Metz. German liberals wanted their national state. Southwest Germans, after 200-odd years of recurrent invasions, wanted insulation from another fit of the *furor francese*. German Catholics, distinctly unhappy about the way things were stacking up against them, were happy to be reinforced by two new provinces where Catholics constituted 80 per cent of the population.[13]

There was even a dramatic economic bonus. In 1870 French and German iron and steel production, the linchpin of contemporary power, had been virtually equal. By 1910, thanks in considerable part to the acquisition of the ores and industry of Lorraine, German production outstripped French by factors of up to 4:1.[14] But despite much *post facto* speculation, there is little evidence that iron, at least, had been on Bismarck's mind.[15]

The indigenous population had the choice of taking or leaving it. The choice was familiar enough by the standards of the seventeenth and eighteenth centuries, and even quaintly humane by the standards of the twentieth. But for many people, particularly the Alsatian bourgeoisie, the choice was difficult and even tragic. Most stayed on. But whether for reasons of family, business, patriotic loyalty, or some combination of all of them, a startling number left rather than become, officially, German. It was estimated that 480,000 emigrated between 1871 and 1914, about 300,000 of them to France. The figure is remarkable for provinces whose aggregate population at the time of the annexation was only about 1½ million, and that had reached little more than 1.8 million forty years later.[16] About 30 per cent of the emigrants left during the transitional period directly after the war, but the emigration obviously continued. Displaced persons from the lost provinces continued to be conspicuous in French public life through the German period, among them a Dreyfus from Mulhouse — though his conspicuousness was not intentional. Others married the first available Frenchman, took out Swiss citizenship or married their daughters to Swiss.[17] Between 1871 and 1905 the emigrants were replaced by an estimated 176,000 Germans from the other side of the Rhine.[18] They came to be known as 'Old Germans', not only by the Alsatians but in reference to themselves.

Theoretically, and even practically, non-fraternisation was the order of the day. Liberated brothers or not, official Germany was disposed to treat them as unreliable, a position that was both objectively defensible and self-fulfilling. Administrative responsibility passed only reluctantly and ambiguously from a military governor to an imperial governor, a *Statthalter*, literally a viceroy. As late as 1902 the governor's arsenal still included a 'dictatorship' paragraph. It authorised him to take any appropriate step to restore or preserve order without declaration of martial law or the risk of contravention by the Reichstag. The emperor was, and remained, sovereign.

Symptomatically the first governor, Manteuffel, was a professional general of impeccably conservative Prussian origin. It was typical of his situation that his shrewd efforts to find conservative common ground with the local notables, who constituted the Alsatian establishment, were regarded with distrust by his military colleagues. They suspected him of being soft on Alsatians.[19]

Bismarck, one of the great masters at viewing with alarm, found grounds for concern as far afield as Ireland. The Catholic danger was everywhere, he told the Reichstag in 1873. With the passing of the anti-Catholic *Kulturkampf* in 1878, the basis of the argument naturally shifted. But the presumable danger was the same. In effect the defence of the Upper Rhine began at the Irish Sea. German diplomats, including Bismarck's son Herbert, continued to take a dark view of any imaginable step towards Home Rule as a threat to the Alsatian domino.[20]

Their position was mirrored by British Conservatives. 'My alternative policy is that parliament should enable the government of England to govern Ireland', Salisbury declared in 1886. 'Apply that recipe honestly, consistently, and resolutely for 20 years and at the end of that time you will find that Ireland will be fit to accept any gifts in the way of local government or repeal of coercion laws that you may wish to give her.'[21] Heard from behind a screen, the speaker could have been an imperial governor in Strasbourg.

In the event, the twenty-year prognosis was just about right – at least in Alsace-Lorraine. The press law was successfully liberalised in 1898 after an abortive attempt at repeal of the 'dictatorship' paragraph by the Reichstag in 1895. The emperor himself repealed it rather abruptly in 1902. Provincial administration was liberalised in increments. Successive chancellors made constitutional reform a legislative priority, including provision for some degree of home rule.[22]

But this did not mean the provinces had been Germanised and/or pacified, any more than it implied that conservative Germans had come to take a more tolerant view of their regional peculiarities. People frequently see what they want to see – and also hear what they want to hear, to judge by the extraordinary sensitivity of German ears to the slightest whisper of the 'Marseillaise' or the occasional provocative shout of 'vive la France' that persisted throughout the entire period of German administration. It was inevitable that Prussian officers would feel uneasy about a population so Catholic, so liberal, so bourgeois, so egalitarian, in any case so different from themselves; that dedicated nationalists would resent people so cold to what they considered their secular accomplishment.

Self-parody came easily, but perhaps a little more easily to the Germans. They had more reasons, but also more opportunities, to make themselves look silly, whether in the discharge of their official duties or in what they viewed as their patriotic mission. 'In those days it was impossible for a sparrow to fall off a roof without getting entangled in a flag', one Alsatian recalled.[23] Perceived and even addressed by Germans as 'the natives', Alsatians replied with the snobbery and contempt that tend everywhere to be the weapons of the weak. 'They lived the way the Greek colony used to live in Muslim Anatolia', an Alsatian said of his fellow countrymen. Business was one thing. Marriage was something else again. *'Commercium, sed non connubium.'*[24]

The Germans Germanised as best they could with differential results, and indifferent success. The anomalous constitutional status of the provinces was itself a concession, both to German domestic opinion and to the indigenous population. If autonomy was out of the question, so was military government. Annexation of the provinces by the adjacent German states of Baden and Bavaria, let alone by Prussia, was guaranteed to provoke massive resistance on both sides of the Rhine.[25] Sanctions continued to apply in German law, and also in the French law that antedated it. But they were invoked only rarely and then as though it were a kind of tantrum. Nothing in the history of the press or public life suggests very conclusive deterrence of whatever it was that was supposed to be deterred. There were infrequent squabbles about language, including the local dialect. But there are also indications that German schoolmasters were less zealous about their patriotic mission than has traditionally been assumed.[26]

The authorities went to some trouble to preclude any ambiguity of citizenship.[27] In an age of almost unbelievably casual travel and immigration,[28] they imposed special requirements on foreign military personnel, including retired officers in mufti, and even applied them to their Austrian allies.[29] On grounds of national security they periodically denied visas and hunting licences. Petulance seems a more plausible reason. Rather than accept a French consulate in Alsace-Lorraine, they rejected foreign consulates altogether. Anybody who wanted to see a French consul had to go to Kehl on the Baden side of the Rhine.[30]

But thousands of people also crossed the borders to tour the Vosges, visit their relatives, conduct their business, pursue their studies. Local correspondents reported to French papers. There was even a presentable French-language press.[31] The press was a good index, not only of the intellectual life of the provinces but of the reluctant tolerance of an administration unwilling to face the risks involved in once again trying to make things tough.

In 1913 the government presented Bills and amendments in the Reichstag intended to restrict both freedom of association and the foreign-language, that is, French, press. But nothing more was heard of them.[32] Newspaper circulation increased substantially faster than the population. In 1908 Alsace alone boasted forty-four dailies, a number of them of considerable quality and individuality.[33]

Despite understandable misgivings, the authorities endured active local chapters of the Souvenir français, an organisation whose concern for French war graves and patriotic statuary went well beyond antiquarian or aesthetic interest.[34] In the years immediately before the First World War there was also an active French cultural life with imported lecturers of some distinction.[35] A German General Bullmoose deplored the way Alsatian bourgeois families continued to send their daughters to private schools, where they learned French from the nuns. 'Things have already reached a point where French is spoken in Protestant pastors' homes even in pure German districts in Lower Alsace', he added darkly, 'just because the lady of the house thinks it "nicer".'[36] For both German and French chauvinists it was an article of faith that in every Alsatian there was a Frenchman or Frenchwoman struggling to get out.

But the reality was more subtle. The protest movement of the earlier years receded, not only for reasons of intrinsic futility, but because of its own internal problems. Intransigence gave way to what one local observer called 'liberal opportunism'.[37] The 1876 election was a clue to what followed. The francophile liberal bourgeoisie abstained. As a result six of the eleven deputies elected to the Reichstag were Catholic priests. The Germans, who had first conquered, caught on fairly early that they could also divide. They first threw their weight in one direction, then the other. What catalysed Manteuffel's nominal dovishness was the concern of local notables to preserve an oligarchical status quo. There was a last spasm of protest in 1887, the year of General Boulanger, the darling of the French *révanchistes*, and the *Septennat*, the long-term military budget whipped through the Reichstag in the course of the war scare that followed. But the Alsatian tides had long since shifted to autonomism. Even this was understood with caution. One recent student finds only a single Liberal reference to autonomy between 1879 and 1900.[38] If direct election and home rule were to mean the triumph of *M. le Curé*, the Liberals preferred to take their chances on the status quo, the quasi-advisory Landesausschuss with its fifty-eight indirectly elected deputies, and its clubby, but thoroughly informal, relationship to the German administration.

By the 1890s, the shape of Alsatian politics had become increasingly remote from radical France. But it was no mystery to any observer of southern Germany. Politics was triangular. Liberals testified to the persistence of a pre-industrial republican tradition. Socialists profited from accelerated industrialisation, successful resistance to Bismarck, and their institutional hostility to the imperial status quo. As in Bavaria, political Catholicism met the needs of both domestic conservatism and local patriotism. Anti-secular and anti-Protestant, it was anti-Prussian practically by definition. The wavering integration of the Centre Party in the empire only reinforced Catholic particularism in Alsace-Lorraine. It was only in

1906, while France still glowed from a prodigious binge of anti-clericalism, that various groups merged to form a Centre Party at the provincial level.[39]

With neither a native gentry or a Protestant clientele to support it, indigenous Conservatism was marginal. As usual, the exception proves the rule. Zabern, the only Alsatian constituency with a Protestant majority, elected an indigenous Conservative to the Reichstag until 1912. He then lost in a run-off to a coalition of Liberals and Socialists, who had dumped their own candidate after the first round in order to support the eventual Liberal winner.[40]

In the long run, the convergence of Germany and Alsace-Lorraine was favoured by at least two fundamental factors. Impervious to specific vagaries in the Franco-German relationship, geography had been one all along. Of all the self-appointed Moseses who appeared over the centuries between Louis XIV and Bismarck to lead the provinces into one or another promised land, Napoleon had been right in ways he might himself have underestimated. Geography really was the province's destiny — or a good-sized piece of it. Historical chance had made Alsace a ping-pong ball instead of a Swiss canton. But it was, and remained, an Alemannic province largely interchangeable with any other. Paris might theoretically be the city of Alsatian dreams, Berlin the city of their waking humiliations. But Strasbourg was not much like either of them. It was like Freiburg in Baden, or Basle in Switzerland. The exodus of francophile Alsatians, the influx of Old Germans, only reinforced a social and demographic structure already there. There were plausible and legitimate reasons why Alsatians should feel that the German Reich was 'they', not 'we'. But neither incompatibilities of social structure nor politics were really among them.

Economic development was a second major source of convergence. Even Alsatians acknowledged it as one of the Reich's accomplishments. If political integration was partial and problematic, economic integration was rather successful. The Reich was one of the era's economic success stories. Alsatians enjoyed their share, for all that they contested its equity. Strasbourg, the provincial metropolis, doubled in population between 1870 and 1900. By the admittedly modest standards of urbanity of both German and French demographers, 53.2 per cent of Alsatians were urban in 1910, that is, lived in communes of over 2,000, compared to 44 per cent of Frenchmen. While agricultural employment fell from 45.2 per cent to 37.4 per cent between 1882 and 1907, industrial employment rose from 36.2 per cent to 38.6 per cent, tertiary activity from 18.6 per cent to 24 per cent, a near facsimile of the all-German averages of 34 per cent, 40 per cent and 26 per cent respectively. By contrast, the French agricultural sector, that employed 49.3 per cent in 1876 and 45.3 per cent twenty years later, still employed 43 per cent in 1906.[41]

The provinces periodically protested economic discrimination. The liberalised Caprivi tariffs of the early 1890s were demonstrably hard on Alsatian wines. The anticipated benefits of a domestic tobacco monopoly never materialised. Domestic heavy industry still had an uphill struggle against the steel producers of the Ruhr. Alsatian producers felt characteristically victimised when a Swiss—German treaty liberalised the import of fine thread already produced in Alsace, but not otherwise produced in Germany. From 1900 on, there was understandable indignation about the development of Kehl, the Rhine port on the Baden side. Construction of a Mosel canal remained a gleam in the eyes of local patriots, its repeated frustration by Prussian interests a source of heartburn.[42] In fact the canal was only opened in the 1960s, though then in the presence of both the presidents of France and West Germany.

But Alsatians also enjoyed the advantages of German growth, just as they also felt the consequences of French protectionism. Immediately after the annexation, Alsatian textile producers had opened new mills in France to exploit Germany's liberal tariffs while avoiding France's relatively stiff ones. Subsequent German tariffs also protected Alsace. The Méline tariffs of 1892, on the other hand, cut painfully into the Alsatian textile industry. Local growth industries – heavy machinery, chemicals, electrical equipment – held their own in the German market.[43]

Railways are the best index of contemporary infrastructural development. Like the school system and the extension of the Reich's exemplary social welfare system, they testify to the relative advantages of German administration. Between 1871 and 1913 rail mileage in Alsace-Lorraine more than doubled. Railway density, which was over 15 per cent greater than the Reich average, was over 40 per cent greater than in France. It was also clear where the trains were going. In 1913 about 26 per cent of the freight carried was internal. About 23 per cent was in transit to other destinations from other places of origin. But over 46 per cent of the freight was en route to, or from, Germany. Under 5 per cent was en route to, or from, France.[44]

Of course man does not live, nor are hearts and minds won, by freight trains alone. But even taking the darkest possible German view, economic integration should logically have been preferable to no integration at all. On the other hand, like everything in Alsace-Lorraine, this had a logic of its own, whose premises went back to 1871. Was Alsace a bridgehead and a fortified glacis aimed at the French, or a liberated German province? Was the Reich a federally constituted German national state or the extension of Prussia by other means? The questions remained distressingly familiar. But the answers varied, evidence again of how things changed while seemingly remaining the same.

A famous test case took place in Grafenstaden in spring 1912. Contemporaries were to recall it typically as 'the affair' after the assertion of high principle, as so frequently happened, had turned an otherwise insignificant local incident into a matter of national interest.

What was at stake was a Prussian locomotive contract with a large local plant. The issue was the undeniable francophilia of a company executive, who had allowed the 'Marseillaise' to be sung and the tricolour to be displayed at a company picnic. He had also discriminated almost totally against the employment of Old Germans in a workforce of nearly 2,000.

Contrary to provincial suspicions, there was no official action until a maliciously motivated protest from an Old German printer in town reached the Prussian Railway Commission in Berlin. But what followed was both firm and predictable. The government of Alsace-Lorraine was asked to investigate. The contract was cancelled, contingent on dismissal of the offending executive. Provincial politicians protested. The emperor got angry. The Reichstag got excited. The Chancellor tried unsuccessfully to be conciliatory.

In the end, the executive was transferred to a sister plant in French Belfort, business resumed and the source of the complaint went broke as the result of a boycott. Everybody assumed something important had been learned in the meanwhile, but differed on what it was. Official Germany was prepared to buy, not beat, Alsatians into co-operation argued the one side. Therefore things change. Alsatians were congenitally unreliable or Germans were congenital autocrats, argued the other side. Therefore things remain the same.[45]

An alternative test was the latest round of the recurring debate on the Mosel canal in early 1914, that is, after the pandemonium over Zabern. The Prussian Minister of Public Works took the traditional position that what was good for Alsace-Lorraine was not necessarily good for the country. The canal was bad for national security, he said. It would jeopardise supply of southwest German industrial areas. It would encourage what was already a regrettable intimacy between France and Luxembourg, and presumably with adjacent Lorraine.

He was challenged not only by Georges Weill, a Socialist deputy from Alsace, but by Bassermann of the National Liberals, and even by Nobis, the official representative of a provincial government the emperor still appointed. Weill, the spokesman of Alsatian labour, argued that the canal would be good for Alsace-Lorraine. Bassermann, the spokesman of patriotic German management, argued that it would be good for Germany. Appealing to *noblesse oblige*, Nobis argued that opposition to the canal was politically bad for Prussia.

Indignant about the substance, but still more about the form, the Prussian minister turned to Bethmann for aid in the prevention of any further such embarrassment. Bethmann only played the incident down. Nobis was supported from Strasbourg by return mail. It was regrettable that a confrontation between Alsace-Lorraine and Prussia should have taken place in the Reichstag rather than the Bundesrat or in the respective state legislatures, the Alsatian under-secretary, Count Roedern, conceded coolly. But it was 'obvious' that Alsace-Lorraine's position in the matter should be different from Prussia's. The only issue was where and when the question should be discussed.[46] Things remained the same: Alsace-Lorraine was governed, as it had been since the 1870s, by an imperial governor. Things changed: in 1914 a governor who knew what was good for him looked after the economic interests of his involuntary constituents, for his own sake as well as theirs.

Like almost anything else in Alsace-Lorraine, this was nowhere near as simple as it appeared. On the face of it, economic development of the provinces was a corollary of political integration. But depending on circumstances, it was also an alternative to political integration. Under the rather special circumstances of 1914, it was, in fact, the only alternative readily available to an administration momentarily, and perhaps definitively, at the end of its tether.

Both the German and the provincial dilemma again went back to the annexation. It was reflected in the very fluidity of the provinces' constitutional status. The governor's office was an index of German ambivalence. Devised in 1879 as an alternative to government from Berlin, it resolved existing ambiguities at the cost of new ones. Theoretically the governor was sovereign, or close to it. He was a direct appointee of the emperor and 'responsible', like the chancellor, for administration of the provinces under his authority. Theoretically he also remained subordinate to the Bundesrat, where Alsace-Lorraine had no votes, and to the chancellor who was responsible for legislation affecting the empire of which Alsace-Lorraine was understood to be an integral part. As elsewhere, the special constitutional status of the army added an extra degree of complication. By its nature Alsace-Lorraine was an area of particular military interest. In theory the civil and military authorities might be equal. But to an even greater degree than usual in imperial Germany, there was the inevitable question of what this might mean in real life.[47]

In practice, the complexities of theory could often be fudged. Beginning with Manteuffel himself, successive governors and/or their lieutenants both claimed and achieved a degree of autonomy, despite the conservative opposition of the military and civilians. Manteuffel enjoyed the heft of a retired Prussian field-marshal. But his successor, Hohenlohe-Schillingsfürst, was Bavarian, Catholic and a former ambassador to Paris, all characteristics that testified to a changing perception of the job. His arrival was viewed as a symbolic test, and subsequently as a symbolic victory — or defeat, depending on the point of view. He was met at Strasbourg station by the commanding general and the military authorities. The sentries, who were posted at the gate of the governor's palace during Manteuffel's incumbency, remained there under Hohenlohe.[48]

During the Boulanger scare of 1887, the course was reversed or at least suspended. Hohenlohe was notified that in the event of war executive authority devolved upon the military. His request for a commission was denied. There was nothing to gain by one anyway, Bismarck informed him a bit disingenuously. He was a general himself, Bismarck said. He still had no authority to proclaim martial law, but could find something to do if war broke out.[49] The governor lived to enjoy his inadvertent revenge. Bismarck, the super-star, retired abruptly to private life in 1890. Hohenlohe, the team player, succeeded to the chancellorship from his Strasbourg office in 1894.

Despite its 200,000 mark salary, the second highest in the imperial schedule,[50] the governor's position was never among the empire's most prestigious, let alone most popular, jobs. The frustrations attendant on service to so many masters can be imagined. The career of Hohenlohe, probably the most undistinguished of the four governors to serve through early 1914, is exceptional for the very fact of his subsequent promotion. One might infer from his memoirs that the way to success in Strasbourg lay in avoiding the place in favour of Berlin, where he spent at least half his time.[51] Like Manteuffel before him, who died in office, his successors seem to have had little to look forward to but honourable retirement. The salary itself reflected one of the intrinsic burdens of the office. This was the obligation to entertain like a head of state, with a corollary obligation to entertain *the* head of state, who considered Alsace-Lorraine to be one of his particularly happy hunting grounds.[52] There was even a supplementary budget for such purposes equal to the governor's salary. In late 1913 the new provincial legislature cut it in half in a demonstrative gesture of thrift and institutional self-assertion. But while there were innumerable complaints about the governors, it was hardly ever claimed that they were getting rich. (In a note to Bethmann of 5 December 1913, Delbrück reported that a prominent Alsatian politician believed Hohenlohe-Schillingsfürst's successor had used his entertainment fund to pay off mortgages on his personal estate.[53] But there seems to be no further evidence for the charge.)

If anything, the very risks and burdens of the office favoured a certain level of competence and even independence. Between 1879 and early 1914 three of the four governors were from the higher nobility, two had held high military rank, two had held major diplomatic assignments. Three had assumed office at 65 or older, the fourth at 62. These are ages at which men can usually be assumed to be beyond ambition, if not beyond all care. By training, income and social disposition, all could be regarded as *grands seigneurs*, a term Germans often used. They were comparable in many ways to ambassadors, rather different from the usual bureaucratic run of the emperor's ministers. A worldly 65-year-old with an inherited fortune may be any number of things, including conservative. But under normal circumstances he is unlikely to be deferential.

From an Alsatian point of view a good governor was a contradiction in terms. But even here bad could be distinguished from worse. Each governor realised in his own way that intransigence was relative. Mutual interest was the last best hope of German administration. Earlier administrations sought it in the socio-economic self-protectiveness of the local bourgeoisie, even though this was the population most susceptible to francophilia. By the beginning of the twentieth century smart German officials went to some trouble to satisfy the bread-and-butter yearnings of the provincial pseudo-Parliament, the Landesausschuss, in informal consultations, and find jobs in the courts and administration for deserving native sons and nephews. With the arrival of Count Wedel, probably the most attractive and successful governor, the course was reversed in 1907. Wedel's administration decided that the more promising constituency was the majority of the population who were neither bourgeois nor francophile. Their arguments were democratic and populist. But there was a second irony. Support for Alsatians who were neither francophile nor bourgeois, that is, those with an arguable long-term interest in the German connection, still meant support for Alsatians who opposed the status quo.

No matter what side they favoured, the logic of the Strasbourg scene favoured self-government. From the 1890s on, German administrators inclined to the view that 'not against us is for us'. They based their policy, and even staked their careers, on it. But things looked different in Berlin.

In a voluminous private memo to Bethmann in March 1914, Berlin's police chief, Jagow, reviewed the history of the provinces in authentic conservative perspective. What he saw, predictably, was rack and ruin going back to Manteuffel. Wedel, he implied, not only tolerated the provinces' 'social' and 'cultural' differences. They were all he reported.

Jagow's pulse jumped again as he reported the advice of a senior official in Strasbourg for a newly arrived member of his department. 'You have to develop a more liberal position', the man said. 'We can't go on governing Alsace-Lorraine like a police state.'

'And this after a mere 40-year occupation of a territory whose population was politicized to the finger tips by the French', Jagow roared. He conceded that self-government might be possible in another forty years — naturally assuming the provinces could be isolated from external contamination, that is, France. As might be imagined, Hohenlohe-Schillingsfürst, the most cautious imperial governor, was Jagow's favourite. 'Unfortunately he had to leave Alsace-Lorraine to become Chancellor', Jagow noted.[54]

The history of those most German institutions, the university, the army and the political system itself is an instructive index of the successes and failures of the Berlin—Strasbourg connection.

By its nature and the relative constancy of its mission, the army's experience was the most consistent. While contingents of all four federal German armies were represented in Alsace-Lorraine, the Prussian army, as always, was more present than the rest. There was a startling lot of army in the provinces in general, particularly in Lorraine, where 35 per cent of the population of Alsace-Lorraine but 55 per cent of the large provincial garrison, were located. In 1912 about a sixth of the entire German army was stationed in the provinces.[55] In the German Empire in 1905 there was an active soldier per 100 population and 45 males. The equivalent ratios in Alsace-Lorraine were 4 or 5 soldiers per 100 population, one for every 11 males.[56] In 1910 military personnel constituted 8½ per cent of the population of Strasbourg, 17½ per cent of the population of Metz.[57] As with any peacetime garrison, the impact was mixed. There was that much more business for local suppliers, merchants, barkeepers. There was that much more annoyance for farmers whose fields and crops were periodically stomped by manoeuvring troops. There were that many more bar-room and dance-floor squabbles on a Saturday night to be recorded in the police column of Monday's paper.

There was more to the friction than numbers. Nobody had asked the German army to come to Alsace-Lorraine. The population regarded it as 'their' army practically by definition. But the nature of the garrison increased the distance. In 1907 the ratio of Protestant to Catholic officers and military officials was virtually the reverse of what it was in the local civil population in a country where this mattered.[58] Natives constituted only about 8 per cent of the garrison. The disproportion increased with rank. NCOs, who comprised nearly 20 per cent of the German army in 1912, made up fewer than 8 per cent of the contingent recruited in Alsace-Lorraine.[59] Officers from the provinces were all but unknown in the German army. In the French army they were rather common. One source cites seventy-six French generals of Alsatian origin at the brigade or divisional level in 1910.[60]

This, of course, was part of the problem. Nobody denied that there was an Alsatian military tradition. What Germans had against it was that it was the wrong one. Alsatian pacifism, a fact of prewar life, was largely asymmetrical.[61] As late as 1887 there were large numbers of people in the provinces only afraid there might not be another war. By 1913 still larger numbers were only afraid there would be one. 'The Alsatians are neither better nor worse than other people, but their situation is basically difficult', an intelligent Old German, Friedrich Curtius, wrote to Alexander von Hohenlohe-Schillingsfürst, the old *Statthalter*'s son, in early 1914.[62] 'They are not only asked to take a friendly view of Germany, but a hostile one of France, and this is something that cannot decently be asked of them.'

There was a degree of accommodation on both sides. If nearly half the French Foreign Legion consisted of emigrants from Alsace-Lorraine, recruited at 500 a year between 1890 and 1914, it was also a fact that evasion of the German draft declined from nearly 25 per cent in 1879 to 8 per cent in 1904.[63] Unlike other armies, including the French, who made a point of sending recruits away, the Germans decided in 1903 that 25 per cent of a given year's recruits from Alsace-Lorraine could serve at home. But in 1912 about half the 14,000 troops from Alsace-Lorraine were in fact serving in their home provinces.[64]

The accommodation none the less remained crisis-prone. Only honour was at stake. But this was again the problem. What might have been local squabbles elsewhere became 'affairs' in Alsace-Lorraine, amplified by circumstances, military obstinacy and the provinces' odd constitution to a kind of malignant silliness.

The 'affair' of Mulhouse was both magnificent and typical. It began in 1909 when a customer at the town's best hotel paid the band five marks on a Saturday afternoon in November to play the 'Marseillaise', which was a deliberate provocation. The band prudently followed with the German anthem 'Heil dir im Siegerkranz'. The audience, already feeling fine, intervened with shouts of 'Vive la France'. A number of German officers then walked out, and the proprietor lost his licence to have a band on Saturday afternoons. The military authorities declared the hotel off-limits. Early the next morning the local military band played 'The Watch on the Rhine' in full public earshot.[65]

Even assuming a comparable fracas between citizens and garrison happened anywhere else in the empire, the very density of public administration tended to be a kind of circuit-breaker, confining the incident to the immediate locale. But in Alsace-Lorraine the intermediate levels were missing. Army—emperor, prefect—governor—emperor: in Alsace-Lorraine the normal administrative channels led abruptly to the top, and vice versa. So the Mulhouse 'affair', apparently forgotten, revived abruptly in May 1911. The emperor's brother, who was planning an exhibition flight, declared his intention to spend the night in Mulhouse, where the military still regarded the best hotel as off-limits. The police chief and city council demanded that the local commander reverse his decision. The local commander, a major-general, marched out of the meeting in protest. He was supported by his superiors. The city officials then turned to Wedel. He demanded the transfer of the major-general. The military countered by demanding the transfer of the chief of police. The emperor himself inevitably became the arbiter. As was often the case, guiding and constraining his natural impulses required enormous effort and ingenuity from the stoical Bethmann. By November Wedel threatened to resign. The incident was finally liquidated with an elaborate compromise: transfer of the major-general and the police chief. But the police chief went first. The general was not only transferred to a Guards regiment. He became the first brigade commander to be honoured with a conspicuously high decoration, the Order of the Red Eagle, Second Class, with crown and oak-leaf cluster.[66]

'Is the Military Cabinet so short-sighted as to overlook the risks of the precedent they created here?' Wedel wrote to Valentini, the emperor's chef du cabinet, in the aftermath. 'It positively encourages military eager beavers [*Streber*] to get tough and provoke conflicts with the civil population in the hope of cashing in on honours and commendations.'

Valentini underlined the passage. He even wrote 'right!' in the margin.[67] Sanity was not uncommon in imperial Germany, even at the administrative summit. But no matter how high it was, it invariably seemed to have an uphill fight.

The history of the university was an interesting variation. Like the army, the new University of Strasbourg was 'their' institution too. By the standards of the time it was an extraordinary and very German place, a temple to the flame of 'pure' secular science and scholarship that distinguished the German university so advantageously, if problematically, from anybody else's. Even the inscription over the main entrance, 'Litteris et Patriae', in that order, testified to the institutional self-image and mission. It also testified to a mini-victory over Bismarck, whose priorities were different. Both pioneer élan and official favour glowed in its corridors. The new university enjoyed the most advanced physical plant existing, and a conscientiously recruited faculty fifteen years younger than the German average, and up to a quarter-century younger than the faculty in Berlin.

Both Alsatians and foreigners appreciated the university for what it was, a particularly well-developed specimen of the German academic style. This was what the Alsatians had against it. In its first decade the university enrolled one foreigner for every 7.5 Germans, compared to the German average of 1:20. But the enrolment from Alsace-Lorraine was about equivalent to the enrolment of foreigners. Without the Protestant theological faculty, Alsace's only real surviving link with German culture, it would have been still less.

Like the relationship between the inhabitants and the German administration, this gradually changed. From the 1880s on, half or more of the enrolments in medicine and pharmacy were local. Unlike law, both specialties were attractive for their freedom from state control of jobs, access to indigenous patients, privileged draft status, and the opportunity to work in local hospitals under their consistently anti-German staffs. By the beginning of the century, as Alsatians began to eye jobs in the German administration, local enrolment reached about 50 per cent universitywide, though indeterminate numbers were presumably the offspring of Old Germans.

The shifting enrolments were arguably a testimonial to the virtues of

German administration. They were not so obviously a homage to the
virtues of German scholarship. As local enrolment increased, academic
autonomy visibly declined. The original solidarity of the official German
community faded. The introduction of a Catholic theological faculty was
a characteristic breach. Subject to veto from Berlin, candidates were
nominated by the Bishop of Strasbourg. Professors with outside offers
left uncontested. Early on there had been protests from Berlin about
a critical dissertation on the situation of the working class in Mulhouse.
As far back as Manteuffel there had been professional opposition to the
official policy of conciliating the Catholic bourgeoisie and local industrialists who constituted the provincial establishment. In 1902 there was
something of a *cause célèbre* when Berlin invented unrequested chairs in
history and philosophy in order to fill them with Catholics. The history
chair went to Martin Spahn, who was not only the son of a prominent
Centre deputy, but only 26. The faculty appealed to the emperor without
reply. There was a vigorous protest from the venerable Theodor Mommsen,
but relatively little from other Prussian professors.

Like other provincial institutions, the university changed again under
Wedel. He was sympathetic both to the particularism and the germano-
phobia it now represented. Natives still resented the discrimination, real
or imagined, in faculty hiring just as Germans took the darkest possible
view of a francophile student club, the Cercle des Etudiants, whose very
aggressiveness might have reflected apathy among the majority of their
fellow Alsatians.

But the university had measurably ceased to be a foreign body. It had
instead become a good provincial university, the first in the world with
a million volumes in its library. Its very provincialisation worried occasional perceptive members of the academic community. The faculty,
which had long since ceased to be interchangeable with the civil service,
was increasingly divided within itself. Pierre Bucher, one of the paladins
of a francophile 'double culture', found serious academic support. As
early as 1901, Fritz Van Calker, a sometime National Liberal politician
and professor of law, publicly endorsed full autonomy for Alsace-Lorraine
within the empire. At a rally in 1907 he expressed a desire to see the
provinces become 'a crucible in which the Germanic and Latin civiliza-
tions could blend'.[68] This was hardly a typical view. But it also seems not
to have been a particularly daring or dangerous one, even for a National
Liberal with tenure and a claim on a Prussian pension.

The crucial test of political integration was politics itself. The difficulties
of constitutional reform anywhere in the empire were proverbial. But
reform in Alsace-Lorraine was a special dilemma. It was more difficult than
most if only for the particular intensity and immediacy of the military
opposition. But it was also more necessary than most, if only to pre-empt
still more drastic initiatives from sources beyond government control.

Bethmann's disposition was favoured by a particularly fortunate conjunction of circumstances. French pressure since the Moroccan crisis of 1905 increased the sense of urgency. The goodwill of both the Social Democrats and the provincial administration offered reassurance that the risks might pay off. William II got along well with his new governor, Wedel. The emperor had been well received on a provincial tour in 1910. There was a happy consensus between the emperor and the centrist parties of the Reichstag on the need to maintain the emperor's basic prerogatives in the annexed provinces irrespective of other constitutional changes.[69]

The reform that followed was widely regarded then and after as a masterpiece in the art of the possible. 'Alsace-Lorraine is to be regarded [*gilt*] as a federal state', the first article of the new constitution stipulated with deliberate ambiguity. But much really was possible, as even the domestic opposition acknowledged. 'Without having independence, Alsace-Lorraine basically has the principal attributes of an autonomous state, and among its prerogatives the outstanding one is budgetary ratification and legislation by a state legislature', declared the Abbé Wetterlé. An intransigent anti-German, he had been in jail only a year or two before for insulting the principal of the Colmar Gymnasium.[70] There were doubts about the motives and substance of reform. 'Your political and civil liberties will be augmented in the degree that you efface your natural character which, however, we respect', was how a French paper caricatured the German position.[71] Like all good caricatures, it included a bit of authentic portrait.

But there was enough in the final package to make a lot of people feel not only that something important had changed, but that there was a real possibility of getting something better. Contrary to Bethmann's plans, the draft that emerged from the Reichstag included universal, direct, equal, secret, male suffrage for a real Lower House. The new legislature could interpellate at will and enjoyed a budgetary sovereignty save only as increases required ratification by the provincial government.

For the consolation and reassurance of conservatives on both sides of the Rhine, there was also an Upper House. Half of it was indirectly elected. The other half was appointed by the emperor, who also retained his authority to appoint the governor and suspend the constitution in case of emergency.

An ingenious compromise resolved the intricate constitutional dilemma of how to grant Alsace-Lorraine votes in the Bundesrat without automatically increasing the Prussian majority. It was agreed that the delegation from Strasbourg would abstain on the issues of war, treaties and constitutional amendment, or in the unlikely event that Prussia had no majority without them.[72]

Everyone understood that this was neither home rule nor parliamentary democracy. But it was closer to home rule than Alsace-Lorraine ever got before or after, and as close to parliamentary democracy as anything in the German Empire. If it was clear that the people of Alsace-Lorraine did not govern themselves, it was also clear in law as well as fact that no imperial administration could govern without or against them. Large numbers of Irish would imaginably have been happy with a similar package. Despite intense 'nationalist' agitation, there was little evidence of general dissatisfaction in Alsace-Lorraine.

As though born to the exercise, 81 per cent of the eligible electorate turned out in November 1911, a week after the resolution of the second Moroccan crisis, to elect their first and last state legislature, endorse particularism, and wallop the 'nationalists', who failed to win a single seat. The Catholic Party won 42 per cent, the Social Democrats 32 per cent, the various liberal democrats 21 per cent, the 'nationalists' barely 4 per cent. Only Daniel Blumenthal, the 'nationalist' major of Colmar, survived to take a legislative seat. But it was the one in the Upper House, to which a fair but oligarchical indirect election process entitled him.[73] The Reichstag election two months later confirmed that the 'nationalist' defeat had been no fluke. This time the turnout was almost 85 per cent, the Social Democrats ran only 2 per cent behind the particularist Catholics, and the traditional clerical, anti-German contingent was a record low.[74]

At least in conservative perspective, a 'nationalist' defeat was still fundamentally different from a German victory. The provinces might be prudent, realistic. In their way they might even be loyal. They were not demonstrably grateful. They were certainly not Prussian. This compounded Bethmann's and Wedel's dilemma, but also their own. Understandably suspect when they seemed to behave like Frenchmen, they were only a little less suspect when they merely behaved like Alsatians, Old German immigrants included. The key was again in the empire's problematic foundations. Domestic politics had always been a campaign and a holding action against those whom Bismarck himself declared 'enemies of the empire': Progressives, Catholics, Social Democrats. Between them, these were the parties that monopolised politics in Alsace-Lorraine. The nominal Germanisation of the provinces only reflected and reinforced the increasing pressures for democratisation in Germany.

'I have no doubt at all that the integration of Alsace with a democratic Germany would have been easily achieved, that it will only be complete when there has at least been a basic liberalization of customs, public institutions and governmental methods in the Empire', a Mulhouse pastor noted in early 1914.[75] In their respective ways, official Germany had reached the same conclusion all the way to the emperor himself, but more in anger than in sorrow.

The emperor was infuriated by the civic officials of Mulhouse. He was enraged again by the factory directors of Grafenstaden. He was bitter again when the new legislature censured the Strasbourg government for allegedly neglecting provincial interests in favour of pan-German nationalism, Ruhr competitors and their own Prussian superiors in their treatment of the affair. In Strasbourg a week after the censure resolution, a small group heard the emperor declare in the presence of the mayor that he had had enough. He was ready to smash the new constitution and solve the problem for good and all by annexing Alsace-Lorraine to Prussia.[76]

Since the emperor's moods notoriously came and went, this was not necessarily to be taken as a literal statement of intent, let alone policy. Within a month, Wedel was again expressing 'great optimism concerning the present situation'. But, he prudently added, it was 'admittedly tempered with scepticism that a sudden change could bring a set-back'.[77]

References

1   See Jean Schlumberger's introduction, *La Bourgeoisie Alsacienne* (Strasbourg and Paris, 1954), pp. 12–15.
2   See John Eldon Craig, 'A mission for German learning' (unpublished dissertation, Stanford University, 1973), pp. 407ff.
3   Franklin L. Ford, *Strasbourg in Transition* (New York, 1966), pp. 205–6.
4   The text is cited by Ford, op. cit., p. 258.
5   Franz Schnabel, *Der Aufstieg der Nationen* (Freiburg, 1964), pp. 314–15.
6   Dan P. Silverman, *Reluctant Union* (University Park, PA, 1972), p. 75.
7   Jack G. Morrison, 'The intransigents' (unpublished dissertation, University of Iowa, 1970), p. 80.
8   *King Henry V*, V.ii.
9   Cited by Karl Marx, 'Zweite Adresse des Generalrats über den Deutsch-Französischen Krieg', *Ausgewählte Schriften*, Vol. 1 (East Berlin, 1953), p. 468.
10   See Jean-Marie Mayeur, *Autonomie et politique en Alsace* (Paris, 1970), pp. 29ff.; Morrison, op. cit., pp. 155ff.
11   Cited by Morrison, op. cit., p. 157.
12   Michael Howard, *The Franco-Prussian War* (London, 1961), p. 447.
13   See Silverman, op. cit., pp. 34–5; Morrison, op. cit., pp. 12ff.; Otto Pflanze, *Bismarck and the Development of Germany* (Princeton, NJ, 1963), pp. 473–9.
14   See J. H. Clapham, *The Economic Development of France and Germany* (Cambridge, 1961), pp. 248–85.
15   See Silverman, op. cit., p. 27.
16   Morrison, op. cit., p. 17; Joseph Rossé *et al., Das Elsass von 1870–1932* (Colmar, 1936–8), Vol. 4, pp. 43, 48.
17   Robert Redslob, 'La Bourgeoisie Alsacienne sous le régime allemand', in *La Bourgeoisie Alsacienne*, op. cit., pp. 443ff.
18   Rossé *et al.*, op. cit., p. 48.
19   See Silverman, op. cit., pp. 36ff.
20   Felician Prill, *Ireland, Britain and Germany* (Dublin and New York, 1975), pp. 6ff.
21   ibid., p. 58.
22   Morrison, op. cit., pp. 90–2; E. R. Huber, *Deutsche Verfassungsgeschichte* (Stuttgart, Berlin, Cologne and Mainz, 1969), Vol. 4, p. 440; Silverman, op. cit., p. 87.

23 Rossé *et al.*, op. cit., Vol. 1, pp. 144–5.
24 Redslob, op. cit., pp. 443–51.
25 See Huber, op. cit., p. 438; Silverman, op. cit., pp. 34–5.
26 Silverman, op. cit., p. 76.
27 ibid., pp. 68–70.
28 See A. J. P. Taylor, *From Sarajevo to Potsdam* (London, 1966); Theodor Heuss, *Erinnerungen* (Tübingen, 1963), p. 154.
29 Report to Chief of Imperial General Staff, 20 January 1914, Gstb., Nr. 227, HHStA and Kriegsarchiv, Vienna.
30 Rossé *et al.*, op. cit., Vol. 1, pp. 157ff.
31 See Morrison, op. cit., pp. 195ff.
32 Bundesrat, Session 1913, Nr. 63, 'Entwurf eines Gesetzes zur Ergänzung des Vereinsgesetzes vom 19 April 1908' and Nr. 64, 'Entwurf eines Gesetzes betreffend Einführung des Reichsgesetzes über die Presse vom 7 Mai 1874 in Elsass-Lothringen'.
33 See Mayeur, op. cit., p. 19.
34 See Morrison, op. cit., pp. 266ff.
35 See Mayeur, op. cit., pp. 40ff.
36 Lt. Gen. (Ret.) E. v. Liebert, 'Die Zukunft der deutschen Westmark', Schwäbischer Merkur, 19 January 1914.
37 F. Eccard cited by Mayeur, op. cit., p. 14.
38 ibid., p. 15.
39 See Morrison, op. cit., pp. 126ff.
40 Rossé *et al.*, op. cit., Vol. 4, p. 80.
41 See Mayeur, op. cit., p. 16; Rossé *et al.*, op. cit., Vol. 4, p. 44; Clapham, op. cit., p. 159; Fritz Croner, *Soziologie der Angestellten* (Cologne and Berlin, 1962), p. 196; Carlo M. Cipolla, *The Economic History of World Population* (Harmondsworth, 1965), p. 28; Charles P. Kindleberger, *Economic Growth in France and Britain* (Cambridge, 1964), pp. 215–16.
42 See Silverman, op. cit., pp. 177ff.
43 ibid., pp. 165ff.
44 Rossé *et al.*, op. cit., Vol. 4, pp. 183–5.
45 ibid., Vol. 1, pp. 166ff.; Morrison, op. cit., pp. 386–98.
46 Memo from Prussian Minister of Public Works, 3 March, 1914, letter from Secretary of State Roedern, 9 March 1914, reply from Bethmann, 10 March 1914, Rep. 84a, 6340, GStA West Berlin.
47 Morrison, op. cit., pp. 30–5; Silverman, op. cit., pp. 36ff.
48 Friedrich Curtius (ed.), *Denkwürdigkeiten des Fürsten Chlodwig zu Hohenlohe-Schillingsfürst* (Stuttgart and Leipzig, 1907), Vol. 2, p. 371.
49 ibid., pp. 408–9.
50 Silverman, op. cit., p. 48.
51 See Morrison, op. cit., p. 87 and fn. 42, p. 117.
52 RK 158/1, ZStA Potsdam; RK 158/1, ZStA-II Merseburg.
53 RK 158/1, ZStA Potsdam.
54 Jagow to Bethmann, returned 31 March 1914, I–A, Els.-Lothrn., Nr. 4 (Geheim), Bd. 1–2, AA Bonn.
55 Silverman, op. cit., pp. 72–3.
56 Rossé *et al.*, op. cit., Vol. 4, p. 43.
57 Silverman, op. cit., pp. 72–3.
58 Rossé *et al.*, op. cit., Vol. 4, p. 229.
59 Silverman, op. cit., pp. 72–3.
60 Fritz Jaffé, *Zwischen Deutschland und Frankreich* (Stuttgart and Berlin, 1931), pp. 342–5.

61 See Gilbert Ziebura, *Die deutsche Frage in der öffentlichen Meinung Frankreichs von 1911–1914* (Berlin, 1955), p. 23.
62 Letter of 3 February 1914 in Nachlass Hohenlohe, BA Koblenz.
63 Silverman, op. cit., pp. 68ff.
64 See Hans-Günter Zmarzlik, *Bethmann-Hollweg als Reichskanzler* (Düsseldorf, 1957), pp. 87–8; Silverman, op. cit., pp. 72–3.
65 See Morrison, op. cit., pp. 1–3.
66 Zmarzlik, op. cit., pp. 105–9.
67 ibid., p. 109.
68 The discussion of the university is based on John Craig, op. cit.
69 See Zmarzlik, op. cit., p. 102; Mayeur, op. cit., pp. 29ff.
70 Quoted by Rossé *et al.*, op. cit., Vol. 1, p. 136.
71 Quoted by Mayeur, op. cit., p. 61.
72 ibid., p. 112; Zmarzlik, op. cit., pp. 98ff.
73 Silverman, op. cit., pp. 150ff.; Mayeur, op. cit., pp. 167ff.
74 See Morrison, op. cit., pp. 353–4; Mayeur, op. cit., p. 182.
75 C. Scheer, *Zum Verständnis der elsässischen Seele* (Marburg, 1914), p. 15.
76 *Verhandlungen des Reichstages*, Vol. 285, pp. 2,054, 2,072.
77 Cited by Silverman, op. cit., p. 164.

5 What Happened in Zabern

All my life I've noticed that nothing else reveals a person's character so surely when all else fails as a joke he takes amiss. (G. C. Lichtenberg)

The change came in Zabern. As a contemporary observer was to recall almost wistfully, it incidentally 'made our town world-famous'.[1]

The 99th Prussian Infantry regiment had been garrisoned for twenty-five years in Zabern. But this in itself was only a proximal cause of the subsequent commotion. Zaberners were old hands, even connoisseurs, at garrison life. Their experience went back to Julius Caesar.

Periodically the experience had its hazards. There had been a legendary slaughter in 1525 when an incumbent Duke of Lorraine mowed down the town's peasant garrison. During the Thirty Years War Zabern had been attacked by the Swedes and again by the French. In the War of the Austrian Succession a contingent of Hungarians, Croats and Slovenians were garrisoned in the cellar of the local chateau, the palace of the Archbishop of Strasbourg. They were known collectively as 'pandours', and had been recruited a few years earlier to fight against the Turks. The cellar, now a museum of local Roman antiquities, continued to be known as 'pandour cellar' after their departure.

But the town also had its sunny side. On the eve of the revolution, Rohan-Guémené, the Cardinal-Archbishop of Strasbourg and Zabern's leading citizen, was triumphantly received home after being acquitted in law, if not in honour, for his part in the affair of the necklace, the *ancien régime*'s last great scandal. The old chateau burned down in 1778. Construction of a new one began two years later.

The revolution interfered with this as it did with many other things — Zabern was a party to the revolution too. This was hardly to be avoided in an Alsatian town where the bishop had traditionally appointed the city government. But anti-clericalism was not really Zabern's style. Under outside pressure there was a mini-terror in 1792 in which various clerical paraphernalia and churchbells were destroyed, and Jews rounded up to remove gravestones from the local cemetery. Things resumed their normal course after Thermidor. Like the rest of Alsace, Zabern coexisted with Napoleon, then with his successors. In 1848 Zabern favoured the republic. It also favoured the presidential candidacy of Louis Napoleon. Once in power, he reciprocated in his way. Zabern enjoyed the glow of early industrial prosperity in Alsatian German, its native idiom. It even got funds at last to complete the new archepiscopal palace – in time, as it turned out, for a German garrison to make themselves at home in it.[2]

But the trauma was evidently minimal. The Alsatian writer René Schickele subsequently described Zabern as the town quickest to reclaim its German past after the war. This even included a declaration of loyalty addressed to Bismarck.[3] Known at least to its chamber of commerce as the 'city of roses' and 'pearl of the Vosges',[4] though to Baedeker as 'a dull town with 8,300 inhabs.', it was known to German papers as 'the most German town in Alsace-Lorraine'.[5] As the only district in the conquered provinces to return a Conservative to the Reichstag, it was honoured as early as 1890 by an official visit from William II. The local historian, a transplanted eastern German who had joined the Alsatian judiciary in a flush of élan in 1871 and quit in protest against continued oppressive government from Berlin ten years later, none the less recalled the visit as a signal event.[6] Almost uniformly, officers recalled Zabern as a good, if unprestigious, post where the garrison figured prominently in local social and also commercial life. Like the widows of French civil servants before them,[7] Germans, including a number of ex-officers and at least one former regimental commander, found Zabern a comfortable place to retire.

The relative frequency of native Alsatians in the local administration – the prefect, the postmaster, the presiding judge of the district court – testified to a considerable degree of political integration. Social integration was a different story, though class and culture interacted rather too intimately to permit any easy inferences about the immediate source, or even quality, of the differences. The garrison was obviously perceived, and perceived itself, as a foreign body several times over – for its Prussian Protestant officers, for its Rhenish Catholic enlisted men, even for simply being strange to a small town where people are inevitably sensitive to strangers. There was evident sensitivity, though no apparent hostility, to Germans. Yet Stieve, the local historian and lawyer and a strong believer in Alsatian autonomy, obviously felt at home. So did Wiebicke, the émigré Saxon, who published one of the two local papers.[8]

Social integration was not so obvious where the army was concerned. For officers Zabern was an assignment, not a personal choice. At least some of them seem to have regarded resident civilians as a necessary evil. In December 1913 Georg Mahl, one of three natives among the provinces' twenty-four prefects, reported to his superiors in Strasbourg that a drunken major had informed him at a party the previous January that civilians had only been invited by accident. There were subsequent apologies though only one subsequent invitation, Mahl noted, and he had then been the only civilian present. But whether the garrison snubbed Alsatians, civil officials, civilians as such or Mahl in particular was unclear from the report.

If any imaginable Alsatian could meet conventional German expectations, it should surely have been Mahl. He was a graduate of German universities, life member of one of the classiest German fraternities, and a recently retired first lieutenant in the reserves. His relations with the army were good, Mahl said. He participated in parades, military church services and 'the other patriotic occasions'. His relations with the regimental commander, Colonel von Reuter, were 'correct'. In the general tradition of small towns, there was speculation that they might have been still better had Mrs Reuter, the vice-president of the Women's Patriotic League, not felt upstaged by Mrs Mahl as president. The ladies' social rivalry spilled over into their husbands' official relationship in August, Mahl admitted, when the Alsatian Youth Development League, of which Wedel was patron, asked Mahl to help with a membership drive. He wrote to Reuter. But his office neglected the honorific 'esquire' in the salutation, and Reuter had brusquely sent back the note. He was not a subordinate of the prefecture, Reuter said. Mahl reported that he had acknowledged Reuter's objections 'especially politely'.[9]

Given the familiar complexity of the German–Alsatian relationship, such nuances of social pique, like Mrs Mahl's reported preference for French couture, schools or governesses,[10] were invariably invested with tribal significance. A half-century later, Marie Draude, a Zabern native, recalled that her papa kept a bust of Napoleon on his desk, and that she had hummed 'Sambre et Meuse' as a child.[11] The extraordinary attention devoted to such seeming trivia testifies only to innumerable misunderstandings, French as well as German, on the nature of bourgeois life Alsatian style. This was reflected again in the custom attending local celebration of the emperor's birthday. Since a regimental commander had discovered an old military regulation conferring on him alone the right to give an after-dinner speech, respectable Zabern commemorated the occasion at separate tables. The garrison held its own dinner, civilian officials and local businessmen another, the teachers yet another, the veterans' association another still.[12]

Writing nearly twenty years later, Willy Höflich, who had been a sergeant in the 99th, recalled Zabern with qualified affection. He admired the Alsatians. He was less sure about the Prussian army of which, in his early 20s, he had been a part. There had obviously been a good deal of mutual provocation. To what extent it distinguished the Prussian army in Zabern from any other contemporary standing army in any other garrison town is hard to say. Manoeuvres, as Höflich described them, were obviously hard on farmers, livestock and the landscape. Training was hard on recruits. There was to be ample evidence for this as it applied to recruits, in general, and Alsatian recruits, in particular.

Weekends could be hard on everybody.[13] Barge traffic on the canal through town carried a transient population that turned up, like soldiers, in Zabern's bars. They were young single men, far from home. With time and a bit of money on their hands and girls in short supply, they did what came naturally. But there was evidently some feeling among the troops that the army, unlike the police, tended to turn the other cheek. The lumps were felt disproportionately by the contingent from the German side of the Rhine. Irrespective of the local virtues, it was not like serving at home, and manoeuvres were no pleasure, Höflich observed. As a reward for voluntary enlistment, Alsatian recruits were allowed to eat at home and receive their friends and families in the barracks. Non-Alsatians were left to look after themselves. Though Höflich refers exceptionally to a local girlfriend and dinner at the family table, there seems to have been little intermarriage between local girls and serving non-Alsatian NCOs. But none of Zabern's bars were off-limits.[14]

Though none of the available evidence, military or civilian, suggests that morale was a particular problem, there were limits to the sweetness and light. There was a notable brawl between civilians and NCOs around the turn of the year 1913–14. It ended with the civilians acquitted or released on their own recognisance, but the soldiers court-martialled. A military report noted other episodes in April and September where the state prosecutor's office failed even to bring charges.[15]

A perceptible threshold of frustration may or may not have tripped the 20-year-old, and only recently commissioned, Lieutenant Günter Freiherr von Forstner in late October. But frustration was unmistakable in the report Reuter filed on his behalf some days later. In its very gratuitousness the episode was a textbook example of what, within months, was to persuade whole European populations that the military was too serious a business to be left to soldiers, Prussian or otherwise.

What started it, according to Höflich, was a slight scuffle on the rifle range, initiated by a recruit with a police record. The ruction provoked Forstner to a speech on military discipline. It was easy to get into a fight in town, Forstner observed. He hoped the offending recruit would have the sense to avoid it. But should he be attacked by some *Wackes*, that is, unfriendly natives, Forstner added in earshot of the man's squad, he should feel free to fight back, side arms and all. 'And if that happens, and you happen to waste one of them, OK', the official report quoted him. 'Behave yourself right and you get 10 marks from me, and nobody says a word.' To which Höflich added, 'And three marks from me.'[16]

Violence, verbal and otherwise, was no stranger to the training camp then or afterwards. It figured noticeably in the Reichstag debates of the prewar period.[17] The army was aware of the problem and not insensitive to it. As it later developed, both Forstner and Höflich had already acquired something of a local reputation for training practices that might have been considered tough by some, but were plausibly considered sadistic by others. One can only guess about prevailing norms elsewhere. But there was no question that they had exceeded the tolerance of their superiors. Höflich was eventually sentenced to eighteen days in the stockade for various episodes during the preceding year. Forstner, the officer and gentleman, drew four weeks of house arrest.[18]

But the significance of the *Wackes* episode lay in the word itself, one of those symbolic bone-breakers that can hold its own with sticks and stones. In contemporary usage the word was both discriminatory and derogatory. It was an open question whether it could be understood to apply to all Alsatians. But it was agreed that it applied only to Alsatians, and was therefore among those tribal and regional epithets only rarely used, and still more rarely heard, with affection and respect. Though common enough in the German, as in any other army, such expressions were officially frowned on. They even led to periodic sanctions. An officer had already been transferred under William I for calling his troops 'Oldenburg oxen'.[19] The 'oxen' might have been acceptable; 'Oldenburg' was obviously not.

Even in local usage *Wackes* tended to be pejorative. In all likelihood it was a remote cousin of 'vagabond' via a common Latin source, though other etymologies were current, including one that associated it with 'Vosges'.[20] Various apologetic German commentators, with personal experience in Alsace, could remember hearing it used neutrally, even affectionately. But this was exceptional. In normal circumstances even Alsatians used it only with care, and non-Alsatians at their peril. Intemperate use had led to litigation, violence, even criminal convictions,[21] and the word had been proscribed by regimental regulation since 1903.[22]

Rather remarkably in a town of 8,000, where soldiers and civilians lived in constant contact and the garrison itself was a major social institution, it took over a week for the story to get into the local papers. But gamey as it was to begin with, it had, by that time, acquired an advanced *haut gout*. 'Waste one of those Alsatian *Wackes* and you won't get two months', the paper quoted an anonymous lieutenant. 'For every one of those dirty *Wackes* you bring me, you get 10 marks.'[23] Headquarters in Strasbourg immediately demanded a report. The story meanwhile crept into other papers, first in Strasbourg, then in Paris via a local stringer with a source in Zabern, then in Berlin via Wolff, the German news agency, which had picked up the story from *Le Matin*.[24]

It took headquarters nearly a week to respond publicly, and then there was no denial, but merely a qualification. Forstner had warned against unprovoked aggressiveness in town, but had endorsed self-defence, the statement said. It was clear from the context, the army claimed, that *Wackes* referred specifically to troublemakers, not to Alsatians in general.

But there was little reason to think this would suffice even if it had been said publicly and officially on the spot. Under the best imaginable circumstances, Zabern was not a place where an adolescent Prussian lieutenant, and a baron at that, could easily plead extenuating circumstances. But as it turned out, a previous class of recruits had their own grievances against Lieutenant Forstner. So did the father of a nubile 14-year-old. Or at least he said he did. So did a number of people who had encountered a very drunk Forstner during recent regimental manoeuvres in the country. The combination of symbolic role and public persona precluded Forstner's anonymity. In the weeks that followed, the army's initial omission, and the circumstances that followed it, transformed local notoriety into international fame.

On 8 November Forstner's landlord reported to local police that two strangers had broken into the vestibule of the house and threatened to beat Forstner up the night before. There had also been jeering in the street outside, and stones had been thrown at the shutters.

That night, a Saturday, Forstner and a fellow lieutenant were heckled by a crowd as they sat in the 'Carp', then — and still — a popular restaurant on the main street across from the archbishop's palace. They responded by demonstratively showing their pistols on the table in front of them. Reuter, who intervened personally to extricate them, was heckled too. In the end Forstner was taken home by a military escort. According to the regular schedule, he was to get up the next morning and be duty officer — unless, of course, Reuter changed the rotation, or better still transferred Fortsner to a company stationed in an outlying village.

But this Reuter obviously refused to do. He had filed his report. There had been no reply. To judge by his personal history and subsequent actions, he was not a man likely to opt independently for tactical retreat. Himself the son of a professional colonel who fell at the head of his regiment in 1870, he was conceivably more hawkish than most, profoundly conscious of the justice and even urgency of the cause he served. And so the demonstrations continued.[25]

To complicate things, both the normal Sunday crowds and the general hilarity were further increased by a local election. According to Reuter's later report, Forstner was followed by a crowd of 150—200 as he went about his afternoon rounds, accompanied by the regimental medical officer. About twenty egg-size stones were thrown behind them, Reuter said. About 4.30 p.m. he finally fired off a bristly note to Mahl, demanding the police support he claimed he had requested the day before. Unless the police intervened energetically, he announced, he saw no alternative but a proclamation of martial law. Mahl replied within the hour. He had asked the mayor to alert local law enforcement personnel, he said, railway police and firemen included. He had also called up the local contingent of the state police (gendarmes). In his own report, Mahl notified his superiors that armed military patrols were circulating in the streets too. He added that he had pointedly reminded Reuter that proclamation of martial law was an inalienable constitutional prerogative of the emperor. He expressed the hope that his own measures would prevent further demonstrations 'to the extent the fact that Lt. Fortsner is duty officer might not itself provoke the population still more'. Reuter answered directly. He awaited the intervention of the state police, he said. He was also 'fully aware of his rights and obligations'.

That evening a crowd estimated at from 200 to 300 gathered at Forstner's house, children, adolescents and women included. As a tender of serious purpose, Mahl noted, he had even called out the fire brigade on a Sunday. While police were not asked to break up the crowd because of the women and children present, firemen were ordered to turn on their hoses. But someone in the crowd cut the hoses, which the fire department later displayed as trophies, and because of threatening weather, many in the crowd had brought umbrellas anyway. Meanwhile, Forstner himself stood by in his long overcoat, smiling disdainfully and smoking a cigar. In the end mounted gendarmes were called in, but by that time the crowd was already breaking up on account of rain. Some stones were thrown at the police and there were a few firecrackers. Obviously replying to official queries, Mahl mentioned that he had heard the 'Marseillaise' whistled, though not sung. There had been a shout of 'Vive la France', he added conscientiously. But it came from a bricklayer with a reputation for trouble-making, who was also heard singing the 'Marseillaise' later that night in a downtown bar.[26]

The army claimed two stones were thrown at a passing military column the next morning, and there was another demonstration the next evening on the main street in front of the palace. This time the crowd was estimated at 1,000. Mahl had enlisted school officials to keep adolescents off the street. But the crowds were reinforced by workers from the local factories, and the usual contingent of housewives doing some last-minute shopping. Even the military conceded that perhaps half the crowd consisted of women and children. There were a few firecrackers and some jeering, the inevitable 'Vive la France', and 'Vive la République', not to mention 'Merde la Prusse', included.

Returning to his office Mahl found a note from Reuter proposing a common effort to control the crowds. He suggested that they meet. 'I am available at any time and request notice when Your Honour proposes to come to my office', Reuter said. Mahl replied at 8.15 that evening. He had been directed to keep order by his superior in Strasbourg, Mahl indicated. Should military intervention be necessary 'contrary to expectation', Reuter would be notified. 'I remain at the colonel's disposal, if necessary tonight at the prefecture', Mahl said. He added that he could also be reached by phone.

But it was 8 a.m. before they met on neutral ground at the railway station. They had come to greet Wedel and General Deimling, their respective superiors, who were arriving for the governor's annual hunt. Reuter shook Mahl's hand, then took him aside and bawled him out audibly for failing to appear the night before. He outranked Mahl by two service grades, he insisted. Mahl replied that he would ask for military assistance when he needed it, that it was Reuter who wanted something of him, and that, as head of the civil administration in Zabern, he considered himself Reuter's equal. Wedel supported Mahl's position on his arrival.

During the day Mahl reinforced the gendarmes, though he ordered them to dismount in order to avoid further provocation. He meanwhile asked for the support of outlying factory owners in alerting employees about the risks of any further breach of the peace. He again warned school officials, and had the mayor post a notice that troops were armed with live ammunition, and that demonstrators would be prosecuted.[27]

Assiduous school-teachers did their bit. 'In order to encourage parents to pay attention to their children', they even threatened students from poor families with loss of their book subsidies if they were found at the demonstration after dark. Classes were reminded of how a police record could complicate their military service. Teachers patrolled the streets, herding adolescents away from the square in front of the palace. 'It was unavoidable that there were about 100 students in front of the school between 7 and 7.15 p.m. when classes changed', the superintendent conceded.[28] That night there was another demonstration. Between 7 and 11 November about fifteen persons were charged with disorderly conduct. Then peace broke out.[29]

On Sunday, it appeared, Reuter had submitted his resignation on grounds of health. It was successively approved at the brigade, divisional and army level the following days. On 12 November a moving van appeared before the colonel's quarters at the palace. His successor, a Lieutenant-Colonel Sonntag, soberly set about to mend the fences. With Reuter gone, he conferred with Mahl on what might be necessary and kept Forstner out of sight. He actually thought Forstner should be transferred, it was reliably reported, and assured Mahl at their meeting that he had been appalled by Reuter's performance at the station the day before. The military had threatened to boycott the Zivilcasino, a local social club, unless it cancelled its subscription to Wiebicke's *Zaberner Anzeiger*, the source of the Forstner stories. Officers were allowed to stay though there had been no cancellation. Sonntag was supported without reservation by General von Harbon, the brigade commander in Strasbourg.[30]

Since there were no further demonstrations, Mahl dismissed the gendarmes, though police patrols continued. At Sonntag's suggestion he prevailed on Wiebicke to remove a copy of the paper from his office window. It was widely, and familiarly, believed that the press was the major cause of the disturbance.[31] Mahl was sceptical. The peace since Reuter's departure made him wonder whether the impact of the press might have been overrated — though he also feared that new disorders might accompany a Social Democratic protest meeting scheduled for the following week.[32]

In the meanwhile wheels had turned at army headquarters in Strasbourg. On 16 November Forstner was sentenced to six days of house arrest and Höflich to ten days in the stockade for the *Wackes* episode. But it was early December before this was publicly known. Nor was it publicly reported that Wedel had recommended not only a general ban on the use of *Wackes*, but the immediate transfer of Forstner — 'not least in his own interest', as he said. Given the recent incident in Mulhouse he was not entirely confident. Deimling himself had been the instigator of the hotel ban. But Deimling had also said he planned to request Forstner's transfer at a future date. Wedel noted pensively that the army seemed to feel that an official reprimand, where the military itself had offended local sensibilities, would be bad for its prestige. He inclined to the contrary view.[33]

His darker instincts were vindicated by two events. One was the return of Reuter on 17 November, 'by order of His Majesty the Emperor and King', as the colonel's telegram to headquarters in Strasbourg indicated.[34] It was questionable whether his departure had anything to do with the incidents that were meanwhile making Zabern famous. But it sufficed, as Wedel speculated in a letter to Bethmann, that 'a few imbecile papers' should think so.[35] If Reuter's departure was understood as a signal in Germany, it was hardly surprising that his return was understood as a signal in Zabern.

The other event had again to do with Forstner. In a tactical modification of its traditional policy of direct action against the presumed Social Democratic menace, the army, true to its self-image as 'school of the nation', had introduced morning lectures for recruits.[36] As elsewhere, the chore invariably fell to the most junior officers. It was therefore Forstner who enlightened an audience of seventy-nine recruits on the French Foreign Legion the morning of 14 November. Forstner let it be known that, as far as he was concerned, they could 'shit on the French flag'.

The proposal was ill-advised, not least because of a new Forstner story in the papers. It was widely rumoured that a memorably drunk Forstner had soiled his bed during manoeuvres in mid-September. Forstner wanted to sue the paper that first carried the story. It was in fact untrue — at least in its literal form. The army had diligently solicited an affidavit from the village barber who rented the bed Forstner had slept in. He testified under oath that the lieutenant had left it in appropriate order. But the army also appreciated that public discussion of what had not happened led unavoidably to consideration of what had, for example, that Forstner had got sick in the kitchen, where somebody else had to clean up, that he had no recollection the next day of what happened the night before, and that he had refused to pay his bill. His request to sue was denied. He even got another day of house arrest. But again none of this was publicly known.[37] Meanwhile Forstner, who was already a figure of some notoriety as 'the *Wackes* lieutenant', acquired a new epithet, *Bettschisser*, and the latest episode took only a day to get into the newspapers.

Wedel went directly to Deimling even as Sonntag authorised an immediate investigation. The inquiry began with Forstner himself. He resolutely denied saying what the papers reported. A hasty roundup of twenty-two recruits, thirteen of them Alsatians, produced no evidence to the contrary. According to Joseph Kaestlé, a Strasbourg reporter, they had been rousted out of bed at 10.30 p.m. and were read Forstner's deposition.[38] They apparently concurred, and Sonntag reported reassuringly to Strasbourg that Forstner had referred only to the Foreign Legion. This was promptly published and appropriate authorities in Berlin, including the Foreign Office, were notified by telegram.[39] A court martial in December, where the entire group was called to testify, produced quite different results. This time only 5 recruits spoke in Forstner's favour, 19 testified against him. Ten more were uncertain. Another 44, as the official report noted, 'had nothing of significance to say'.[40]

In the meanwhile Kaestlé, one of the three editors of the *Elsässer*, a little Catholic paper in Strasbourg, was called to Zabern by his local stringer to meet in private with recruits prepared to testify against Forstner. Only one turned up, a 20-year-old office clerk inducted just two weeks before. But he was willing to sign a statement even, he said, 'if I have to go to jail'. Kaestlé promised to protect his source, and the story appeared on 20 November. Two days later the paper demanded Wedel's resignation.[41]

The same evening Wiebicke's office was searched for nearly two hours at Reuter's request by four gendarmes in the presence of the regiment's legal officer. They were looking for the leaks responsible for the flag story. Predictably they failed to find them. Contrary to the law, they also failed to get a warrant from a magistrate, though three were available, and no representative of the civil prosecution was present. The sergeant in charge of the gendarmes was officially reprimanded by his superiors, who also dispatched a stiff note to Deimling, requesting that he order an investigation of the incident.[42]

Wedel dutifully reported the obvious to Berlin. Forstner's behaviour had made a terrible impression even, as he said, in 'Well-disposed germanophile circles'. He felt obliged to tell the emperor that the incidents, and their consequences, were a severe blow to the German position. To make things worse, an Alsatian sergeant and five local recruits were under arrest on suspicion of having talked to reporters — as three of them actually had.

The rest of the Zabern recruits had been transferred to garrisons in Mulhouse, Colmar and Neubreisach. So far as anybody could see, nothing had happened to Forstner. Mahl was worried about new demonstrations, Wedel noted ominously: the transferred sergeant had a father and relatives at a nearby factory. Wedel doubted that the worst would happen, but instructed Mahl to take appropriate steps. If necessary, this included armed force.[43]

What really mattered, Wedel felt, was that the army should take corrective steps instead of covering up. But as he knew, this was whistling in the dark. Deimling was part of the problem. He was pleasant enough. He was even prepared to listen to reasonable arguments. But he was also an eager beaver (*Draufgänger*), particularly in public. Wedel recalled two recent speeches in which the commanding general had exhorted Alsatian recruits to go after the 'red pants', that is, the French, the same way they attacked their red-flagged manoeuvre targets. If this was how the general talked, one could hardly be surprised about his subordinates.[44] He informed Bethmann that he had been to see Deimling about the transfer of the sergeant and the treatment of the recruits. The contrast with his apparently lenient treatment of Forstner was bound to shake confidence in the army, Wedel argued. Deimling just replied that there could be no concessions to newspapers and demonstrators. 'And there we have it', Wedel said.

But, as he also knew, the real problem was elsewhere. It was the emperor himself. The Mulhouse incident proved that he could expect no support from that direction, he sighed. The emperor really believed that his commanding generals knew more about Alsatian politics and how to deal with the population than the government he appointed. 'And so', he concluded, 'provocation is trump.'[45]

Whether and to what extent this might be true was, and remains, an open question. Reuter's return was no coincidence. It was logical to infer that his orders, and Forstner's, were sanctioned, if not directly initiated, higher up. It seems reasonable that people perceived Reuter's actions as escalatory in themselves, as something more than mere reaction. Meanwhile the wheels of military justice were turning. But this was something the army was at pains to hide. Even Wedel seems to have been unaware that there had been any action against Forstner. But even had it been public knowledge, there could only have been indignation about the obvious disparity in the way the army treated its enlisted men and Sergeant Höflich, not to mention civilians, and the way it treated an aristocratic junior officer.

On the other hand, there was little evidence to suggest that provocation was a conscious and comprehensive policy. Forstner and a colleague, the 21-year-old Lieutenant Kurt Schad, seem to have enjoyed the role of *enfants terribles*. Schad regularly and demonstratively appeared in public with a large bulldog. But the fun stopped abruptly when challenges, and even concerned telegrams from the Paris embassy, started to arrive. On 27 November Deimling notified Berlin that Paul de Cassagnac, a Bonapartist journalist, and three other French reserve officers had expressed great interest in a duel. Forstner had orders not to react or even answer.[46]

A report to the Strasbourg authorities the same day from the prefect in Schlettstadt, another Alsatian town, was a guide to what could be done. A newly promoted captain had inadvertently insulted an Alsatian sergeant before the entire unit there, by expressing surprise that half a border unit should consist of Alsatians. He then asked whether the troops were indigenous or Old Germans. Where Alsatians were concerned, the captain indicated, there was always need for caution. The sergeant understandably took this personally. The commanding officer had only recently lectured his officers on good local relations and immediately ordered an investigation. He even managed to get the prefect to intervene with the local papers pending his report. The editors co-operated. The captain clarified his position before the troops on his commander's orders. Reporters were then summoned for an official statement, and asked for their goodwill.[47]

The difference between Schlettstadt and Zabern had less to do with policy than with Reuter, who was meanwhile filing libel charges against the *Zaberner Anzeiger*, and threatening an official boycott of any restaurant or bar in town where customers were even seen reading it.[48] Suspected of calculated provocation, he seems rather to have behaved like a man on the ragged edge. Fully persuaded that the dignity, and even the personal safety, of his troops was at stake, he ordered that Forstner henceforth be followed in the street by an armed escort, presumably to defend him against the jeers that unavoidably accompanied him. The colonel had long since concluded that the civil authorities were a hopeless case. 'What can I do about it?' was how he subsequently paraphrased Mahl's position. 'I can't send out a policeman after every officer.'

This led to another incident on the night of 26 November. Forstner and others were followed home from the 'Carp' by about fifty hecklers. Schad and Forstner were jeered. There were two arrests. According to the police reports, a journeyman baker, aged 20, had been standing in the palace square, chatting with friends, when an officer came by with a four-man escort, armed with bayonets. The friends fled. The baker was arrested. 'You laughed and are under arrest', he was told. Shortly afterwards he was joined by a bank clerk, aged 26. He had been sitting in the 'Carp' himself, the man said. When he heard the racket outside, he ran out to see what was going on and was arrested too. Witnesses confirmed their stories. The police, who were called to take them into custody, released them on their own recognisance. The charges were dismissed the next day by the magistrate.[49]

By now Reuter was running out of patience. 'I already notified the prefect after the incidents of Nov. 8—10 that the military authorities would be compelled to help themselves should local law enforcement officials be unable to protect officers against further jeers and insults from the mob', Deimling informed Berlin. 'I also informed Col. Reuter personally that he was himself to arrest demonstrators, and use armed force in case of resistance, should the jeering not stop, and should the civil authorities prove unable to prevent it and bring the situation to an end.'[50]

Disposed, in any case, to react as a statue might react to pigeons, and congenitally suspicious of Mahl, Reuter was perhaps more legitimately sceptical about the will and capacity of Zabern's finest to pursue rowdy adolescents. The town employed a police force of five, whose average age was 49. They were reinforced by five auxiliaries, but their average age was 53. The captain himself was 72.[51] Reuter must have found the incidents of 26 November, not to mention the dismissal of charges that followed, the last straw.

There was peace the night of 27 November. But the next evening, after an indeterminate number of kids had climbed a wall to watch regimental officers working out in the gym and five officers, including Forstner, had been heckled on their way home, Reuter finally did what he had presumably wanted to do all along. As it happened, the civil authorities were at a particular disadvantage. Mahl had been invited to dinner in Strasbourg by his superior. By coincidence, Deimling was at the dinner too. The mayor, a Catholic member of the state legislature, was sick in bed.

Reuter's lever was an inconspicuous passage in the military regulations, whose obscurity was only compounded by the complexity of its history. Its direct source was a royal Prussian order of 1820 providing for self-authorised military intervention in civil disorders. It had been questioned and challenged on various occasions since, particularly in the constitutional period after 1848. It was none the less retained in successive versions of the Prussian army regulations in 1861 and 1863, and again in 1899.[52]

Most recently reprinted in the 1913 edition, it specified that military authorities were 'permitted and obliged' to use armed force in the repression of civil disturbances and in enforcement of the laws 'when, in the event of disturbance of public order due to riot [*Ausschreitungen*], the military commander observing the demonstrations concludes, in consonance with his conscience and his sense of duty, that the civil authorities are excessively hesitant to request military aid because the forces at their disposal no longer suffice for the restoration of order.'[53]

Despite the regulation's long history, Reuter's action seems to have been the first time it had ever been invoked. The very fact of its existence, let alone its survival into constitutional times, came as a surprise to most people, at least most civilians. There was even some question whether this might not include Reuter himself, whose dark allusions to his 'rights and obligations' were conceivably motivated by tactics. Deimling's report covering Reuter's action is strikingly weak in legal support, though Wedel's refers at least to the 1899 edition of the military regulations.[54] He was fully aware, Deimling conceded, that the laws presently valid in Alsace-Lorraine were a questionable basis for his previous order.[55]

The problem was that the statute in question was not a law at all, but a Prussian military regulation. Prussian officers, as a rule, were not lawyers. But they were believers in positive legality, given like their countrymen to citation of laws and statutes wherever possible. Kleist's 'Prince of Homburg', threatened with execution by his king for countermanding an order even though his contravention had actually won a battle, is a classic figure of German literature. Unlike Kleist's prince, Reuter would probably not have welcomed his impending execution as a matter of honour. But, as a representative of the same tradition, he might at least have looked through his service regulations before acting, and taken seriously what he found there, particularly if it seemed to read in his favour.

In their first reports, the civil authorities in Zabern and Strasbourg acknowledged the existence of the military regulations too, though there was no clue to when and how they had become aware of them.[56] They clearly knew there was a provision for unsolicited military intervention in civil disorders. What they refused to acknowledge was its relevance. There had been no civil disorder, they argued without exception – at least until Reuter provoked one.

Though details varied, eye-witnesses concurred that there had been an incident after the evening work-out in the gym. According to one of the state's attorneys, who testified the next day at the prefect's office, he heard a passing adolescent tell how he planned to heckle Forstner while waiting for a colleague to come out of a bookshop around 7 p.m. As he mentioned this to his colleague, six or seven lieutenants rushed by and arrested a 16-year-old. A military patrol arrived on the scene. The witnesses assumed they had been waiting for just such a provocation. The boy was led away, protesting his innocence. According to some accounts, there were two arrests, and Forstner himself was an active participant.

According to the official report, patrols armed with bayonets then crossed the square, dispersed, and began arresting people, while still other people stopped on the street to stare at the odd goings-on. At this point a detachment of sixty appeared on the palace square, facing the main street, Schad on the right, and Reuter behind. There was a drum roll, as the statutory military practice prescribed, and an order to the crowd to disperse. After a second drum roll, the first column advanced to the left, the second to the right, driving people off the streets or arresting those who failed to respond to their orders. In effect Reuter had declared martial law.

Mahl, who was at dinner in Strasbourg, was in no position to stop him. Successively called to the phone by the mayor and his deputy, he could only appeal to Deimling for help. According to the general's memoirs, Deimling replied that he could hardly intervene without personal knowledge of what was going on. Mahl then asked his superior whether he should return to Zabern. Reassured that there was no riot in progress, that his deputy was competent, and anyway that it would all be over before he could get back, Mahl was persuaded to stay.[57]

It fell to his deputy, Grossmann, to approach the colonel. He was not about to let anybody tell him what to do, the colonel replied. The civil authorities had failed, officers were being humiliated. Wiebicke, the editor of the *Zaberner Anzeiger*, was still not in jail though Reuter was convinced he could only have got his stories by stealing military documents. There was nothing left but self-help, Reuter declared. He was ready for any eventuality. If people continued to insult his officers, obstruct the public square or laugh, the troops had orders to shoot.

'In reply to my contention that such a misfortune must be avoided under all circumstances', Grossmann reported, 'he announced that he would regard it, on the contrary, as good fortune if blood flowed, since things could no longer go on the way they had.' Now he was in charge, Reuter said. To avoid the worst, Grossmann informed him that the police and gendarmerie would be ordered to clear the palace square and main street so the military could return to barracks. He then went away to call Mahl.

The scene on the street as this was going on must have been a combination of *Walpurgisnacht* and the Keystone Kops. Another state prosecutor testified the next day that he had been impressed with the general calm as he left the district court around 8 p.m. But there was a sense of repressed excitement and also of comedy, he said, as 'warriors, armed to the teeth, went into action against harmlessly peaceful by-standers'. The first man was arrested because he happened to be standing in the way, a second because he jeered in response. An adolescent was arrested for laughing. Another man, a 37-year-old father of five, was arrested on his way from work when he tried to break through a cordon of troops. He was hungry and they were blocking his way. He was particularly bitter about the loss of wages the next day caused by his arrest.

Those registered at night-school seem to have been pursued on principle. Various apprentices declared the next day that they had been arrested for no apparent reason. One claimed Schad had roughed him up, breaking a tooth. Several of those detained said they had been out shopping. One was on his way to the fire brigade. One was balefully informed that he had whistled. 'They arrested at random like Cossacks in the streets of St Petersburg', a state prosecutor testified. A cabinet-maker named Levy, who got up from dinner and ran down to the street from his second-floor apartment to see what was going on, was chased back in again by Schad and several soldiers. They scared the daylights out of Levy's 78-year old mother before dragging Levy off too.[58]

Before it stopped, there had been twenty-seven arrests. The suspects ranged in age from Oskar Lerch, 15, to the 43-year-old Levy. But sixteen of them were 20 or under, and only six were over 25. The occupational distribution was both revealing and slightly ambiguous. With the exception of one shop clerk, it consisted of blue-collar − or, as a later French commentator noted, no-collar − workers,[59] six of them job trainees or apprentices of one kind or another. To a point, the distribution only reflected the reality of Zabern or almost any other contemporary town. Blue-collar workers, artisans included, were a majority of the population. They were also physically identifiable, at least on work days. To a point it also reflected the daily social pattern. At 7 p.m., in Zabern or any other contemporary town, workers en route home were likely to constitute a majority of the people on the street. Evening vocational classes and the social habits of single men meeting their friends in town reinforced their number, particularly in the lower age groups.[60]

But there was no doubt about a direct animus, approaching class warfare, in the evening's pursuit. It was a baron's revenge on the common folk, a lieutenant's on undeferential recruits, the army's on refractory civilians, Prussia's on Alsace, all at once. Asked to justify the action, military witnesses could only point to the failure of the civilian officials to defend them against an unceasing stream of verbal abuse. Its source, as they saw it, was 'factory workers of 18 to 20'. But leaving out the special abuse reserved for Forstner, its nature was tribal, 'Prussian pig' or 'Swabian pig', where 'Swabian' applied to Germans in general, and was equivalent to *Wackes*. The issue, as they understood it, was both practical and symbolic: preservation of respect for the army against the 'mob'.[61] This was also Deimling's position. 'I had ordered Colonel von Reuter that he was not, under any circumstances, to tolerate the jeers and insults to his officers by the plebians of Zabern', he informed the Emperor on 5 December.[62]

In practice 'mob' was understood both comprehensively and differentially. Among the people on the street after 7 p.m. were the judges of the district court, who had just recessed a locally celebrated manslaughter trial. One of them said later that he had assumed the crowd on the street was waiting to hear the verdict. By their own account the jurists stood by, puzzled that soldiers were acting like police. Then came the order from the ubiquitous Schad to clear the street. It was more than one of the judges could take. Himself a reserve officer and brother of the editor of a Conservative paper in Pomerania, he advanced on Schad, arrayed in respectability, to inform him that he was violating the law. Schad arrested him too. As he was led away, he was accompanied by three exasperated colleagues.

One of them, who had often frequented the officers' mess and thought he had a good relationship with the colonel, insisted on seeing Reuter. The colonel was predictably unmoved. Perhaps referring to Grossmann's offer to activate the police, Reuter claimed the mayor himself had ordered the crowd to disperse. The jurists demurred. 'This is where jurisprudence ends', Reuter told them, according to one account. 'Mars rules the hour', he added, according to others. It was a citation from Schiller's *Wallenstein*.[63] 'I had the feeling that Col. v. Reuter's initiative was based on a very special view of law and public affairs, and that he was absolutely unaware of any sense of the illegality of his actions', one of the jurists later testified.[64] But alone among those detained, the arrested judge was released within a few hours.

Two non-arrests add more nuances. One of them, identified in the official report as 'editor and newspaper publisher', can only have been Gilliot, a member of the state legislature and editor of Zabern's second, and more respectable, paper. Wiebicke, a natural target for Reuter's fury, would hardly have been on the street. Bourson, the local stringer for *Le Matin* in Paris, later recalled being taken to see him by the light of a pocket lighter in the hand of Charles Frey, later a French parliamentary deputy from rural Strasbourg. They found him hiding out from the patrols behind bales of newsprint. They spent the night drinking kirsch together, and Bourson filed his story from Wiebicke's telephone. Gilliot, on the other hand, had been stopped by soldiers on his way to the post office. He protested to a passing gendarme, he said, and was released.[65]

The second non-arrest involved Wilhelm Kaufmann, aged 21, who said he was detained by Forstner while waiting for his wife to buy a sausage. At Forstner's request, he identified his wife. Forstner hesitated, according to Kaufmann. He then backed off because 'Lt. Forstner had had an affair with my wife's sister, who is only 14, and is currently in Paris'.[66]

Military patrols continued to circulate and block the street until about midnight, while the twenty-seven detainees were held in the 'pandour cellar', the palace's cold, unlighted basement. There was no floor and no sanitation. In reply to their pleas, they were told they could relieve themselves in the corner, they said. It was 11 p.m. before they got blankets, and the next morning before they got bread and coffee. Only then were they led off individually to a magistrate, who released them. Reuter's suspicions about the local judiciary had evidently been confirmed two nights before. Deimling, too, defended holding the prisoners overnight. 'To judge by previous experience, if he had turned the prisoners directly over to the police, they would only have let them go again', the general declared. 'The whole action would have seemed a bad joke and would only have reinforced the mob in its disrespect for the army.'[67]

There were echoes on Saturday, and again on Sunday. In the mayor's absence, an alderman named Guntz had spent Friday night on the street appealing to his fellow citizens for calm. On Saturday morning Schad and four soldiers smashed into his hardware store, claiming an apprentice had shouted a name at them from behind the door. Grossmann, called to the scene, noted that the door showed signs of having been broken in. Schad was assured that the apprentice would be turned over on his return — which he evidently was.[68]

Though order was thoroughly restored on Sunday, Lieutenant Böttcher none the less felt it necessary to run in Emil Meyer, a baker's apprentice of 17, for laughing around 4 p.m. That evening a moulder of 24 was arrested for singing. The official report regrettably neglects to say what. His brother, a painter of 17, who protested by hollering in front of the guard room, was locked up too. The first two prisoners were transferred promptly to the local jail. The latter two were taken there directly.[69]

The official correspondence is a portrait of dedicated Lilliputians doing their best to contain an infuriated Gulliver. Successive telegrams from Strasbourg promised an official inquiry and offered police reinforcements. Mahl was to keep order at any cost, his superiors told him. Mahl informed Reuter of his instructions, and his responsibility for maintaining order. Reuter laconically acknowledged receipt of the message. There was a follow-up telegram from Wedel as late as 2 December, enjoining Mahl to be sure the army had no further excuses to practise self-help.[70]

An official proclamation from Guntz, as acting mayor, passed on the message. Repeating appeals from Mahl to avoid congregating on the street and disturbing the peace, and to observe all police instructions, Guntz also requested citizens with the greatest urgency to refrain from the heckling of military personnel, since the regimental command had announced its intention of proceeding without quarter against any further jeers, shouts or insults.[71]

The proclamation, and the announced arrival of an inspector general from Strasbourg for an official investigation, evidently had their effect. The patrols finally withdrew from the streets and Mahl's report noted the outbreak of peace for the first time in days.[72]

But even this was premature. Before sunrise on the morning of 2 December, as he led his battalion through the outlying village of Dettweiler, Forstner again heard familiar sounds. There was a chase led by a 19-year-old ensign, who heard a threat as he ran and saw someone reach into his pocket. He was accompanied by two enlisted men. The chase produced Karl Blanck, also 19, and en route to his job at the local shoe factory. A club foot made it difficult for him to run, he testified credibly. He had resisted arrest because he was innocent. As he was brought to Forstner he was still resisting — threateningly, according to Forstner. Though Blanck was held in check by the ensign and four men, Forstner smacked him with his sabre, opening a two-inch gash in his head. It was the only time anybody was actually injured during the whole month of incidents.

Investigation of Blanck's pockets produced a sandwich, a wallet, a handkerchief and a pocket knife.

Mahl issued another proclamation 'because of recent incidents in Zabern and Dettweiler', requesting citizens' help in arresting anybody who provoked military personnel. 'Persons assisting will not only contribute to the good reputation of the citizenry', he said, 'but will also deprive the military of any occasion for self-protection.'[73]

The city council had meanwhile fired off appeals to Berlin. After a special meeting on Saturday the Zabern City Council declared its unanimous indignation in telegrams to Wedel, Bethmann and the emperor, protesting against the 'repeated, obviously provocative and entirely illegitimate actions' on the part of Reuter, and urgently requesting 'appropriate measures for the protection of the citizenry they were legally entitled to claim.'[74]

Wedel, whose role was considerably more delicate, expressed his rage too — but also the fundamental ambiguity of his situation. 'Should incidents like those in Zabern go unprosecuted and thus confirm the impression that the population is at the mercy of military arbitrariness for want or evidence to the contrary, they will destroy the work of years, force the friendly elements, too, into the arms of our opponents, and deal an irreparable blow to the German cause', he informed the emperor. Wedel noted that his honour as an officer and a German precluded any public statement that would confirm differences between the army and the civil authorities. But his obligation to the emperor, whose decision he was unwilling to pre-empt and whose name he wanted kept out of the debate, also prevented him from promising any relief. He was prepared to live with this, he said. But he was also aware that it could only cost him the confidence of the local population, and make his position redundant.[75]

By now Zabern had become so famous that even foreign reporters could cause problems. On 4 December, when a photographer from the London *Daily Mirror* tried to get a good shot of Schad and his bulldog, Schad demanded of a passing gendarme that he destroy the plate. The photographer was brought to Mahl, who passed on the man's camera to a magistrate for eventual return, and the offending plate to the state prosecutor. The plate was eventually destroyed, but pictures of Zabern appeared in the big London and Paris picture magazines, and newspaper stories appeared as far away as the front-page of the Bloomington, Indiana, *Daily Telephone*.[76]

In Paris, it was reported, Forstner had inspired a window display in a ladies' shop: a cartoon showing him defecating on the tricolour. It was withdrawn by order of the police.[77] The team of P. Gay and Dickson collaborated on a music-hall tune on the same subject.

Forstner a dit 'je ferai
Mes besoins su'l'drapeau français.'
Mais, mon p'tit lieutenant, faut d'abord pour ça
Avoir le courage de l'prendr' l'drapeau-la.
Et j'crois qu'avant ça, mon bon,
Ça s'rait fait dans ton pantalon.[78]

Perhaps recalling Deimling's earlier campaign against the Hereros in Southwest Africa, Gustave Stoskopf, 'the Alsatian Molière' as admirers called him, was moved in Strasbourg to a parody letter from the Congo. Everything had been fine, he said, until a lieutenant hit a native with a cocunut and called him a Kaffir — which was as bad, he added, as a *Wackes* calling a Prussian lieutenant a civilian. The natives had demanded justice, but only got machine guns instead. Now the natives were turning in their Bibles and prayer books, and wondering whether they ought to return to the old tribal gods.[79]

And on the stationery of the Hotel Woodstock, Times Square East, came an unsigned note for the emperor himself. 'For God's sake, Billy', it said, 'tell 'em to stop.'[80]

References

1 P. Gilliot, 'Ephemeriden zur Zaberner Affäre', *Journal de Saverne*, no. 133 (1923).
2 Léon Bachmeyer, *Pages d'Histoire de Saverne* (Société d'Histoire et d'Archeologie de Saverne et Environs, 1965), *passim*.
3 Quoted by Erwin Schenk, *Der Fall Zabern* (Stuttgart, 1927), p. 5.
4 Brissaud (no initials), *L'affaire du lieutenant de Saverne* (no place, 1929), p. 13; Karl Baedeker, *The Rhine from Rotterdam to Constance* (London, 1900), p. 311.
5 Joseph Kaestlé, *Ein Sturmsignal aus dem Elsass* (Strasbourg, 1933), p. 22.
6 Richard Stieve, *Zabern im Elsass* (Zabern, 1900), p. 238.
7 Brissaud, op. cit., p. 15.
8 Kaestlé, op. cit., p. 24.
9 Wedel report to Bethmann, 14 December 1913, RK 171, Els. Lothr. 6, 'Die Unruhen in Zabern [RK 170–73], ZStA Potsdam; Ricklin speech, *Verhandlungen des Reichstages*, Session of 11 December 1913.
10 See Brissaud, op. cit., pp. 59–63.
11 Marie Draude, *Almanach Sainte-Odile* (Saint-Odile, 1964), p. 101.
12 'Ein Rückblick auf den "Fall Zabern"', unpublished ms., Nachlass Schwertfeger, BA Koblenz.
13 See Wilhelm Hoflich, *Affaire Zabern* (Berlin, 1931), pp. 67ff.
14 ibid., pp. 9–47.
15 Reuter report of 8 November 1913, cited in Arnold Heydt, *Der Fall Zabern* (Strasbourg, 1934), pp. 7–8; see Höflich, op. cit., p. 59.
16 Heydt, op. cit., p. 8; Höflich, op. cit., pp. 67ff.
17 See Heinrich Hasenbein, 'Die parlamentarische Kontrolle des militärischen Oberbefehls im deutschen Reich vom 1871 bis 1918' (unpublished dissertation, Göttingen University, 1968), pp. 93ff.
18 Höflich, op. cit., pp. 196ff.; Heydt, op. cit., pp. 34–7.

19 Schenk, op. cit., pp. 10–11.
20 See Höflich, op. cit., p. 51; Wedel report of 16 November 1913, Rep. 89H, 1 Els.-Lothr. 6, Bd. 2, ZStA-II Merseburg.
21 See 'Ein Rückblick', Nachlass Schwertfeger, BA Koblenz; Kaestlé, op. cit., pp. 27–8.
22 Kaestlé, op. cit., p. 32.
23 *Zaberner Anzeiger*, 6 November 1913.
24 See Brissaud, op. cit., p. 41; Kaestlé, op. cit., p. 24; Paul Bourson, 'Vingt ans après', *La Vie en Alsace* (1934), p. 2.
25 See Decision in the case of Col. Ernst von Reuter and Lt. Kurt Schad, RK 172, op. cit., ZStA Potsdam; Bourson, op. cit., p. 5.
26 Mahl reports of 9 and 27 November 1913, D247/23 and D388/677, AdBR Strasbourg; report of 11 December 1913, RK 171, ZStA Potsdam; decision in the case of Col. Reuter, RK 172, op. cit., ZStA Potsdam; Brissaud, op. cit., pp. 39–40.
27 Reports of 14 December 1912, RK 171, op. cit., ZStA Potsdam; 10 and 12 November 1913, D388/677, AdBR Strasbourg; decision in the case of Col. Reuter, RK 172, op. cit., ZStA Potsdam.
28 Report of 23 March 1914, D388/677, AdBR Strasbourg.
29 Report of 26 December 1913, RK 171, op. cit., ZStA Potsdam.
30 Heydt, op. cit., pp. 11–13, 55–60; Mahl report of 14 December 1913, op. cit., RK 171, ZStA Potsdam.
31 Wedel report of 16 November 1913, Rep. 89H, Bd. 2, op. cit., ZStA–II Merseburg.
32 Mahl report of 13 November 1913, D388/677, AdBR Strasbourg.
33 Heydt, op. cit., p. 15; Wedel report of 16 November 1913, RK 170, op. cit., ZStA Potsdam and Rep. 89H, Bd. 2, op. cit., ZStA–II Merseburg. See Berthold von Deimling, *Aus der alten in die neue Zeit* (Berlin, 1930), pp. 132–3; Deimling report of 12 November 1913, RK 170, op. cit., ZStA Potsdam.
34 Heydt, op. cit., p. 14.
35 Wedel letter of 23 November 1913, RK 170, op. cit., ZStA Potsdam.
36 See Martin Kitchen, *The German Officer Corps 1890–1914* (Oxford, 1968), pp. 170ff.
37 Heydt, op. cit., pp. 41–51.
38 Kaestlé, op. cit., p. 60.
39 Wedel telegram of 17 November 1913, I–A, Els.-Lothr., Nr. 4, Bd. 16–17, AA Bonn; Wedel to Bethmann, RK 170, op. cit., ZStA Potsdam.
40 Heydt, op. cit., p. 24; report of court-martial, 12 December 1913, RK 170, op. cit., ZStA Potsdam.
41 Kaestlé, op. cit., pp. 51–6.
42 Note from Under-Secretary Zorn von Bulach to Deimling, 29 November 1913, Wedel report of 26 December, 1913, RK 170, op. cit. ZStA Potsdam.
43 Wedel report of 23 November 1913, ibid.
44 Wedel letter to Bethmann, 23 November 1913, ibid.
45 ibid.
46 Telegram from Paris embassy, 26 November 1913, I–A, Els.-Lothr., Nr. 4, Bd. 16–17, AA Bonn; Heydt, op. cit., p. 21.
47 Report from Schlettstadt, 26 November 1913, RK 170, op. cit., ZStA Potsdam.
48 Note from Reuter to Mahl, 28 November 1913, D388/677, AdBR Strasbourg.
49 Decision in Case of Col. Reuter, RK 172, op. cit., ZStA Potsdam; report of 29 November 1913, D388/677, AdBR Strasbourg; Wedel report of 1 December 1913, Rep. 89H, Bd. 2, op. cit., ZStA Merseburg.

50   Deimling report of 30 November 1913, RK 170, op. cit., ZStA Potsdam.
51   Report of Zabern police, 9 March 1914, D388/677, AdBR Strasbourg.
52   Memo from Minister of Justice, 6 February 1914, M12/9020, GStA West Berlin.
53   Art. II, Sec. 3, Vorschrift über den Waffengebrauch des Militärs und seine Mitwirkung zur Unterdrückung innerer Unruhen vom 23, März 1899, Berlin 1913.
54   Report of 1 December 1913, Rep. 89H, Bd. 2, op. cit., ZStA Merseburg.
55   Deimling report of 30 November 1913, RK 170, op. cit., ZStA Potsdam.
56   Report to Wedel, 30 November 1913, ibid.
57   Deimling, op. cit., p. 150; see Schenk, op. cit., p. 30.
58   Grossman report of 29 November 1913, D247/23, AdBR Strasbourg.
59   Brissaud, op. cit., p. 68.
60   Depositions of 29 November 1913, filed with Zabern prefecture, accompanying Wedel report of 1 December 1913, RK 170, op. cit., ZStA Potsdam; decision in case of Col. Reuter, RK 172. op. cit., ZStA Potsdam; accounts of trial in *Kölnische Zeitung*, 6–8 January 1914.
61   See testimony in Reuter-Schad trial, cited in *Kölnische Zeitung*, 6 January 1914.
62   Heydt, op. cit., p. 29.
63   See depositions of 29 November 1913, RK 170, op. cit., ZStA Potsdam; Schenk, op. cit., p. 31; 'Ein Rückblick', Nachlass Schwertfeger, BA Koblenz.
64   *Kölnische Zeitung*, 6 January 1914.
65   Bourson, op. cit., p. 10; depositions of 29 November 1913, and Wedel report of 1 December 1913, RK 170, op. cit., ZStA Potsdam.
66   Deposition of 29 November 1913, RK 170, op. cit., ZStA Potsdam.
67   Heydt, op. cit., p. 30; Wedel report of 1 December 1913, RK 170, op. cit., ZStA Potsdam and Rep. 89H, Bd. 2, op. cit., ZStA–II Merseburg.
68   Grossmann deposition of 29 November 1913 and Wedel report of 1 December 1913, RK 170, op. cit., ZStA Potsdam.
69   Report of 30 November 1913, D388/677, AdBR Strasbourg.
70   Report of 29 November 1913, ibid.
71   Prefect's report and mayor's proclamation of 1 December 1913, ibid.
72   Report of 2 December 1913, D247/23, AdBR Strasbourg.
73   ibid.; appellate decision in case of Fortsner, RK 172, op. cit., ZStA Potsdam.
74   Telegram of 29 November 1913, RK 170, op. cit., ZStA Potsdam.
75   Wedel report of 1 December 1913, ibid.
76   Prefect's report of 4 December 1913, D247/23, AdBR Strasbourg; report of 26 December 1913, RK 171, ZStA Potsdam; Tommy T. Hamm, unpublished seminar paper, 19 January 1967, Bloomington, Ind.
77   Brissaud, op. cit., fn. p. 170.
78   ibid., p. 49. Roughly: Forstner said 'I'll lower my pants
                              And go on the flag of France.'
                              But, my lad, to pull off that gag,
                              You must first get your hands on that flag.
                              And if I know where it's at,
                              You'll go in your pants before that.
79   Gustave Stoskopf, *Zabern* (no place or date).
80   Note dated 5 December 1913, I–A Els.-Lothr., Nr. 4, Bd. 16–17, AA Bonn.

6 *What Happened in Berlin*

Four deputies pee at a coach, the coach goes away, and they
pee at one another. (G. C. Lichtenberg)

To complicate things further, Billy had meanwhile absented himself
from the kitchen, leaving the government in Berlin to face the heat.

Official parliamentary consideration began on 28 November with
an interpellation by the deputies from Alsace-Lorraine. What did the
Chancellor have in mind, they asked, to spare troops in the provinces
from insult and the people of the provinces from provocation?

Consistent with the official ethos, Falkenhayn, the new Minister of
War, was first into the breach. There had been no provocation, he declared to jeers from the Centre, the Social Democrats and the deputies
from Alsace-Lorraine. *Wackes* was explained away. 'If every slip of the
tongue by every jolly 20-year-old, and every misstatement in professional
life or duty were to be a matter of public record', he announced to appreciative noises from the right, 'the scandal would be so great that nobody
would know what we were saying.'

Like others before and after, Falkenhayn laid the blame instead on
individual soldiers who had gone public rather than through channels.[1]
It was not a happy performance. A preliminary draft of his remarks in
the Chancellor's files indicates two omissions in what was actually said.
One, a reference to continuing disorders and agitation, was presumably
dropped at Bethmann's suggestion. The other was the unspoken perora-
tion, 'observance of the law by all parties is the basis of any constitutional
order'. If there were to be unsolicited concessions by the government of
the kind this implied, Falkenhayn was evidently not the man to make
them.[2]

An exchange of telegrams between Wedel in Strasbourg and the emperor
at the expansive ménage of his friend Max Fürst von Fürstenberg in
Donaueschingen was a clue and a counterpoint to what was unsaid in
Berlin. 'I report to Your Majesty herewith that my investigation of Zabern
has uncovered such excesses and illegalities on the part of Col. Reuter that
I consider immediate correction an absolute necessity', Wedel wired. He
wanted to see the emperor directly.

'I will hear the Chief of the Military Cabinet about Col. Reuter's actions
as soon as I have the report from general headquarters in Strasbourg', the

emperor wired back. 'Until then I order Your Excellency to confine himself to written reports.'[3]

Karl Georg von Treutler, a professional diplomat assigned to the emperor's entourage and a confidant of Bethmann's, kept the Chancellor informed. He had it from Plessen, the emperor's adjutant, that Wedel would at least be put off tactfully, Treutler informed the Chancellor. But despite Plessen's suggestion that the emperor discuss the matter with Treutler, William was adamant. Treutler was positively grateful for Plessen's suggestion that the emperor receive Valentini, the Chief of the Civil Cabinet. Feeling against Wedel was very bad, he added, and he regarded the presence of Huene, the Chief of the Military Cabinet, as positively disastrous.[4]

It seemed something of a triumph under the circumstances to get William to discuss Zabern with any civilian at all. In Treutler's view it was already a mini-victory to have the support of Plessen. The adjutant kept him informed of what was going on, for example, that Deimling was to be encharged with keeping order in the provinces, while Wedel and Bethmann were to keep at their respective distances. 'I made a strenuous effort to persuade Plessen that the telegram to Deimling was extraordinarily dangerous', Treutler informed the Chancellor, 'and I think that I have at least managed to be sure that Plessen will inform me of any further orders of this kind, and try to see that nothing is done over Wedel's head.'[5]

Wedel wired back that he too wished to see the emperor as soon as possible. He left no doubt that he considered the army to have violated the law. Even Deimling conceded as much. 'I am entirely aware that the existing statutes constitute an unsatisfactory basis' for Reuter's orders, he reported.[6] The situation was bad for the army's reputation and for foreign policy, Bethmann emphasised pragmatically. Briefing Falkenhayn, who was about to leave for Donaueschingen, he informed the War Minister that he considered action by the brigade commander necessary, and suspension of Reuter desirable. He wanted immediate action he could report to the Reichstag.[7]

The next day the Reichstag acknowledged the *cri de cœur* from the Zabern City Council and Bethmann himself implied provisional relief. 'Things of such a regrettable nature have happened in Zabern that I consider it of the utmost importance that the Reichstag and the country be informed of them as soon as possible', he announced, 'in order to avoid any doubt that the law is maintained as scrupulously as public order and the authority of the state's representatives.' An unidentified 'bravo!' answered from the floor.[8]

But again the omissions were interesting. At Falkenhayn's suggestion, the emperor had already agreed to send a general to Zabern for a definitive report, and to inform Wedel of this decision. But he recommended against reporting this to the Reichstag — it would be known soon enough anyway, he said — on grounds that the matter was for the military authorities. '!?' notes a marginal scribble, presumably Bethmann's, on a copy of the memo in the Chancellor's files. In any case, the emperor's spokesman was not to mention it under any circumstances.[9] The same day Valentini's request to appear in Donaueschingen was dismissed,[10] and Wedel's staff report sank among the emperor's inimitable marginalia:

'I fail to see that the police have failed ... (but other people do!!)';
' ... a few adolescent kids called Lt. von Forstner a name' ('!!');
' ... without any significant crowds, let alone demonstrations ...' ('?');
'the course of events showed that the police were entirely adequate to prevent real disruption' ('they didn't do it'); 'Considering the increasingly frequent disposition of the military to intervene in civil affairs ...' ('because the civilians are too soft'); ' ... the impression among the population that they are at the mercy of the military ...' [underlined, '!'] ; ' ... destroy decades of effort, and drive the good elements too into the arms of our opponents ...' [underlined twice, '!'] ; ' ... inadequate protection of domestic interests ...' ('officers too'); ' ... renders my own activity pointless' ('is anyway').[11]

From Berlin Bethmann did what he could to sustain the governor's morale, while incidentally preserving his own. No one was more vulnerable to what happened in Zabern than Wedel, the Chancellor consoled him. It was clear from Wedel's letters that he was on the verge of crucial decisions. Bethmann only hoped that his years of honourable service might be extended by one last contribution: that Wedel for the moment would stay at his post. 'In my opinion, your resignation under these circumstances would be a heavy blow to the provinces and to the empire', Bethmann wrote. He conceded that Wedel could hardly be expected to remain very long. But the how of the governor's resignation was a matter of such importance that he hoped Wedel would at least consult with him before reaching his decision.[12]

A preliminary report from joint conferees of the Justice Department and War Ministry helped prepare Bethmann for the impending debate in the Reichstag. The conferees agreed that military intervention was justified in the event of self-defence or demonstrable inadequacy on the part of the civil authorities. They also agreed that Forstner's — evidently uncontested — reference to enlistment in the Foreign Legion was within the limits of the regulations, that recruits who talked to reporters were not, and that certain individual arrests were covered by statute.

But the actions of 28 November 'were without any legal basis whatsoever', the report continued. The same was true of the interrogation of suspects by the regimental legal officers and incarceration in the local barracks. The commanding general conceded this himself. It was imaginable, the conferees suggested, that Reuter could be charged with any of three derelictions: with exceeding his official mandate, with false arrest or with duress. It was a decision for a military tribunal, with the possibility of appeal to the superior military court (Reichs-Militärgericht) in the event that a court martial failed to act. To be sure, the conferees added presciently, conviction was unlikely since all three charges presupposed conscious intent on the part of the defendant. They argued that the status of military patrols was ambiguous. Patrols were legitimate as part of the military police function, unacceptable as a general obstacle to public assembly. The *rapporteur* from the War Ministry explicitly acknowledged that the now-famous regulation of 1899 – the executive order of 1820 – was illegal. The order had never been published. It had been superseded by the Prussian constitution. He also confirmed that Forstner had been sentenced to six days' house arrest for the *Wackes* incident while Höflich had got ten days in the stockade. But there was to be no public announcement. It was the emperor's view that judicial actions should remain classified 'in the interest of discipline'.[13]

In the meanwhile, General Kühne, the inspector from Strasbourg, was going about his business in Zabern. Peace had again broken out as he arrived. In the next few days he interviewed Mahl and other local officials at length. He even drove out to Dettweiler in Mahl's car to talk to the major. Obviously propitiating the spirits, Mahl reported to Wedel that 'The general repeatedly expressed his satisfaction with what I had done, and also with what I told him.'

'He shared my opinion that there was no question of a nationalist coup', Mahl continued, 'and expressed his own view that I had done my duty in defending the military.'[14]

But this was hardly Kühne's message. In his own report a few days later, Kühne hesitated to go the full route with Reuter, who by now was persuaded of actual conspiracy among former NCOs, the opposition parties and the local papers. In the general's view, the Alsatian soul and its amplification in the local press were explanation enough for the disturbances. The former was 'democratically disposed, conceited and oversensitive, not to mention disrespectful'. The latter was only out to turn the situation to its advantage.

He conceded that Mahl had made a 'relatively energetic' effort to keep order, had kept adolescents off the streets and done what he could to satisfy Reuter's wish that the police at least hold suspects in custody until they could be interrogated. He also tried to reconcile Reuter and Mahl. But he was sceptical as to how long peace would continue, especially after the Dettweiler episode, and given the aggressive propensities of the local press. 'I feel obliged to add', he added, 'that the civil officials believe that only the transfer of Col. Reuter and Lts. Forstner and Schad will calm things down for good.'

Kühne admitted that Reuter's 'rather aggressive manner' was an irritant to so sensitive a population. Even Old German elements had been disturbed by recent events, he reported. He was reluctant to say whether this justified so significant a concession as the transfer of a regimental commander, though a lieutenant was another story. The papers had made Forstner look silly, which was bad for the reputation of the regiment. 'Therefore his early disappearance from here seems desirable', the general concluded. The designated reader underscored every suggestion of journalistic overeagerness and official nonchalance, though he also underlined the recommendation that Forstner should go. 'Very good', William noted at the bottom of Kühne's report. 'So the lousy press *is* 75% responsible.'[15]

But this was whistling in the wind. By now events in Berlin had superseded events in Zabern. On 3 December formal debate began in the Reichstag. By evening, Valentini was referring to a *'dies ater.'*[16] Predictably the debate began with a salvo from the provinces. Alsatian deputies again rehearsed the familiar story of verbal insult, false arrest, military arrogance, and the betrayal of local goodwill. Jacques Peirotes, a Social Democrat from Strasbourg, carried the attack a stage further. While acknowledging local contempt for German militarism — 'a creation unlike the Napoleonic army in the fact that every soldier might at best carry a sandbag rather than a marshal's baton in his backpack', he said — he conceded that the army had been well received in Zabern. He then exuberantly compared recent events with the legendary sixteenth-century slaughter of local peasants by ducal mercenaries.

'Militarism, military dictatorship, high treason!' Peirotes roared. Warming to the subject, he pointed to the discrepancy between the punishment of young recruits and the leniency shown young lieutenants. The chair intervened twice to reprimand him for insults to the War Minister and the Conservatives, and again for an unfavourable comparison of Germany with Mexico and Venezuela. The Social Democrats applauded and the right hissed as Peirotes proposed transfer of the entire regiment, regional autonomy and a 'free, modern state'. Amplifying cues from the previous speaker, Conrad Haussmann, a Progressive, called attention to Deimling, the colonial general and 'hero of Hereroland', whose high-handed appearance before the Reichstag in 1906 still festered in parliamentary memories.

It was only now that Bethmann rose to reply. Characteristically, he advanced straight down the middle. The official transcript tells everything and nothing of what was on his mind. Returning to the first episode, he deplored Forstner's promised bounty, but defended his right to caution against Foreign Legion enlistment. He regretted any resulting insult to 'an army with which we honourably crossed swords more than forty years ago', but assured his listeners that nothing of the sort would be tolerated in the German army. The assurance drew cheers from the right and centre. The Chancellor acknowledged official regret for the use of *Wackes*, but also indicated that 'the officer was called to order and punished, as was the sergeant'. This drew snickers from the left. 'Naturally', Bethmann added, the sources of the newspaper stories would be punished too.

Alsatian feelings had to be respected, he declared, but there was no excuse for insults to military personnel. His resumé of the incidents in November followed Deimling's. The purpose of the arrests was deterrent or pre-emptive, he argued: to avoid the worst in the form of physical attack. He conceded that there was no legal basis for the arrests. He was sceptical that the civil officials had provided adequate support, but fair-mindedly admitted that the civil officials were of a different opinion. The courts would decide the merits of the case and award appropriate compensation. The Chancellor himself abstained from any position.

But, above all, Bethmann declared, 'the king's uniform must be respected under any circumstances'. It was this that concerned the army 'even where the measures taken as a consequence exceeded the limits of the law'. Addressing Peirotes, he rejected the charge of treason with its premiss of guilt pending proof of innocence. There was no evidence of endemic civil–military conflict, the Chancellor insisted. The immediate task was to restore normality, including the normal co-operation of civilians, civil and military officials, and the attendant respect for law and order.

Falkenhayn seemed less self-assured and was certainly less conciliatory. Under steady fire from the left, he denounced 'screaming mobs and yellow journalism' that were even now seeking to exert illegitimate influence on the decisions of responsible officials. Authority, discipline and honour were the essence of the army, he said. The army needed youth. It paid the price for occasional youthful overexuberance and tactlessness. But the army also had means to deal with these, the general declared. Experience merely suggested that sins of omission often weighed more heavily than errors in the choice of means. The previous Friday evening was an example. Even Mahl had conceded the need for self-help. Falkenhayn felt that arrests were at least preferable to manslaughter, and that self-defence was a legitimate prerogative.

Constantin Fehrenbach, a backbench Centrist from Baden and later Chancellor of the Weimar Republic, had originally been considering a few words on behalf of Deimling, a former Freiburg classmate, it was reported.[17] Bethmann and Falkenhayn had changed his plan. He was disappointed with the government, he said. They conceded their regret, but showed no sign of acting on it. Instead they relied on the military for information, while expressing suspicion of the civil authorities. The military would have to respect the law, Fehrenbach declared, or *Finis Germaniae*. Like other critics of military discipline at other times and places, he had no sympathy for arguments about proper channels.[18] Recourse to proper channels under such circumstances only led to harassment, the speaker contended. He regarded this as an extenuating circumstance for the incriminated recruits. Nor did he find the military reaction commensurate with the provocation. Military patrols had nothing to do with shopping for cigars and chocolate, he announced to enthusiastic assent from the floor. The real problem, in his opinion, was the failure to transfer Forstner, and the fault for what had happened was Reuter's. Those who supported Bethmann and Falkenhayn shared the responsibility for driving a wedge between the civilian and military authorities, he argued. They had allowed a local problem to become a general one. There was a thunderous and quite atypical ovation as Fehrenbach sat down. A counter-attacking Falkenhayn affirmed unspecifically that 'the officer has been punished according to the law'. But, as he replied to repeated shouts from the left, he was unable to explain how.

Reportedly, Fritz Van Calker, a National Liberal from Strasbourg where he was a law professor at the university, had also been disposed to conciliation before the debate.[19] But little showed as he followed Falkenhayn to the rostrum. For sixteen years he had been trying to reconcile Germany and Alsace. Was it all kaput, he asked rhetorically? Yes, was the answer. There were shouts of 'Bravo!' from the floor. The Forstner incidents were small potatoes, the speaker insisted. The supersession of the civil authorities was not. The military refused to acknowledge error, Van Calker charged. In fact, it seemed positively proud of having violated the law. What, he typically asked, would have happened in a similar case in England? And how did the government see the future of Alsace-Lorraine? Was military dictatorship to be the order of the day? Replying again for the government, Falkenhayn confined himself to the future of the military. He intended to maintain order in the army, he said.[20]

It had been a turbulent session. Bethmann reported that night in a telegram to the emperor. The left was wild. The mood was grave in the centre and well to the right. There was a consensus that the whole problem could have been resolved with the transfer of Forstner, the Chancellor indicated. He pointed to the warmth of Fehrenbach's reception and his warning about conflict between the country and the army. 'I strenuously rejected attacks on the officers, but had to admit that the measures taken exceeded the limits of the law', he dutifully added. From Strasbourg, Wedel resented Bethmann's failure to report the findings of the civil administration, while relying on information from the military. In Berlin, Falkenhayn charged that Bethmann had underemphasised the actual extent of the provocations, and regretted the Chancellor's request that *Wackes* be proscribed. This implied that other local or regional variants were acceptable, the War Minister complained, which only led to the practical problem of compiling a definitive list of terms to ban.[21]

When the house reconvened the next morning, the Chancellor himself reopened the debate. By now there were fifty-two sponsors for a resolution declaring 'the Chancellor's views on the subject of the interpellation incompatible with the position of the Reichstag'. No, his views on the need for the new constitution in Alsace-Lorraine were unchanged, Bethmann insisted to cheers from the National Liberals. There could be no progress 'until we desist from the unproductive effort to transform south German Alsatians into north German Prussians'.

The situation was grave, he continued, not because of the impending vote of censure — shouts of 'hear, hear!' and general disorder on the floor — but because of the threatening breach between the country and its army. Restoration of harmony between the army and civil administration was the priority of the day. 'Tell that to the War Minister', Georg Ledebour of the Social Democrats shouted from the floor. 'Gentlemen, I am in complete agreement with the Minister of War', the Chancellor retorted as shouts of 'hear, hear!' again resounded. 'You've entirely lost your head', Ledebour shouted back as the presiding officer tried frantically to restore order.

There was no shadow government, Bethmann protested. There was a real government, for which he was responsible to the emperor. 'And when I no longer feel myself capable of this responsibility, you will no longer see me here', he added. Meanwhile the government was of the opinion that without the mutual trust between military and civil authorities, 'that was so regrettably lacking in Zabern', nothing could be done to correct the situation. This had now been inscribed from the very top in the consciences of all parties to the incidents, he contended. 'But not yet effected', the left shouted back. 'Gentlemen', the Chancellor continued gamely, 'there will be compensation for what happened in the past.' For the future, he said, 'we can only restore what was damaged on the basis of law and justice'. This time there were 'Bravos!' from the right and hisses from the left.

The inevitable Conservative spokesman finally rose in nominal support of Bethmann. For a man of Alsatian sensitivity, Peirotes had been casual enough about insulting East Elbians and proclaiming officers traitors, he announced. Turning to Fehrenbach, he brushed off the reservations about official channels. Unlike earlier NCOs, the current generation no longer got away with what they used to, he noted revealingly. He then brought the right to their feet with a testimonial to the honour of the army.

There was another interlude as an acerbic Polish grandee, loyally cheered by his tiny party, enumerated horror stories of military arrogance and discriminations against his countrymen exceeding any on the Upper Rhine. A German grandee countered that the Zabern police had deliberately practised benign neglect in order to embarrass the army.

But the day's last speeches again turned the fire on the government. Georg Weill of the Alsatian SPD drew attention to the embarrassingly obvious: that the military had been called to the royal presence in Donaueschingen. The Chancellor had not. To the delight of the left, Ludwig Haas, a Progressive lawyer from Baden invited the government to try the shoe on the other foot. Supposing, he asked, that officers had been arrested by civilians? His only reservation about the civil authorities in Zabern was that they had failed to exploit their prerogative of demanding military assistance against Reuter and his officers. There was a storm of hilarity and applause on the left.

Turning towards Falkenhayn, Eugen Ricklin of the Alsatian Centre agreed that the army had conquered Alsace-Lorraine and built the Reichstag. 'But I tell him today that it is also the German army that has lost Alsace-Lorraine to the German Empire', he continued to cheers from his colleagues. Bethmann was no longer speaking for himself, he implied. He had changed his position since that hopeful affirmation of the law earlier in the week. 'It is not the law that he has protected', Ricklin declared. 'What he has protected is the military administration, while leaving the civil authorities in the lurch.' There were more cheers from Alsatians. *Wackes* was a disgrace. Recruits no less than officers had honour to defend. In any case, there had been no question of Zabern's loyalty, no evidence of endemic hostility to the army. Bar-room scuffles were not political incidents. They also took place elsewhere. Ricklin called attention to the absence of government representatives from Strasbourg in the chamber, and the rumoured resignation of Wedel. It was fine that Bethmann wanted to be liberal, Ricklin agreed. But could he be liberal, with respect to Alsace-Lorraine? It was a fair question.

With that, the House proceeded to vote on the censure resolution. But the outcome was never in doubt. For the right, as for the rest of the house, the question was one of symbol and principle. But the principle in this case was 'My emperor's Chancellor, that is, the constitutional status quo, right or wrong.' As it turned out, this was worth fifty-four Conservative votes even from members already punning on the Chancellor's name: Bethmann-Sollweg, that is, Bethmann must go. In a rare show of solidarity, the rest of the house, 293 deputies from the Social Democrats on the left to the National Liberals somewhere on the moderate right, voted for censure. Four deputies abstained. One ballot was invalid. It was the second censure in the same year, the second in German parliamentary history.[22]

Again ironically, it was widely believed that Bethmann himself had snatched defeat from the jaws of victory. Gustav Stresemann, who was later to have his own experiences with the bloody-minded right as Chancellor and Foreign Minister of the Weimar Republic, was forthright about the Chancellor's role in a long, defensive letter to an obviously indignant National Liberal correspondent in Dresden. The Reichstag resolution, Stresemann emphasised prophylactically, was not directed at the army but at the Chancellor. But had he been a deputy, he would have supported the resolution too, Stresemann admitted. He had found Bethmann's remarks in the Reichstag, like his position in the whole affair, to be inadequate. He considered the Chancellor's statements too little and too late. They seemed to say that nothing had been done about Forstner, and said nothing at all about how to improve the relationship between the civil authorities and the military. Stresemann considered Falkenhayn's statements, no less than Bethmann's, an expression of unqualified help-lessness.[23]

The Social Democrat Albert Südekum rhetorically conceded the Chancellor 'certain residual inhibitions that prevented the worst, a vestige of self-respect that precluded explicit confirmation of the *de facto* capitu-lation to military dictatorship'. But what genuinely surprised him, he wrote to Morris Hillquit in New York, was the unanticipated civil liber-tarian indignation of the middle-class parties.[24]

Had it not been for Bethmann, and of course Falkenhayn, the Bavarian representative in Berlin was convinced that the middle-class parties would, in fact, have gone along with the government. 'And the remarkable thing', he added, 'is that the Minister of War actually had no intention of offend-ing the Reichstag.' He assumed that Falkenhayn was a victim of simple inexperience.[25]

There was no comparable explanation for Bethmann's failings. Von Salza und Lichtenau, the Saxon representative in Berlin and a notably shrewd observer, could only puzzle at the Chancellor's retreat into details nobody has asked of him, and his reluctance to affirm the basic principle that neither he nor the emperor would tolerate military impropriety. It was understandable that the Minister of War should defend the army, Salza said. But the Chancellor had only made things worse.[26]

There were innumerable explanations for Bethmann's disappointing performance, some plausible, some frivolous. Personal indisposition was one conceivable factor. His son's debts and wife's terminal illness seem also to have been on his mind.[27] Sincerity was another explanation. Bethmann actually believed in the imperial system. Sober, intelligent, tenacious and honest, he was neither a crypto-reformer nor a cynic. His defence of the system, ill-advised and ambiguous as it may have been, actually meant what it said. The same could even be true of his omissions. 'I learned today why the Chancellor neglected to read aloud the imperial order of December 2', that is, the order to send Kühne to Zabern, the Bavarian minister credibly reported after the debate. Bethmann had wanted to avoid the impression that he was trying to buy off the impend-ing censure vote. He also wanted to avoid any impression that he was hiding behind the emperor.[28]

Bethmann's dedication was, in fact, a thing of wonder even to his closest associates. 'What you say about Bethmann and his remoteness from the specifically military temperament is very interesting', Wahnschaffe, the director of the chancellery, was to write to an aspiring Bethmann biographer years later, ' ... and yet he was profoundly convinced that the Prussian-German state lived and died by its military.' The result, Wahnschaffe acknowledged, was 'that it had misled him in the Zabern business, where, contrary to my advice, he went much too far in defending the army's errors.'[29]

But the contingencies of imperial politics were explanation enough for the Chancellor's performance. The army's confidence had been an inevitable factor in any chancellor's calculations since Bismarck. The Countess Spitzemberg was as puzzled as thousands of her plebian fellow citizens by the failure to resolve the problem by simply dismissing 'the dumb lieutenant'.[30] But neither she nor they were operating under Bethmann's restraints. It was a practical reality that the Chancellor was virtually helpless without the support of the Reichstag. But his job was impossible without the support of an emperor who, as recently as March, had provoked Bethmann to snarling rage with a clipping from the London *Daily Graphic* on the subject of 'fearful, meticulous bureaucrats, who hate doing anything and are only plagued into activity by the experts'. As though this were not enough, Bethmann was then instructed to pass it on to the War Ministry and the General Staff.[31]

'The very factors that are supposed to make things easier, His Majesty and the Conservatives, complicate things for me with all their strength and cunning', Bethmann had written to his friend Eisendecher, the Prussian minister in Baden, in early October. He regretted not having quit in July, he told his friend. The only reason he stayed at all, he said, was because of the difficult diplomatic situation and the domestic hangover following the spring's compromise on the military budget.[32]

The functional relationship between the army's confidence and the emperor's confidence was particularly hard to overlook. Even as the melancholy Chancellor bore the emperor's fardels on the government bench, and suffered the slings and arrows of outraged parliamentarians, the emperor remained intransigent — well, nearly intransigent. 'I am continually left out', Treutler reported from Donaueschingen. 'His Majesty obviously does not want to talk with me about Zabern.' Nor, despite Plessen's urgings, did William want to return to Berlin. He had at least agreed to see Wedel the next day before lunch, but only in the company of Deimling.[33] The emperor himself confirmed the message. He informed the Chancellor that he had ordered Wedel and Deimling to report in person so that he could impress on both of them the absolute need for co-ordination. He wanted to remind the general once again to stay strictly within the limits of the law. 'Actually that ought to be self-evident anyway', the telegram added.[34] A follow-up message from Treutler expressed hope that the Chancellor was satisfied with the latest arrangement. If so, Treutler urged the Chancellor, he should notify the emperor accordingly. He should also make sure the telegram arrived before Wedel, and before the emperor again changed his mind.[35]

Bethmann complied. He had tried to square things with the Reichstag, he informed William. He was unable to say whether he had succeeded. In the surviving draft, an extended passage is crossed out. The Chancellor had wanted to urge the emperor to reject Wedel's resignation if it were offered. It was a possibility Bethmann clearly took seriously. 'Were he to leave under the present circumstances', he had wanted to warn William, 'there would be no way to avoid the impression that he had been sacrificed to a military that actually did behave illegally in its excitement.' He conceded that a new Alsatian government was called for, but asked that decisions be deferred pending his arrival in Donaueschingen. In place of all of this, a supplementary note in Wahnschaffe's hand expressed the Chancellor's insistence that he be present for the interview with Wedel and Deimling and emphasised that his familiarity with the situation in Berlin was necessary in dealing with the case.

That evening Bethmann left for the south.[36] But the decisions were reached before he got there. Only Deimling has left notes on the actual meeting, though contemporary picture magazines published photos of bearded men conferring earnestly in the Fürstenberg palace garden.[37] Deimling walked up and down in front of the palace after being warned against any further *faux pas*, he recalled in his memoirs. He then proposed that the 99th be transferred to its exercise grounds outside Zabern, both to avoid further friction, and to remind the town of its economic interest in the troops. Both Forstner and Reuter should go along. After their pending trials, they could then be transferred to new regiments. The emperor had no objections, and issued orders accordingly.[38]

On Bethmann's arrival, emperor, Chancellor, governor and general, marched off to lunch with the rest of the house guests, including members of the Austrian aristocracy. 'With or without their monocles and lorgnons, they subjected me to a crossfire of glances', Deimling remembered. 'A couple of countesses looked at me half in curiosity, half in terror, as though they obviously regarded me as a kind of Gessler', that is, the villain of Schiller's *Wilhelm Tell*.[39] The emperor vanished after lunch and Bethmann reported the morning's decisions to Berlin. They had been reached before his arrival, he indicated loyally, 'in order not to tie my hands'. The disciplinary measures against Forstner were to be announced only after the fact. Falkenhayn was to be notified that Wedel had made Reuter's transfer a condition for staying at his job. Wedel's threatened resignation was obviously not to be announced either.[40]

Bethmann then returned to the capital, stopping *en route* in Stuttgart, where Weizsäcker, the Württemberg Prime Minister, expressed relief about the emperor's decision and anxiety about the parliamentary situation. He also assured the local diplomatic corps that the Chancellor had no intention of resigning.[41] There was more relief in neighbouring Baden. The royal family had been informed by the emperor himself that he considered the people of Zabern at fault, the military reaction legitimate, and 'far more drastic military measures' imaginable. They were only afraid he meant it. They were accordingly pleased when William informed the grand duchess of his decision to transfer the regiment out of town.[42]

While Bethmann was away, Wahnschaffe, like innumerable government spokesmen before and since, 'clarified' the government's position. But before meeting non-Socialist deputies on 5 December, he prudently cleared his remarks with Falkenhayn. There had been some misunderstandings, Wahnschaffe told the deputies. Certain members had also misunderstood on purpose, he intimated. Basically the Chancellor had already said everything that mattered. He understood the Parliament's concern, Wahnschaffe qualified, to the extent that 'it derives from a sense of justice'. He had also repeatedly made clear that justice would be done — but 'violation of the law can only be pursued in accordance with the law'.

Wahnschaffe summarised the incidents in Zabern with at least a marginal bow to Falkenhayn's handwritten emendations. He then summarized the steps already taken, tidying, but not overtly misrepresenting, the relations between the responsible authorities. 'His Majesty impressed on the commanding general that the military must unconditionally respect the law', he noted emphatically. He called attention to the Chancellor's first statement in the Reichstag about how the law would be upheld, and his statement in the debate that followed on how 'the actions, beginning with the clearing of the square', had been illegal, and that 'reparations must be made'. The deputies were informed of the Donaueschingen decisions: that the regiment was to be transferred, and that pending litigation was to have priority. That should preclude any further friction between the army and the people of Zabern, Wahnschaffe concluded. Later he also received the editor of the *National-Zeitung*, an evening paper with National Liberal connections, for an off-the-record interview.[43]

News of his parliamentary briefing appeared in the next day's papers. It was followed by clarifications of the clarification — presumably for one indignant and all-important reader in Donaueschingen. He had only been explaining the government position, Wahnschaffe informed Treutler. He had not disavowed Falkenhayn. There had been no reference to Forstner or Reuter. The editor of the *National-Zeitung* denied leaking his interview. He had learned of the briefing from his parliamentary correspondent, he said, and only called attention to what was not said. Testifying eloquently to the state of National Liberal nerves, Bassermann volunteered to confirm that reports of Wahnschaffe's briefing had been inaccurate. The offer was gratefully accepted.[44]

The pragmatic optimism in Berlin contrasted with the gloom in official Strasbourg, where Wedel brooded over his successive humiliations. In Berlin 'an absolutely reliable source' had already informed Axel von Varnbüler, the Württemberg minister, that Wedel himself could have prevented the whole affair had he only been more persistent in threatening to resign when requesting an audience with the emperor.[45] Directly or indirectly, the source was presumably Bethmann. Wedel was bitter. He had neither the occasion nor the right to demand an audience with the emperor, pending completion of staff reports on Zabern, the governor maintained. By that time, the emperor had already gone over his head. In any case, he demanded of the Chancellor, would his staff report have made any more impression on William than it did on Bethmann, who neglected to mention it in the Reichstag debate? Now his hands were tied by *faits accomplis*, the local press was unhappy, and his decision not to resign had been a superfluous sacrifice. The cracks were plastered over, but 'half-measures avenge themselves', he added darkly.[46]

A man of considerable natural dignity with little more to lose in the affair than self-respect, Wedel none the less carried on the good fight. Scarcely back from Donaueschingen, he found a report from the prefect in Saarburg. The senior veterinary of the local regiment had called a proletarian customer *Wackes* while drunk, was sentenced to eight days' house arrest for drunkenness, and was now awaiting trial before a court martial on charges of assault and insult. Local editors had been persuaded to keep the episode quiet.

The case impressed Wedel as symptomatic. 'At the end of my most humble report of 16 November, I expressed the reverential wish that Your Majesty might most graciously accede through the royal ministry of war to ban the use of *Wackes* by all troops in the provinces', he reminded the emperor in tactical prose. 'Especially after the incidents in Zabern, such an expression of royal opinion, in which no one could see any indulgence, would be gratefully regarded as an act signifying a magnanimous sense of justice.'[47] In a statement to the official news service on the Donaueschingen meeting, the governor even referred to the emperor as the guarantor of justice and constitutionality.[48] No ban on *Wackes* followed. But there was no repudiation of the interview either, though Bethmann expressed some concern about the unsolicited invocation of the emperor's authority.[49]

A further complication in Wedel's life was a published interview with his under-secretary. Hugo Zorn von Bulach was the first native Alsatian to have reached so lofty a rank in the provincial government. He denounced the lieutenant and the excesses of the military, and denied that the civil authorities had been under the influence of the army. The interview embarrassed Wedel, but outraged the emperor. William thought it bad enough that Zorn had subordinated his official role to his local feelings. He found it even worse that the under-secretary had smeared the army in an interview with the *Berliner Morgenpost*, a democratic paper. The imperial outrage was communicated to Lyncker, the Chief of the Military Cabinet, who passed the message to Valentini, the Chief of the Civil Cabinet, who informed Wedel. Thoroughly shaken but manfully standing his quaking ground, Zorn assured Wedel that he had only meant Forstner, and that he appreciated the need for civil–military co-operation. There had been no intention of putting his superior on the spot, or anticipating the decisions of the courts, he insisted. He had only wanted to say his piece after four weeks of intense heat from fellow Alsatians. He had assumed that the Donaueschingen decisions had finally relieved him of the need to remain officially silent. Wedel loyally defended him in his report to the emperor.[50]

On 9 December the Reichstag resumed its debate on Zabern. Speaking for the Social Democrats, Philipp Scheidemann criticised the Donaueschingen decisions. He considered the removal of the troops an economic hardship for the town, and a practical hardship for the enlisted men. He was incensed by the discriminatory punishment of the recruits. He believed that the Chancellor should resign like a French or British prime minister. Bethmann's continued tenure in office, Scheidemann argued, corresponded to the decision to keep the offending officers in Zabern — not that he meant to compare Bethmann with them in any other way, he added. The officers remained at their posts in the interest of military authority. The Chancellor presumably remained in the interest of the monarchy. He questioned the Chancellor's diplomatic capacity, and the wisdom of appropriating funds while the Chancellor remained in office. 'Either the Reichstag draws some conclusions from its resolution of last week, or it indicts itself for an ill-considered resolution', Scheidemann contended.

His self-esteem and diplomatic capacity were matters for himself to decide, Bethmann replied. He charged Scheidemann with misrepresentation of the constitution and denied any intention of resigning. 'The majority of the German people had no intention of subjecting the imperial authority to the coercion of the Social Democrats', he added to laughter from the left and applause on the right.

Peter Spahn of the Centre and Bassermann of the National Liberals were quick to concur. 'We fund no budgets and write no legislation for the Chancellor or the Ministry of War', Spahn declared. 'We appropriate money, we write laws, we sit in the Reichstag in the interest of our empire and our people.'

Count Westarp, the paladin of the Conservatives, denied that the military had acted illegally at all. Self-defence had not merely been legitimate but obligatory, in Westarp's view. 'The way people are, a resolute personality makes a greater impression than the letter of the law', he proclaimed to approbative noises from the right. 'An officer's authority would be in jeopardy if he were to leave the defence of his honour to a lawyer's pen rather than pull his dagger in the event of insult', Westarp continued. He saw the previous week's efforts as a consistent attempt to democratise the army, subordinate it to the press and the mob, and to carry on the 'revolutionary assault' of the previous spring. He decried Zorn's interview and Wedel's official statement as unjustified assertions of victory over the military, and fired away at Mahl. 'Great balls of fire!' ('*Ja, zum Himmel-donnerwetter!*'), he roared to screams of mirth from the floor, 'when I was a prefect ... ' (continued laughter and shouts from the left, shouts of 'very good!' from the right.) The speaker had to intervene to restore order. 'Gentlemen', Westarp declared, 'the state is a matter of power' ('Hear, hear!' from the Social Democrats, 'Matter of law!' from the National Liberals).

Otto Wiemer, from the Progressives, challenged all the preceding speakers on the significance of the censure. In the process, he confirmed the isolation of the Social Democrats. They had not demanded the Chancellor's resignation after the censure vote of the previous January, he noted. It was inconsistent that they should demand it now, particularly when Polish policy was still unchanged, whereas the government had actually taken some action on Zabern. The point of censure was to strengthen Parliament, he argued. He was himself in sympathy with the goal, prefer-ring parliamentary government anytime to 'the pseudo-constitutionalism we have today'. But there was no obligation to resign. Parliamentary government meant that the opposition parties were themselves ready to form a government, Wiemer added pointedly. He was unsure whether this applied to the Social Democrats. 'Our colleague Frank is nodding', he noted, referring to Ludwig Frank, a lawyer from Baden and one of the party's young stars, who was a consistent revisionist in a party prover-bially dominated by the heavy hand of Marxist orthodoxy. But it was questionable whether Frank's party would go along with him, and whether Kautsky and Rosa Luxemburg, the pillars of the party's centre and left, would concur, Wiemer said. In effect, there was nothing more to do: the censure resolution had had its effect, though he regretted that the Reichstag had not been officially informed of the executive's decisions. The Reichstag had none the less made its point, that is, that illegality would not be tolerated.

Replying for the government, Falkenhayn defended the government's silence. There could be no public statement before the investigation was complete and disciplinary action had been confirmed, he maintained — though without further details. To do otherwise would compromise the autonomy of the responsible commanding officers. As for the incon-veniences attending on the regiment's transfer out of town, the purpose was to reassert order, the minister emphasised. The inconveniences this caused were irrelevant. Bethmann had little to add. One side of the House supported the army's position, the other the civilians, he noted officiously. The judicial process was underway. He refrained in the meanwhile from categorical judgements, and denied that there had been either a shift or a retreat in the government's position as had been claimed respectively by Wiemer and Westarp. The debate had been a useful exercise, the Chancellor added. It illuminated the differences between the parties, and demonstrated the isolation of the Social Democrats, which, he hoped, would continue indefinitely.[51]

The same day there were two new reports from the Reich department of justice, confirming that the legal situation was obscure. Prussian regulations obviously applied on Prussian territory. But Alsace-Lorraine was another case. The specific regulation in question was in conflict with the Prussian constitution anyway. The Chancellor was urged to avoid any public statement on the matter, and to consider instead whether 'the difficulties arising from the present juridical situation might not be met by a new version of the military regulations'.

A supplementary memo added that the military regulations applied neither to the civil population nor to the civil authorities. There was no recourse to article 61 of the imperial constitution either, with its stated intention of extending the Prussian military regulations to the other states of the empire. Military intervention was therefore a matter of whatever law prevailed in the provinces, and not of the Prussian regulations, the memo continued. This meant French laws of 1791 and 1848, which permitted autonomous military action only in self-defence or when the armed forces were otherwise unable to defend their positions, and a related German law of 1872, which failed, however, to cover military intervention for purposes of maintaining public order. The other basis for military intervention was a situation so serious that martial law was required. But there was no question of any such emergency in Zabern, the memo stated. Nor, 'to the extent the situation is known here', could one be assumed.[52]

Renewed debate in the Reichstag, a week after the censure resolution, opened with attacks on Falkenhayn's evasiveness and Bethmann's omissions, and continued with an important speech by Matthias Erzberger, a rising star in the Centre. Erzberger was contemptuous of the argument that the military's action was justified by extenuating circumstances. Carried to its logical conclusion, this meant that the commanding general of the Guards detachment could arrest the Chancellor and the whole Wilhelmstrasse, Berlin's Whitehall, if he felt the Chancellor was about to cause trouble by an untoward speech in the Reichstag, Erzberger declared to appreciative snickers. He emphasised the significance of the censure vote. 'It is perfectly clear that a mature people with universal education, universal military service and a universal tax obligation, cannot be governed only by senior bureaucrats', Erzberger proclaimed to shouts of assent from the Centre and left. It was not true that nothing would come of the censure resolution. The Reichstag could accomplish as much with it as it wished ('Right!' from the Centre and left). It could not be ignored.

The Donaueschingen decisions were unlikely to have been reached without it, Erzberger continued. Alsace-Lorraine had calmed down as a result of it: 'Without regard to party, the population of the provinces has been reassured to know that while military revolt and dictatorship might dominate Zabern for a few hours, the Reichstag is a defender of our rights', Erzberger thundered. 'This is a gain for the entire German Empire, not only for the provinces, for which I personally have an especially high regard.' At the same time, he repudiated the Social Democratic threat to force the Chancellor from office by withholding funds. Budgetary blockade was the last resort in Erzberger's opinion. But it was a hollow threat from a party without majority support, and that incurred no risk. What the Reichstag had said was simply that it expected the Chancellor to do something.

Successive speakers only confirmed the remarkable ambiguity of the situation. Haussmann pointed to the ambiguity of the Chancellor's situation: the breach between Bethmann and the military, which was now compounded by the breach between Bethmann and the Reichstag. But he confirmed the parliamentarians' ambiguity too. The Social Democrats wanted to force the Chancellor out of office. But they were unable to do what inevitably followed from their position: organise the compact majority that could support another government. If the Chancellor were consistent about remaining in office, Haussmann continued, he would logically dissolve the Reichstag. But he knew how a newly elected House would look. 'Very good!' and 'Right!', echoed the left and centre. Given the intransigence of the military and the inaccessibility of the emperor, Haussmann rhetorically acknowledged extenuating circumstances in the Chancellor's situation. 'The Chancellor not only needs to ask: how will I explain it to the emperor, but where will I say it to the emperor?' The left and centre tittered with appreciation. 'He has to study the timetable and ride the train for thirty hours to present his case in a moment of weakness.' 'Right!' echoed again from the left.

Again replying for the government, Falkenhayn begged the outstanding questions: Christmas furloughs had not been cancelled, retention of the regiment in Zabern was not an issue, investigations were still underway. Georg Oertel of the Conservatives rose reflexively to the government's defence. 'Any number of things we have been accustomed to regard as stable in the German Empire are beginning to quake', he announced darkly to cheers from the right. 'Forces that we have been accustomed to regard as reliable supports of the constitutional prerogatives of Crown and people are beginning to fail us.' He hoped the army was not among them.

As the day ended, Bethmann himself returned to the rostrum. Censure, he declared, was a parliamentary declaration of war, the equivalent of attack on a military position. There was no breach in the army, he insisted. Nor was there a fundamental breach in his own position that justice must be done according to due process. 'Have I opposed this process or have I participated in it?' he asked to shouts from the Social Democrats. He noted the variety of motives contained in the censure resolution. Only the Social Democrats, he argued, were actually using it to attack the constitution and the prerogatives of the emperor.[53]

He had, in fact, made his point — or the House had done it for him. The debate wandered off in a general discussion of the Krupp case, with much attention to the role of the Social Democrats' Karl Liebknecht on the investigating committee. Finally the House recessed until mid-January for the Christmas break. As the members adjourned, the speaker announced the agenda: women's suffrage and the official boycott of taverns owned or managed by Social Democrats. Like all recent military debates, it would be an occasion to air grievances of many kinds, Zabern again included. In the meanwhile, Bethmann was out of the woods. Paradoxically, his very weakness had combined with the weakness of the House to produce his victory. The majority of the Reichstag was unprepared to join the Social Democrats.[54] There was little likelihood of new elections, which would only increase the anti-government majority. The emperor could hardly throw his Chancellor to the Conservative wolves without damage to foreign opinion, and the likelihood that the gesture would be read as a sacrifice to the parliamentary lions. Besides, as the emperor well knew, there was no credible candidate to succeed the Chancellor anyway.[55]

While the deputies returned to their constituencies, and the government to the relative security of their in-baskets, the judiciary ground on in the provinces. On 11 December a military court sentenced Kaestlé's sources, the Zabern recruits, to six weeks in the stockade for leaking their story of Forstner's various capers contrary to regulations. They were represented by a civilian attorney. The judges considered their inexperience and their naïveté *vis-à-vis* a city slicker from Strasbourg to be extenuating circumstances. As the prosecution had asked for seven months for one defendant, and three months for the others, the sentences were generally regarded as lenient — at least for enlisted men.[56]

On 19 December another military court found Forstner guilty of aggravated assault and sentenced him to forty-three days in the stockade, the minimum penalty for the offence.[57] The decision was immediately appealed. A resumé submitted by Wedel at Bethmann's request the day after Christmas reported disorderly conduct charges pending against some fifteen inhabitants of Zabern for alleged offences between 7 and 11 November; no charges at all against the suspects of 26 November; a total of thirty-one arrests the night of 28 November; a charge of 'revolutionary incitement', based on a law of 1822, against a Zabern worker accused of singing the 'Marseillaise' in November; an additional arrest for unseemly conduct ordered by a local magistrate on 3 December; dismissal of charges against three adolescents who had again been heard to shout *Bettschisser* in early December; and a delay in the proceedings against Blanck. The Dettweiler factory-hand, while accused of threatening noises, was inaccessible to prosecution in a pre-xerox age because the relevant documents were needed by the military courts or a government facing questions in the Reichstag.

Libel charges were meanwhile being considered against the *Zaberner Anzeiger*, the *Elsässer* and the *Strassburger Neue Zeitung* for the flag story. Höflich, Forstner's sergeant, had actually brought charges against several papers on his own behalf. Damage suits were pending from an officer of the state police, indignant because Wiebicke had peddled postcards of his colleagues looking unconcerned, and from a house painter named Oberle, who was suing the army, the local police and the state police for false arrest on 30 November. Schad's complaint about the London photographer had been resolved by destroying the exposed plate. A handbill from *Simplicissimus*, the satirical weekly, was under investigation in Munich, where the magazine appeared. The authorities were considering charges of *lèse-majesté*. The case against Kaestlé, the Strasbourg reporter, was also delayed while the military court used the relevant papers. Finally the state police sergeant responsible for the search of Wiebicke's office had been officially reprimanded — there had been an official protest to the army from the Strasbourg government as well — and most of the arrest victims of 28 November were suing Reuter and Schad for false arrest. The suits against the officers were a fact of vast symbolic importance, but hardly recognisable as such in the tidy bureaucratic symmetry of the official report. In a cover letter, Wedel noted Conservative screams for disciplinary action against Mahl. He saw no reason at all for it, but added that Mahl had conscientiously filed charges against himself.[58]

In the world outside the government offices, there was a thunder of public meetings, resolutions, opinion campaigns, and expressions of concern, both domestic and foreign, from as far away as Sweden and Tunisia, where the local consul suspected resident Alsatians of a campaign to subvert native confidence in Germany.[59] Reactions were generally predictable. Few could be surprised by a tide of critical editorials in the liberal press, mass meetings in Social Democratic Hamburg, south Germany or Alsace itself, or whole columns of reports from their Berlin correspondents in major foreign papers like *The Times* or *Le Temps*.

The parties of the centre tended to reticence. There was also a chorus, not entirely spontaneous, from the right. The subsidised Anti-Social Democratic League fired off its own salvo in the escalating war of pamphlets. Between extravagant subheads and torrents of exclamation points, they conventionally denounced parliamentarians, francophiles and 'undisciplined punks' (*zuchtlose Burschen*).[60]

The pressures on the government, aggressive, obsequious, opportunistic, but also genuinely concerned, were reflected in the Chancellor's files. The military lost no opportunity to warn of the slippery depths of Alsatian hostility. Was it true, Falkenhayn wanted to know, that the French flag had been wildly cheered in a Strasbourg theatre when carried on stage by a trained dog? Was it true that the German flag had been hissed while police stood by without acting? No, Wedel replied in response to the Chancellor's query. Nor was it any affair of the military, he added tactfully but firmly. If there were any explaining to do, it was a matter for himself and the emperor.[61] A few weeks later, Falkenhayn passed on a friendly editorial from a Heidelberg paper, calling attention to the emperor's characteristically emphatic marginal notes. 'Press and Reichstag in the trap of francophiles', a headline read. 'Right!' the emperor wrote. 'Submission to the tyranny of the mob', said another headline. 'Right!' the emperor wrote again. 'Bravo!' he added. Falkenhayn thought the Chancellor would like to take note.[62] The week before Christmas he forwarded a year's volume and fourteen individual copies of Zislin's bitterly anti-German *Dur's Elsass*.[63]

Private correspondents included the director of a major Bavarian bank and the editor of *Das Grundeigentum*, the house organ of the landlord's association. Both expressed sympathy with the Chancellor. The editor included an editorial from his latest edition, denouncing the Reichstag for its attention to trivia — presumably meaning Zabern — rather than devotion to genuine problems like door-to-door peddling.[64] An outraged Conservative called Bethmann's attention to the insults and humiliations regularly visited on Germans in Alsace. His solutions included posting Alsatian recruits as far from home as possible, and definitive annexation of the provinces by the adjacent states or Prussia alone.[65]

There was also a brochure entitled *Zabern and the King's Uniform* from one Gerd Fritz Leberecht, who was actually a retired first lieutenant named Adolf Stein.[66] Stein approached the War Ministry immediately after the first Reichstag debate, requesting access to the Zabern files as material for what was obviously to be a pro-government pamphlet. Within a week, an edition of 30,000 was in circulation, and a new edition of 100,000 in the works. Stein forwarded copies to both Bethmann and the emperor. He expressed the hope that the Landeskriegsverband, the veteran's organisation, might take 'several thousand' more. A cover letter to Bethmann referred to 'the pathological arrogance of the natives' of Alsace. It tactfully refrained from further comment on grounds that 'in my view, no patriotic German should even be allowed in the present circumstances to criticise the Chancellor, who is trying to overcome the 'gap''. An official reply acknowledged that the emperor had noted the brochure with interest, and speculated on the possibility of helping find readers. It turned out, however, that even in imperial Germany, patriotism had unanticipated limits. The Prussian Kriegsverband wanted nothing to do with the brochure. It was contrary to policy to circulate or recommend literary materials, a spokesman declared. The organisation's board had also been distressed that the brochure, contrary to their by-laws, attacked not only Social Democrats but other parties too. And finally, even at bulk rates, the price seemed extraordinarily high.[67]

There was a counter-flow of letters from the Alsatian establishment. In late November, Baron Hugo von Türckheim wrote to Bethmann, protesting at the 'devastating, occult power of the pan-German military party'. Türckheim emphasised that he was on social terms with the German administrators — though he had been unable to see Wedel, 'a man who dislikes consulting people from here'. Like 'thousands of the best' of his countrymen, he had concluded that the military commanders were in charge. By comparison, he informed the Chancellor, the situation Bethmann had known as a reserve lieutenant in Alsace thirty-eight years earlier could be considered a golden age. Türckheim blamed it all on Deimling. Germanisation was in visible decline, he informed the Chancellor. He wondered whether the whole business had been arranged as an excuse to rescind the new constitution, and feared a definitive break with France. Bethmann passed the letter on to the emperor.[68]

A few days later Türckheim's views were indirectly confirmed by Puttkammer, a senior German official in Colmar. He was appalled by Bethmann's reliance on the military reports. 'No one here, including Old Germans and civil servants', he wrote to Wahnschaffe, 'has the slightest doubt that the military has committed a flagrant illegality with no compelling reason, and is still at it.' Even a few officers shared his view, he said. He insisted that there was no significant hostility to the army. He conceded that news reports were irresponsible. But it was the army that had managed in a few days to damage the German cause in ways that would require a decade of recovery — or do you want to introduce a military dictatorship?' he asked. It was 'Nothing personal, but we German officials are in a state of total consternation', he informed Wahnschaffe. Replying three weeks later, a tired Wahnschaffe could only concur.[69] 'There have been a number of inexcusable stupidities in Zabern', he wrote to a hawkish colonel in Alsace who had requested material for Reuter's impending trial. He conceded that Reuter might be decent. But Wahnschaffe hardly found him 'calm and judicious', notwithstanding the claims in the colonel's letter. On the contrary, Wahnschaffe found his treatment of the civil officials 'petty and *kommissig*', that is, military in the most pejorative sense.[70]

Among the most interesting items in the Chancellor's files were reports from the prefect of Strasbourg, who happened to be his cousin, and an unidentified, but obviously shrewd and well-connected, 'Old Alsatian Hand' who had sounded out local opinion in early December. Things had calmed down dramatically since the transfer of the 99th, the relatively lenient decision against the recruits and the stiff decision against Forstner, the cousin reported. Should the impending decision on Reuter vindicate local feeling, and the regiment return to Zabern, he could even see the affair turning out for the best. He indicated general admiration for the solidarity of Old German immigrants and the Reichstag majority. The innumerable protest meetings had been unexceptionably decorous. He had even been able to call off police surveillance of them, the prefect informed the Chancellor. Meanwhile he had been assured by his brother-in-law, the liberal Reichstag deputy Gerhart Schulze-Gävernitz, that the censure resolution was actually aimed not at Bethmann but at Falkenhayn. What was needed in the provinces, the prefect wrote, was a new governor, dedicated to the 'Bismarckian programme of German schools, German army and a benevolent administration'. Nothing but the best would do, he added, and Bethmann himself was the most frequently mentioned candidate for the job.[71]

The 'Old Alsatian Hand', identified only as a resident of Strasbourg between 1874 and 1902, reported extensively on conversations with all kinds of people 'except Social Democrats'. He concluded that the real local issues had nothing to do with Zabern, which was neither a question of party nor nationality, save as Germans made it one. The real issue was particularism. As he saw it, a sensible German policy would aim at separating the particularists from the 'chauvinists', that is, the advocates of reunion with France. Official toughness was no way to go about it.

Proceeding to diagnosis, the commentator identified the difficulties: opposition had unquestionably increased with the coming of universal suffrage, a directly elected legislature and mass political participation; there was unquestionably competition for jobs as natives, too, began pursuing them; there were feelings of economic discrimination and administrative impotence *vis-à-vis* Berlin. He recommended home rule, assimilation of the Old Germans, jobs for Alsatians in the Berlin administration, and unsubsidised local operation of the provincial railways. Responsibility was a salutary thing, he argued. There was a strong pitch for administrative competence in Strasbourg, letting the chips — in this case Zorn von Bulach — fall where they might. There was another strong pitch for meaningful Germanisation. Why, the commentator wondered, should the entrepreneur of a Strasbourg department store have to go to Paris for money?

Finally there was the problem of 'the military' party and Deimling's relentless confusion of particularism with chauvinism. 'In general, the relationship between the population and the army, which is to say the officers, is very good', the commentator confirmed, 'if only because the officers are good customers.' Nothing could do more damage to the government's reputation than the suggestion that it was impotent with respect to the army.

Zabern itself, the commentator insisted, was purely a legal question. He regretted the failure of the Strasbourg government to resign if Reuter and Deimling remained at their posts; regretted the effect of suggestions that Bethmann had been indisposed in the Reichstag; regretted the implication that Zabern was an attack on the army. 'Alsatians have told me "It would all have been OK if the lieutenant had stayed home for two weeks, voilà tout" ', he reported. As things stood, they were bitter — and likely to be more bitter still if Zabern lost its garrison. The commentator urged the immediate transfer of Reuter and Deimling, followed by the retirement of Zorn. 'Rarely has Alsace felt itself so German as when the Reichstag supported it with all its force', he said. He believed that the government could exploit this before the provincial legislature convened in January.[72] The report was classified 'top secret', and surviving files are silent about its distribution.

In the meanwhile the campaign for Alsatian hearts and minds was diverted by action on the flanks. On 23 December, Traugott von Jagow, Berlin's chief of police, published a letter in the *Kreuz-Zeitung*, the Conservative house organ, aggressively defending Forstner, in particular, and an army that had to operate 'almost in enemy territory', in general. It was unclear whether he was referring to the proximity of France or the situation in the provinces. Either way the letter hardly made life easier for the government. There was an official denial of any official responsibility and an immediate disavowal of Jagow's views by Prussian officials. Wedel, whose howls were audible from Strasbourg, was authorised to inform the legislature that he had protested against Jagow's statement, and that there had been no intention of provoking the French. The Prussian government meanwhile regretted any misunderstanding. Bethmann added that Dallwitz, the Prussian Minister of Interior and Jagow's superior, had reprimanded the police chief. In a plaintive note to Dallwitz, Jagow replied that he had written only as a private citizen with a law degree and some experience with public order. He wanted attention, he conceded. He wondered whether Dallwitz might like to cover his *démarche* with a statement on academic freedom. Not even the left could object to that, Jagow contended. In a letter to Wahnschaffe a few days later, he regretted the government's disavowal. Ever tactful, Wahnschaffe acknowledged Jagow's right to speak out on behalf of the army, but found himself unable to regard Jagow's letter as a gesture of support for the Chancellor. '*Ceterum censeo*, enough of this unpleasantness', he concluded affirmatively. 'Make yourself a good New Year's punch!'[73]

A few days later, Jagow's bugle call was followed by an echo from the crown prince in Danzig. On 29 December it was widely reported that the heir apparent had twice wired support to Deimling a month before. A long visit with the Chancellor followed. It was followed by the inevitable clarifications. *'Immer feste druff'*, ('Hit 'em again'), one telegram was reported to say, though this was subsequently denied.[74] The crown prince himself told interviewers that he was merely expressing personal views. There had been no intention of prejudicing cases under adjudication or of exposing autocratic sympathies he solemnly denied he held.[75]

An intensive search failed to find the telegraph clerk believed to have leaked the message. Subsequent investigation revealed it was Reuter himself who had confidentially passed on the news to several of his officers and superiors in Strasbourg. In early January the search was quietly called off.[76]

'The year's bad end provoked Your Majesty's justified outrage, and we can expect the assults of democracy in the year to come', Bethmann wired the emperor on New Year's Eve. 'At the same time, Your Majesty can look back on 1913 with satisfaction in the fact that confidence in Your Majesty's exalted personage is so firmly established in Germany and the world that the people's sense of purpose will recover.'[77]

A seasonal greeting to his friend Oettingen carried a different message. 'I suppose I don't qualify as a politician', Bethmann wrote. He found the constitutional apparatus hopeless, but was reluctant to lead a charge against the emperor. Since the recent Moroccan crisis, the alternative was to hang on under rightwing fire and hope to save an occasional chestnut.[78]

Meanwhile the troops of the 99th hung on in their winter exile, where packages of socks, sausage, cigars and even some M3,000 in cash contributions had reportedly arrived from all over Germany.[79] In reply to a parliamentary inquiry, an official spokesman denied that their transfer had been a punishment. Höflich, who was there, took a different view. 'If he thought camp life in winter was no punishment, I only regret he didn't have to live out there himself', he recalled in his memoirs.[80]

References

1   *Verhandlungen des Reichstages*, XIII. Legislaturperiode, I. Session, Vol. 291 (Berlin, 1914).
2   Undated drafts of Falkenhayn's reply to Zabern interpellation, 29 November 1913, RK 170, Els.-Lothr. 6, 'Die Unruhen in Zabern [RK 170–73], ZStA Potsdam.
3   30 November 1913, ibid.
4   ibid.
5   Telegram of 30 November 1913, I–A Els.-Lothr., Nr. 4, Bd. 16–17, AA Bonn.
6   Report of 30 November 1913, RK 170, op. cit., ZStA Potsdam.
7   30 November 1913, ibid.
8   1 December 1913, *Verhandlungen des Reichstages*, op. cit.

9   Treutler to Bethmann, 1 December 1913, I–A Els.-Lothr., Nr. 4, Bd. 16–17, AA Bonn.
10 Telegrams of 29 and 30 November 1913, Rep. 89H, 1 Els.-Lothr. 6, Bd. 2, ZStA–II Merseburg.
11 Wedel report of 1 December 1913, ibid.
12 Bethmann to Wedel, 2 December 1913, RK 170, op. cit., ZStA Potsdam.
13 ibid.
14 Mahl report of 11 December 1913, RK 171, op. cit., ZStA Potsdam.
15 Kühne report of 12 December 1913, RK 170, op. cit., ZStA Potsdam.
16 Valentini diary, Nachlass Thimme, Vol. 26, 17–19, BA Koblenz.
17 Report to Hertling of 5 December 1913, BHStA Munich.
18 See 'Nomination of John D. Lavelle *et al.*', *Hearings before the Committee on Armed Services*, US Senate (Washington, 1972), pp. 156–95.
19 Report to Hertling of 5 December 1913, BHStA Munich.
20 Session of 3 December 1913, *Verhandlungen des Reichstages*, op. cit.
21 Memo from Falkenhayn to Bethmann, 3 December 1913, RK 170, letter from Wedel to Bethmann, 7 December 1913, RK 171, op. cit., ZStA Potsdam.
22 Session of 4 December 1913, *Verhandlungen des Reichstages*, op. cit.
23 Letter to Kommerzienrat Max Rüger, 11 January 1914, Nachlass Stresemann, Vol. 138, AA Bonn.
24 Undated draft of December 1913, undated letter to Hillquit, Nachlass Südekum, BA Koblenz.
25 Report of 4 December 1913, Abt. II, Geheimes Staatsarchiv 78163, 'Die Vorgänge in Zabern', BHStA Munich.
26 Report of 8 December 1913, Saxon StA Dresden.
27 See Eberhard von Vietsch, *Bethmann-Hollweg* (Boppard, 1969), p. 168; James W. Gerard, *My Four Years in Germany* (New York, 1917), p. 86; report of military attaché in Berlin of 23 February 1914, Austrian Military Archive, Vienna; diary entry of 4 December 1913, Hildegard Baronin von Spitzemberg, *Tagebuch* (Göttingen, 1961).
28 Report to Hertling of 4 December 1913, BHStA Munich.
29 Wahnschaffe to Georg von Mutius, Nachlass Thimme, Vol. 28, 22a, BA Koblenz.
30 Spitzemberg, op. cit., p. 563.
31 Bethmann letter to emperor of 20 March 1913, Rep. 89H, Bd. 3, ZStA–II Merseburg.
32 Bethmann to Eisendecker, 1 October 1913, I–A Els.-Lothr., Nr. 4 (Geheim), Bd. 2, AA Bonn.
33 Telegram of 4 December 1913, ibid.
34 ibid.
35 ibid.
36 Bethmann to emperor, 4 December 1913, RK 170, op. cit., ZStA Potsdam.
37 Even these led to an amusing flap. A doctored picture of the emperor evidently turning his back on Bethmann and Wedel appeared in *L'Illustration* in Paris on 27 December. In fact, he had been turning from them towards a second group, consisting of Deimling and General Lyncker of the Military Cabinet. The photographer was Heinrich Hoffmann of Munich, later to achieve a certain reputation as Hitler's photographer. Fürstenberg had asked that the plate should not be published, and the police confiscated it. But Hoffmann, who agreed voluntarily to withhold it, persuaded them to return the plate, which was then reportedly stolen from his Munich studio. Letter from Chemnitz publisher, 7 February 1914, RK 172, op. cit., ZStA Potsdam.
38 Berthold von Deimling, *Aus der alten in die neue Zeit* (Berlin, 1930), p. 160.
39 ibid., p. 161.

40 Bethmann to chancellery, 12 December 1913, RK 170, op. cit., ZStA Potsdam.
41 Report from Bavarian minister in Stuttgart, 8 December 1913, BHStA Munich.
42 Reports from Prussian minister in Karlsruhe, 5–6 December 1913, I–A Els.-Lothr., Nr. 4, Bd. 16–17, AA Bonn.
43 Wahnschaffe minutes of 6 December 1913, RK 171, op. cit., ZStA Potsdam.
44 Bethmann to Treutler, 6 December, Bassermann to Wahnschaffe, 7 December, editor of *National-Zeitung* to Wahnschaffe, 9 December 1913, ibid.
45 Spitzemberg, op. cit., diary entry of 6 December 1913.
46 Wedel to Bethmann, 7 December 1913, RK 171, op. cit., ZStA Potsdam.
47 Report to Wedel, 6 December; Wedel report to emperor, 7 December 1913, RK 171, op. cit., ZStA Potsdam.
48 Cited by Westarp in session of 10 December 1913, *Verhandlungen des Reichstages*, op. cit.
49 Bethmann to Wedel, 10 December, Wedel to Bethmann, 11 December and Wahnschaffe to Wedel, 11 December 1913, RK 171, op. cit., ZStA Potsdam.
50 Zorn interview of 7 December 1913, note from Lyncker, 9 December, report to Wedel, 15 December, Wedel report to emperor, 16 December, and emperor's reply 22 December 1913, Rep. 89H, Bd. 2, op. cit., ZStA–II Merseburg and RK 171, op. cit., ZSTa Potsdam.
51 Session of 10 December 1913, *Verhandlungen des Reichstages*, op. cit.
52 Reports from Reichsjustizamt, RK 171, op. cit., ZStA Potsdam.
53 Session of 11 December 1913, *Verhandlungen des Reichstages*, op. cit.
54 See report of 9 December 1913, Saxon StA Dresden.
55 See report of 12 December 1913, BHStA Munich.
56 See *Kölnische Zeitung*, 12 December 1913; Kaestlé, *Ein Sturmsignal aus dem Elsass* (Strasbourg, 1933), pp. 100ff.
57 Appellate decision of January 1914, RK 172, op. cit., ZStA Potsdam.
58 Wedel to Bethmann, 27 December 1913, and report of 26 December RK 171, op. cit., ZStA Potsdam.
59 Report of 13 November 1913, I–A Els.-Lothr., Nr. 4, Bd. 16–17, AA Bonn.
60 Undated pamphlet, ibid. See 'Zabern! Militäranarchie und Militärjustiz' (Frankfurt, 1914).
61 Falkenhayn to Wedel, 9 November and Wedel to Bethmann 17 November 1913, RK 170, op. cit., ZStA Potsdam.
62 Falkenhayn to Bethmann, 8 December 1913, RK 171, op. cit., ZStA Potsdam.
63 Falkenhayn to Bethmann, 18 December 1913, ibid.
64 Letters to Bethmann, 14–15 December 1913, ibid.
65 Letter from Anton Theodor Stoll, 1 December 1913, RK 170, op. cit., ZStA Potsdam.
66 See Gerd Fritz Leberecht, *Zabern und des Königs Rock* (Berlin, 1913).
67 Stein to Bethmann, 13 December 1913, RK 171, op. cit., ZStA Potsdam; letter from Stein, 11 December, acknowledgment of 19 December 1913, letter from Landeskriegsverband, 10 January 1914, Rep. 89H, Bd. 2, op. cit., ZStA–II Merseburg.
68 Letter from Türckheim, 25 November 1913, Rep. 89H, Bd. 2, op. cit., ZstA–II Merseburg.
69 Puttkammer letter, 4 December 1913, RK 170, and Wahnschaffe reply, 30 December RK 171, op. cit., ZStA Potsdam.
70 Letter from Col. Oppen, 17 December and Wahnschaffe reply, 27 December 1913, RK 171, op. cit., ZStA Potsdam.
71 Letter of 28 December 1913, RK 171, op. cit., ZStA Potsdam.
72 Unsigned, undated report of December 1913, ibid.
73 Jagow to Dallwitz, 24 December, Jagow to Wahnschaffe, 28 December,

Wahnschaffe to Jagow, 28 December, Wedel to Bethmann, 30 December 1913, Bethmann to Dallwitz, 1 January, Bethmann to Wedel, 2 January 1914, RK 171, op. cit., ZStA Potsdam.
74   See Paul Herre, *Kronprinz Wilhelm* (Munich, 1954), p. 133.
75   See *The Times*, 9 January 1914.
76   Valentini to Bethmann, 29 December 1913, Wahnschaffe to Bethmann, 7 January, Bethmann to Valentini, 8 January 1914, RK 171, op. cit., ZStA Potsdam. Valentini to Bethmann, 29 December 1913, Bethmann to Valentini, 8 January 1914, Rep. 89H, Bd. 2, op. cit., ZStA–II Merseburg.
77   Bethmann to emperor, 31 December 1913, Rep. 89H, Bd. 3, ZStA–II Merseburg.
78   Cited by Vietsch, op. cit., p. 169.
79   Hermann Ays, *Die Wahrheit über Zabern* (Strasbourg and Kehl, n.d.).
80   Wilhelm Höflich, *Affaire Zabern* (Berlin, 1931), pp. 191–2.

7 *And Yet It Moves*

I'd really give something to know for whom the deeds were
done of which it is publicly said that they were done for the
fatherland. (G. C. Lichtenberg)

On 5 January a military court, resplendent in decorations and dress
uniforms, convened under a major-general in Strasbourg to hear the cases
against Reuter and Schad. By the standards of the era, it was an authentic
media event with reporters from Germany and abroad and the courtroom
filled to overflowing.

During the trial's three days 134 witnesses were called, 125 of them
under oath. The first was Reuter himself, 'a tall, narrow-chested, small-
headed man, with close-cropped grey hair, a heavy moustache, a small
forehead, a large nose, protuberant cheekbones, and large outstanding ears',
as Wickham Steed helpfully described him for readers of *The Times*.[1] The
colonel, claiming full responsibility for November's events in Zabern,
impressed even his French colleagues with his professional standards. 'If all
the colonels in the German army have the same taste for responsibilities,
that first condition of initiative, then the German army is well commanded',
wrote the commentator of *France Militaire*. All but melting in the sun of
Gallic recognition, the editor of the *Militär-Wochenblatt* reprinted the
French commentator's remarks in full and in the original. He wanted 'to
make every expression clear as no translation could', he said.[2]

Reuter's position was widely shared by those present. What divided
them was whether Reuter's responsibility was also culpable. Opinions on
this divided predictably on civil—military lines. Newspaper accounts, the
only surviving resumé of the proceedings, virtually imply that the witnesses were talking about different times and places. Starting with Reuter
himself, some sixty military witnesses, and even the judges, testified to
their conviction, real or disingenuous, that the civil authorities had been
derelict, the crowds large and hostile, and the press incendiary. 'And so
you offered your full co-operation only when Colonel Reuter was prepared to shoot', the presiding officer, Pelet-Narbonne, half asked, half
told the mayor's deputy Grossmann. Successive military witnesses cited a
whole anthology of opprobrium in testifying to the humiliation that had
been heaped on them. 'Silk bunny', 'death's head', 'sow Swabian', 'sow

Prussian', 'rag bag', they said they had been called. There had been 1,400 anonymous cards and letters after the flag incident alone, one reported, 400 of them from Zabern. There was laughter in the courtroom.

Civilian witnesses denied everything. 'And so the spectator leaves with the feeling that the forces of good have contended, without the wise hand that might, with affectionate understanding, have untangled the knots for the common good', reported the correspondent of the *Kölnische Zeitung* in a wistful attempt at objectivity. The judges and prosecuting attorneys of the Zabern district court were especially memorable in their indignation. 'The soldiers just went around arresting people, like the Cossacks in the streets of St Petersburg', a state prosecutor declared in a skirmish with Schad over the peculiar circumstances that had led to the arrest of District Judge Kalesch. In reply to a question from the bench, Judge Beemelmann denied having had any impression that a revolution was in progress. 'I have lived in Alsace since childhood', he added. 'I have repeatedly heard from Alsatians that, with things as they are now, only the emperor can help.' There was a pause to restore order in the courtroom.

Only four civilians appear to have testified for the military. One was the Old German proprietress of a cigar store opposite the palace square. She claimed to have heard rumours of 200 reinforcements recruited from Mulhouse on grounds that 'southern blood' was necessary for any serious demonstration. She reported rather more plausibly that her business had recently been suffering. The second friendly witness was her schoolboy son. The third was a teacher of Prussian parentage, whose testimony was singled out for praise in the verdict a few days later. The fourth was a governess employed by the family of one of the regimental officers.

The rest, natives and Old Germans, pensioners and adolescents, professionals and manual labourers, were adamant in denying the soldiers' claims. Without exception they denied that the 'mob' referred to by the military witnesses had ever existed. Even an Old German witness concurred. She had heard an adolescent shout *Bettschisser* before fleeing from Forstner, had then seen a policeman arrive and heard a crowd of perhaps fifty, drawn by the policeman's presence, laugh and shout 'we're not in Russia'. But there had been no question that the crowd was under control. 'At home in the Palatinate it would not have been that peaceful', she added to peals of hilarity from the spectators.

In the end, the prosecutor called for dismissal of the first charge against Reuter, pre-emption of the police authority. He asked for a week's imprisonment on the second, false arrest, on grounds that the prisoners should have been released at the request of the civil authorities after Grossmann's declaration of intent to maintain law and order. He proposed three days' imprisonment for the 19-year-old Schad for assault. He recommended dismissal of the concurrent charges, false arrest and breaking and entering. The defence, unsurprisingly, asked for acquittal. 'It is unacceptable to send a deserving officer to jail for defending the reputation of the German army after thirty-five years of unexceptionable service', the defence declared in a final statement. Reuter in a final statement of his own, added that he had only been doing his duty. Schad denied any recollection of hitting a prisoner.

On 10 January, after a day's recess, the court reconvened for the verdict. 'In order to appreciate the facts of the case, it must be emphasised that the state has a considerable interest in protecting the representatives of its authority and sovereignty', the court explained by way of introduction. This included officers. 'They wear the king's uniform and have superior rank in the nation's army that must be ready at all times to take up arms for the existence and honour of the state', the verdict continued. The court found that the officers had been jeered and insulted, though there was no reference to actual attack or injury. It conceded that Reuter's threat of martial law was illegal, but it had at least made the civil authorities aware of his feelings. There had none the less been no adequate response until Reuter himself took action. Reuter's appeal to the military regulations caused the court no problems. Any military organisation had to maintain regulations 'without regard to juridical debate', they agreed. They also agreed on the continuing validity of the ancient executive order, and its appropriateness to the situation in Zabern. 'Confronted with repeated insults to the honour of his officers, Colonel Reuter found himself in a kind of emergency, even if it was something different from the state of emergency defined in the criminal code', the court declared. But since he was acting not only as senior military commander but also, in effect, as a senior civil official responsible for law, order and regular administration; since, moreover, he was subjectively unaware of any illegality in the regulations he invoked, the court found him justified in his action. Reuter was acquitted. Schad, who was presumed to be acting in good faith and in hot pursuit as duty officer, was acquitted too.[3]

The verdict was met with despair and jubilation. It was reported that Reuter alone got some 65,000 congratulatory cards and letters.[4] The day after his acquittal Reuter himself wrote to Bethmann to inform him of the torrents of sympathy. He had no political intentions, he wrote, nor did he mean to indulge in vanity or overconfidence. But he believed, after all the excitement of early December, that the Chancellor would like to know about the response. Wedel was understandably appalled. He regretted the acquittal not only 'for our sake', he emphasised, but 'for the sake of the army'. He could only assume that the Social Democrats would profit from the unfortunate impression left by the verdict at home and abroad. Was there no way, he asked in his own capacity as a retired Prussian general, that Bethmann could appeal against the decision? But there was no appeal, and instead Wedel's government submitted its resignation.[5]

As the Strasbourg court announced its acquittal, the military appellate court was meanwhile reversing the court-martial decision on Forstner. The arrest in Dettweiler had been justified, the judges concluded. They also found Blanck's claims credible. He had not intended to attack Forstner and the lieutenant was therefore not acting in self-defence. On the other hand, the ruling argued resourcefully, the lieutenant did have reason to believe he was in danger when he saw the powerfully built Blanck lunge forward with a free arm. 'To avoid this hazard, and effect a meaningful defence of his person, use of his weapon was the only available means', the judges declared. 'It would have threatened others deserving of protection if the defendant had sought to avoid attack, for example, by stepping back, and, especially where the defendant was an officer in full view of his unit, this concern deserves special consideration.' So Forstner had reason to act, after all, in 'putative self-defence'. Nor was there any question of negligent assault. Forstner's means were appropriate: 'restrained blows with a light blunt weapon' were an effective deterrent that none the less caused Blanck no serious harm.[6] Some weeks later and now fully lost to public view, Forstner and Höflich again found themselves before a court for training-ground abuses that had been incidentally discovered and reported since November. According to Höflich, Forstner was found guilty and sentenced to a month of house arrest. Höflich got eighteen days in the stockade.[7] Meanwhile Bethmann informed Wedel of orders to transfer Forstner and Reuter elsewhere, and Schad to an outlying town, if and when the regiment returned to Zabern.[8]

As the military courts convened to announce their verdicts, Bethmann was passing through fires of his own. Like the courts, the Prussian Upper House had convened for a rare Saturday session. The agenda consisted of a resolution submitted by Count Yorck von Wartenburg, a kind of Junker Lord Salisbury or J. C. Calhoun. It requested 'His Majesty's government to exercise its influence in the empire in such a way that Prussia's historical position as well as its relative weight should not be lessened by a transposition of the constitutional balance to the disadvantage of the respective states.' There were eighteen sponsors.

The session, which lasted less than an hour and a half, effectively consisted of two speeches. Yorck's was an extended indictment of an administration that had already opened the door of 'unitarism' so that democracy could enter. He appealed to Bismarck, 'the greatest statesman the world has seen since Richelieu'. In Yorck's view, only the Bundesrat remained as a levee against the democratic flood. He found it intolerable that the Reichstag already presumed to decide the fate of the Prussian government by censuring the Chancellor, and increased its power over the states by appropriating military funds at the cost of 'disgusting debates'. Tax reform figured prominently in Yorck's litany of decay. So did a law of 1906 allowing Prussian deputies, who served concurrently in the

Reichstag, to draw their *per diem* only when the Reichstag was adjourned. Yorck saw traditional jurisdictional limits between Prussia's ministers and the empire's secretaries of state falling too. The next step, he anticipated with a shudder, would be genuine imperial ministries. While he piously affirmed his aversion to criticise the emperor, he saw the King of Prussia losing more than the Emperor of Germany gained. (Shouts of 'Right!') The consequence, he insisted, was erosion of the executive branch and, self-evidently, of the army. The Reichstag, after all, already questioned a regimental commander's newspaper ban, the appropriations committee considered uniforms, and legislators, with the acquiescence of the War Ministry, debated promotions, retirement, perquisites, vacations, disciplinary reform and the reduction of the number of adjutants.

Bethmann was conciliatory but unyielding. Defend the status quo? It was exactly what he was doing, he argued. It was dear to his heart, and not incompatible with the new Alsatian constitution. The Prussian king and German emperor, who instructed both Prussian and Alsatian representatives in the Bundesrat, would see to it that Prussia's position was uncompromised and that there was no parliamentary interference with the executive and judiciary branches, the Chancellor assured his listeners to cheers from the floor. There were precedents for mixed committees like the new committee on arms acquisition. And of its forty-two members, only ten were parliamentary deputies, he reassured them. The law would continue to be upheld in Zabern as elsewhere in the German Empire. He drew more cheers with an emotional testimonial to the army — vindicated, he added, in 'countless letters that I receive daily from all walks of life, but especially from the common people'. There was a short discussion about whether passage of the resolution might not itself be regarded as a vote of no-confidence. 'Gentlemen', one member announced, 'what people say outside should be a matter of complete indifference to the House of Lords.' A bit of fitful opposition from what was quaintly referred to as the 'left' of the House was followed by a roll call vote. The resolution was carried by 148 to 20, with 3 abstentions.[9]

January being universally the opening of the legislative season, the barrage continued the following week, but now it was a cross-fire. In Munich, a Liberal deputy asked the Bavarian Minister of War whether there was anything like the Prussian executive order among Bavaria's military regulations. 'No', the minister replied. Under Bavarian law, military intervention required the request of the civil authorities.[10]

In the Prussian Lower House, that proverbial monument to universal unequal manhood suffrage, the debate smouldered for three days before turning inconclusively to the familiar questions of electoral reform, taxes and the expropriation of Polish land. It was an opportunity for Bethmann to regain a bit of ground. It was incidentally an opportunity to score a few easy points off the National Liberals, who by now seemed afflicted with a critical, even terminal, case of ambivalence.

'I see my vocation now, and in the future in expressing the idea of the Prussian state in the affairs of the empire, the affairs of the entire German nation', Bethmann declared to reassuring assent from the right, 'for if this is not done, then Prussia's effort in the unification of the German Empire since the beginning of the last century will have been in vain, and she should not be a part of it.'

Parliamentary speakers rehearsed what by now were familiar, and basically defensive, positions. Conservatives deplored the government's acceptance of support from the 'party of sedition', that is, the Social Democrats, on the 1913 tax reform and the Alsatian constitution. They raged about taxation and ostensible threats to the monarchy, the erosion of military autonomy, un-Prussian softness in the administration of Alsace-Lorraine, and the price of appeasement. Johannes Bell, the Centrist spokesman, who was to be a reluctant signatory to the Treaty of Versailles five years later, unburdened himself of the inevitable denial of complicity with the Social Democrats and disavowal of designs on the executive autonomy of the army. He still deplored the government's handling of the Zabern arrests and thought there was a need for consistency in the empire's military regulations.

The Progressive Wiemer defended the Alsatian authorities, particularly Mahl, and patiently denied any incompatibility between reform and military effectiveness. Change would come, he insisted. It was the right that wanted a fight, and was doing its best to provoke one by threatening constitutional safeguards.

National Liberal spokesmen fidgeted uneasily between the fronts, declaring a ritual devotion to 'Prussian iron in German blood', and calling for a reconciliation of the Prussian state with the German spirit. It was the Alsatian administration and the Chancellor's caution that were at fault, they claimed. They wanted the law clarified, but they also wanted Alsace-Lorraine governed by a firm, Prussian hand. Their position was easy game for Bethmann. He resented criticism of his performance as Chancellor of the empire in the halls of the Prussian diet, he replied. But he wanted to reaffirm that he had acted in good faith. He had relied on military accounts of events in Zabern, though their validity had been strenuously denied. Had the National Liberals been better informed when they joined the majority in 'that vote', that is, the censure resolution? There was a storm of hilarity from the floor. In the Chancellor's opinion, the decision of the Strasbourg military court had vindicated his judgement.[11]

As Bethmann held off the wolves in Berlin, Wedel's administration faced the fire in the Lower House of the Strasbourg legislature. What, the Centre asked, had the government done to spare the citizens of the provinces from further insult? What was its position on illegalities by the army in Zabern? What future steps were planned to prevent further pre-emption of the civil authority by the military, and illegalities by its commanders? What had the governor done, the deputies from Lorraine added, to require respect for the law, and to avoid further violations? What, the Social Democrats wanted to know, had the governor done to prevent excesses by officers, and what guarantees could the government offer of non-recurrence? What could the governor tell about the reassertion of the civil authority, the Progressives wanted to know, and what guarantees had the government received that the military would observe its official limits?

The hapless Zorn von Bulach was sent to answer for the government at the end of a six-hour session. Already a dead duck, if not yet a lame one, and mindful of his recent brush with his constituted superiors, Zorn was laboriously even-handed. 'Gentlemen', he noted with rueful understatement, 'it is not a pleasant thing to be a member of the government.' He reminded his audience that while there had been provocations and official investigations in Zabern, it was necessary to avoid interference in the army's affairs. Civil–military relations in Zabern had been good. Anti-militarism was not the cause of what happened there, and Zorn regretted exploitation of the Zabern incidents as an excuse for attacking the army.

The House replied with a voluminous draft resolution. It affirmed the conscientiousness of the civil authorities in Zabern and denied that there had been any reason for military intervention. It censured the government for inadequate effort to exact satisfaction from the army and provide reassurance from the population. It accused the government of inadequate assurances that the illegalities would not be repeated. 'The House asks the Reichstag, which it thanks for its energetic support on behalf of the people of Alsace-Lorraine, to continue its struggle for the defence of the law', the resolution continued, 'and to carry on its struggle for (1) a modern, nationwide separation of powers, (2) a reform of the military code and (3) further development of our constitution in the direction of complete federal autonomy.'

Replying for the government, Deputy Under-Secretary Petri went further than any government spokesman yet to meet the legislature halfway. Perhaps, the Bavarian minister in Berlin speculated, it was because Petri and his colleagues were on the way out anyway, and he had nothing more to lose.[12] In any case, administration of justice was Petri's job. He addressed himself to the defence of the judiciary with a warmth that was at once liberating and self-destructive. The judiciary had been insulted, Petri agreed. He had authorised three state prosecutors to testify before the military court and notified the presiding officer that all were prepared to testify against Reuter. He had meanwhile ordered reports on the contested cases. Contrary to Reuter's claim, he had established that everything was in order. Petri was cheered at each point. It was simply not true that soldiers were convicted while civilians were let off, Petri continued. No charges had been brought against civilians, and the soldiers had been convicted for military offences. If local judges dismissed charges against suspects turned over by the military, it was because arrest required a legal basis. The same applied to the warrantless search of Wiebicke's office, Petri declared, and army headquarters in Strasbourg had been informed accordingly. There were more cheers.

In contrast to Petri, his colleague Mandel, the other deputy undersecretary, tended towards defensiveness. He felt that his decision not to send Mahl back to Zabern the night of 28 November had been vindicated by Grossmann who had done everything possible. But he was unapologetic about his silence in the Reichstag in early December. It was the military, not the Strasbourg government, that was under attack, he said — there were some hecklers at this point — and it would have been embarrassing for a native of the provinces like himself to contradict the Chancellor. He defended his nods of acknowledgment when Ricklin, the Centrist deputy from Alsace, enlightened the Reichstag on the overtones and undertones of *Wackes*. The press, too, shared responsibility for the flap, Mandel argued. They could have taken the position that the population was immune to insult by an inexperienced lieutenant, though appropriate measures were expected. But the papers were determined to have their sensation. He supported Wedel's public silence. Imperial Germany was not a banana republic, Mandel declared. A senior official was supposed to file his appeals through appropriate channels.

Mandel defended his colleagues against the claim that the military was in charge. He also defended the provinces against the charge of antimilitary sentiment, estimating that as many as 75 per cent of the provinces' 300,000 to 400,000 Old Germans would concur. 'We had reason to believe this would be an idyllic legislative session this year', he sighed, 'and it would have been had things not gone wrong in Zabern.' Seven hours had passed by the time the House adjourned.

Before the vote the next day, the deputy Schlumberger invited the government to resign if it could not do better, while his colleague Peirotes drew laughs with an invitation to forget Zorn's performance in the previous day's debates. The resolution passed unanimously.[13]

A few days later, the Upper House, half of it directly appointed by the emperor, followed with a debate and a resolution only a few degrees cooler. It included an earnest declaration of loyalty to the indigenous population by Friedrich Curtius, a Prussian Protestant and father of the polyglot literary historian Ernst Robert. Paul Laband, Professor of Constitional Law at the University of Strasbourg and one of the few speakers to defend the army's action at Zabern, was disavowed by Rudolf Schwander, Strasbourg's mayor and a former student.

The resolution regretted the events in Zabern, and the impression they engendered of how the provinces felt, especially about civil–military relations. Conceding civilian excesses and journalistic irresponsibility, it also affirmed that the incidents could have been avoided by public announcement of disciplinary action against Forstner, and declared that the commanding officer, despite his conviction of good faith, had antagonised the population by his violations of official prerogatives. It demanded guarantees against any repetition, and announced firmly that local garrisons would have to abide by the law. The first of four paragraphs passed unanimously, the others by thirty-three to three with two abstentions.[14]

It had been a bad day for Zorn, Wedel confirmed in his report to Valentini. He had already urged his deputy to resign. Zorn agreed but wanted to stay on until the emperor's birthday a few days hence because he needed the money. Wedel hoped the emperor would understand. Meanwhile Wedel wanted Mandel to stay on because he was an unusually useful member of the administration.

Petri, as a native Alsatian, understandably wanted to resign too. Wedel looked forward to a thorough housecleaning and then, finally, his own retirement.[15] Two days later he asked that a draft statement on his impending resignation be leaked to the *Norddeutsche Allgemeine*. The key word in the release was 'renewed', Wedel added. That is, he wanted an explicit reference to his previous threat of resignation 'since our honour depends on it'.[16]

From across the river in Baden, Bethmann's friend Eisendecher reported general sympathy with the Alsatians. Opinion of the acquittals was generally critical, a view that Eisendecher evidently shared. If the first verdict against Forstner was found to be 'rather severe', acquittal, too, was considered inappropriate. Local Conservatives, dependent on the Centre, were keeping their peace, the minister wrote. But the Prussian military were understandably satisfied and younger officers, especially, lost no opportunity to express their opinions. Several regiments had cancelled their subscriptions to the *Karlsruher Tageblatt*, 'generally quite a reasonable, liberal paper', as Eisendecher characterised it. The editor had approached him for help, but the commanding general defended the cancellations.[17]

Oettingen's diary was a guide to the Chancellor's frame of mind. Oettingen had come for a visit a few days after the Alsatian debate. He found the Chancellor in good spirits, cheerfully quoting from Zelter's correspondence with Goethe which he was reading for the first time. Tea was interrupted by the appearance of Wedel. When Bethmann returned, his good humour had vanished. He reported that Wedel was too decent to throw his colleagues to the wolves, and that he wanted to make his own incumbency contingent on theirs. Apparently grateful for a friend to talk to, Bethmann then proceeded to his own situation. It was stronger than ever, he felt ('although one always had to reckon with the emperor's sudden inspirations'), but he had none the less had enough and doubted that he could go on much longer.

The Reichstag censure was insignificant, Bethmann continued. Everybody realised it was a mistake. On the other hand, none of the parties were on his side either. Unlike his predecessor Bülow, who had promised everything to everybody, the Chancellor felt his own error was a failure to cultivate any party or anybody. He considered the enmity of 'that conceited Bassermann' and the Conservative Heydebrand the result, and returned their contempt. In Bethmann's opinion, there was no one of stature or character in any of the parties – save for a few Social Democrats, whom he admiringly described as *Mordskerle*, wonderful fellows. He had also neglected to cultivate the press.

There was no way to govern Prussia without the Conservatives, the Chancellor acknowledged, 'and these shameless, chronic harassments from all sides' were getting on his nerves. Oettingen tried to cheer him up. With the forces of democratisation pouring over the walls, he could, and had, to stay, his friend told him. He then reported how civil servant X had recommended the purchase of Gobelin tapestries for the Reichstag speaker's official reception room. The motif consisted of 'comedians and Orientals – the real Reichstag', Bethmann found this terribly funny.[18]

Writing to his friend Eisendecher the next day, Bethmann himself surveyed his troubles. He regretted the resistance of Bavaria and Württemberg to a unitary reform of the military regulations, with its implication that they were in conflict with Prussia. The Prussian Cabinet order, he conceded, had to go. He especially regretted Eisendecher's gloomy news about the state of Prussian military morale in Baden. 'It is not going to be any better here', he added. 'On the contrary: military circles are dominated by a boundless, howling arrogance directed against the plebs, and the irresponsible policy of the Conservatives only makes it worse.' The Conservatives had concluded a short-term ceasefire with himself, he reported, but were scheming against him behind his back with the support of Admiral Tirpitz, who was, Bethmann implied, out for blood. Meanwhile the Chancellor worried about Russian aggressiveness – it was lucky France was peaceful, he noted – and British intransigence in the Middle East. 'Life could be quite pleasant if only people weren't so unreasonable', he sighed.[19]

By now the Reichstag, too, was back in session. Respect for the law was an acceptable common denominator, especially for legislators. The question was which and how. On 19 January, the Progressives proposed a Bill permitting military intervention only at the request of the civil authorities. Specific administrative guidelines would be left to the Bundesrat, an obvious concession to the empire's federal realities. The Bill also stipulated that the military was entitled to carry out its duties without interference; that, aside from self-defence, it was entitled to use armed force only to deter or overcome attack, disarm opponents, protect persons or property already in custody, or prevent their loss or escape; and that existing provisions for martial law would continue in force.

On 21 January the Alsatians and Poles proposed a resolution of their own. Considering the conflict between the civil and military authorities resulting from Reuter's action, as well as the differences of opinion on the validity of the Prussian regulations, and the dangers to civil liberties resulting both from the uncertainty and the discrepancy between Prussian and Bavarian usage, they said, they wanted the Chancellor to submit a Bill standardising military practice, and assuring that the military could intervene only on request of the civil authorities.

On 22 January, the Social Democrats proposed a more drastic resolution. It demanded that the Chancellor submit a Bill eliminating the jurisdiction altogether, and placing military personnel entirely under the civil jurisdiction. A variation from the Centre proposed instead that the Chancellor approach the Bundesrat about a common solution 'that would assure the autonomy of the civil administration'. The same day, the National Liberals, predictably cautious, filed a draft resolution, asking the Chancellor to do nothing much at all. The proposal simply acknowledged the review of the military regulations currently in progress, and asked that the Reichstag be informed of the outcome.

On 23 January, the Social Democratic and Progressive resolutions emerged from the parliamentary bedchamber, where they had obviously spent a connubial night. The new version asked that the Chancellor submit a Bill subjecting military personnel to the civil jurisdiction if they were charged with 'offences other than military crimes or derelictions'.[20] At the end of a day's debate, the Progressive Bill and the Alsatian resolutions had been referred to a committee artfully composed of six Centrists, including Franz Haegy from the virtually autonomous Alsatian Centre, six Social Democrats, three Conservatives, three National Liberals, two Progressives and a Pole. The National Liberal and Centrist motions carried with Progressive and Social Democratic support on the ground, as the Social Democrats' Hugo Haase conceded, that they could do no harm.

The debate itself continued from noon until after 8 p.m. There was occasional hilarity, ritual enthusiasm, and a good deal of acrimony. Ludwig Frank of the Social Democrats drew first blood with a reference to the Chancellor's isolation. 'He will soon, perhaps even today, be standing there alone like King Lear, and I believe even Cordelia Bassermann will soon forsake him', Frank announced to the general delight of the House. Fehrenbach drew laughs with a reference to 'a near miracle: the Alsatian government was in agreement with the Alsatian Parliament'. Beginning with a specific question of constitutionality, the debate addressed itself, in the course of the day, to virtually all the hopes, fears, dilemmas, compromises and disappointments of the past half-century. Successive speakers struggled for historical analogies — 1848, the Prussian constitutional crisis of the 1860s — or conjured up the heroic ghosts of 1870. Liberals of all colours and even the Centre, represented by Fehrenbach, celebrated the national state and its army, while some appealed for the vindication of its elected representatives.

'We on the left favour a parliamentary government', Friedrich Naumann declared, though he immediately qualified that it must be something different from a British copy. 'Every people and state seek their own development, and this is also true of Germany', Naumann continued, 'and the Reichstag cannot remain forever in its present state as the insignificant organ of control it tends to be.' He was cheered from the left. Conservatives, on the other hand, looked around them and saw the slippery slope. Westarp confirmed the obvious, that the Conservatives found Progressive and Social Democratic proposals unacceptable. But they felt the same way about the proposals of the Centre and the National Liberals. 'In our view, they represent the first step in a direction we fundamentally oppose, a first step, whose consequences cannot be anticipated.' He was cheered from the right, but successive motions to adjourn from the right and centre were withdrawn because of Social Democratic objections.

Instead, the House heard Ledebour advance from an attack on the military justice system to one on the taste and companionship of the crown prince. 'The problem is that a gentleman like this can one day attain a position of the greatest possible influence in the German Empire, and this is the worst kind of danger', Ledebour proclaimed as the right shouted back and the Conservatives demonstratively left the room. Germany was threatened with military dictatorship, he proclaimed. 'The status quo in the distribution of political power, the division of Germany among the various states, is petrified in the state of incompletion left behind by the peace treaties of 1866 and 1870', Ledebour declared. But the process was still underway. Prussia had to be absorbed in Germany, the social revolution had to proceed, 'and this obviously includes the elimination of military dominance that actually exists in Germany notwithstanding the cover of parliamentary institutions'.

Clemens von Delbrück, the director of the imperial Department of the Interior and Deputy Chancellor, expressed gratitude for Ledebour's candour in confirming that it was not Zabern but a blow to the monarchy and army that was on Social Democratic minds. He was, incidentally, the only government representative present, a fact that even exasperated Conservatives. The majority of the House struck the scheduled debate on funds for the Department of Interior in protest,[21] while the speaker reprimanded Ledebour for his attack on the crown prince, for his *ad hominem* argument and for his diction.

The heady days of early December, when a demonstrative 'no' had produced a moment of euphoric consensus, were already receding into nostalgia. The draft Bill and three resolutions on the floor testified in themselves to the limits of parliamentary consensus. Even the Social Democrats had passed the initiative back to the Chancellor. Bethmann, supported in the crush like the passenger in a rush-hour bus, exploited his minimal space with skill and self-assurance. Military intervention at the request of the civil authorities only was the norm in all German states, he declared, and certainly in Prussia. The Prussian constitution allowed certain exceptions, contingent on a law that had, in fact, never been passed. He doubted that this precluded intervention where, for example, self-defence was called for or a state of emergency existed. The question at issue was a special provision on unsolicited intervention. The problem was that it had apparently never been challenged or — since 1820 — even invoked. ('Hear, hear!' shouted the right, 'Ha, Ha!' shouted the left.) But the provision had never been a secret. Nor was there any need to review the Reuter decision, the Chancellor continued, since without a statute Reuter's only alternative was to observe existing regulations. 'But whether statute or regulation, where questions exist — I repeat this — there must and will be clarification.' This, he announced, and this alone, was the issue of Zabern.

In any case, Bethmann added, he considered Zabern vastly exaggerated. It was not typical of Alsace-Lorraine, nor was it justification for a cold war between northern and southern Germany ('Bravo!'). He particularly resented partisan exploitation of the case with the goal of subverting the military command structure or inciting workers. 'I ask you', he declared, turning to the Social Democrats, 'what does Zabern have to do with the labour question?' (Laughter from the Social Democrats.) He was not about to see crowds incited in order to provoke requests for military intervention, said the Chancellor. The army was too important for that ('Bravo!' from the right). He also resented the way the foreign press had misrepresented Zabern, not to mention the echo effect produced when Social Democrats quoted foreign papers in German debate. Only Germans quoted the foreign press as an argument against their own government, the Chancellor charged, and then claimed that their government had disgraced them abroad.

Above all, Bethmann defended the army and the nation's need for it if Germany were to maintain and preserve its place in the world. 'We won't let them take that away from us, gentlemen', the Chancellor emphasised, 'just because — well, gentlemen, because in one certain place in the great German Empire certain things happened that no one wants to see repeated.' There was extended applause from the right and the National Liberals, and hissing from the Social Democrats.[22]

The debate passed without incident, Bethmann informed the emperor that evening, save for some unacceptable Social Democratic criticism of the crown prince. The Chancellor added that he had replied energetically. He was otherwise impressed to see the Centre, the National Liberals and even the Progressives trying to extricate themselves from their liaison with the Social Democrats. Bethmann thought the Social Democrats, concerned as they were with holding the coalition together, had actually behaved rather temperately. He had called this to the attention of the House and enjoyed their evident approval.[23] 'A hopeful nation, not to be confused, thank God, with its political parties, looks to Your Majesty', Bethmann wired the emperor on his birthday a few days later.[24]

From Karlsruhe, the assiduous Eisendecher confirmed that the Chancellor's latest performance had even gone down well in liberal Baden. 'People are just tired of Zabern', he reported. Even the opposition was gaining confidence in 'Your Excellency's just and conscientious appreciation of the possible and necessary', he added, though he expressed fears that the 'military party' was feeling both vindicated and self-assured in ways that might cause as much trouble in Baden as they did across the river. 'Cases like Zabern are not at all impossible', Eisendecher wrote, 'and are even supposed to have happened here, save that the exemplary co-operation of civil and military authorities permitted their discreet resolution.' Eisendecher wondered whether the same might not have been accomplished in Zabern. He considered it an error now to get tough with the provinces and punish them indiscriminately for what had happened. But according to what he heard in Baden, he said, it was only the officer corps that favoured a tougher line anyway, and everybody agreed that their views only reflected their political inexperience.[25]

Meanwhile the parliamentary wheels turned, confirming and vindicating Bethmann's calculations. In late February, with the revision of the military regulations now before the Bundesrat, the Centre moved, seconded by the National Liberals, to adjourn the Zabern committee *sine die* after a week's deliberation. The Social Democrats and Progressives proposed instead that the committee consider the first paragraph of the Progressive Bill with its stipulation that armed force only be invoked at the request of the civil authorities. The Conservatives then declared their opposition to adjournment as a matter of principle. In their view, further discussion, no matter what the terms, was an incursion on states' rights and the autonomy of the military. Their support for a motion to adjourn could only be understood as acquiescence when the committee reconvened. Against an improbable majority of Conservative, Progressive, Social Democrat, Polish and Alsatian votes, the adjournment motion lost thirteen to eight. Shifting sides, the Conservatives then joined the Centre and National Liberals in refusing to debate the Progressive Bill. Submitted to a vote, the Bill's first paragraph lost eleven to ten. The subsequent paragraphs were withdrawn. In successive votes, the Polish–Alsatian resolution and the connubial Progressive–Social Democratic motions were also

defeated eleven to ten. Support for the Social Democratic motion predictably came only from the Social Democrats.[26] 'And so we see again that
the bourgeois parties would ten times rather endure the excesses of the
junkerised, bureaucratic, militarist system than make the slightest concession to parliamentary democracy', the *Vorwärts* wrote in its editorial
the next day.[27]

But in imperial Germany, the more things remained the same, the more
they also changed. The problem was recognising it. While the parliamentarians fumbled towards mutual frustration, the government was concerned
that the parliamentarians might actually beat them to the punch. 'If the
new service regulation could be released before the committee considers
the [Progressive] Bill and before the military budget comes up in the
appropriations committee, it could only strengthen the position of the
government', Bethmann signalled in a memo to Falkenhayn.[28] But it was
late January before this was generally known. On 31 January, an article
by a Göttingen law professor in the liberal *Vossische Zeitung* confirmed
that the review of the military regulation was in progress. The Chancellor
hoped to find a common formula, the author informed his readers. But
he was sceptical that correction of the problem of unsolicited military
intervention would be the result. While grateful for the emperor's initiative
in authorising the review, he regretted the exclusion of the Reichstag
from the process, particularly where he believed that legislative imple-
mentation of constitutional provisions was involved.[29]

The professor's apprehensions were shared in tendency, if not detail,
by Bernhard Dernburg, the former Colonial Secretary. In a memo for
Wahnschaffe, Dernburg considered that the re-examination of the military
regulations was too important to leave to the Ministry of War. Zabern
itself was no longer the issue, he declared. By now the conflict embraced
not only Alsace-Lorraine, but the civil—military relationship and the
north—south relationship. In Dernburg's view, people wanted law and
justice, civil liberties, confidence in the honour and reputation of the
army, clarity in the legal code, and a greater sense of responsibility on the
part of both the army and the civil authorities. He even proposed executive pardon for the imprisoned recruits, if only to anticipate parliamentary
pressure to release them anyway. Reuter had been acquitted on grounds of
subjective good faith and Forstner for 'putative' self-defence, he noted. If
intentions were the issue, he thought the ineptitude (*Dummheit*) of the
recruits should also constitute an extenuating circumstance. 'I believe this
most urgent matter could thus be resolved, and that the bourgeois parties
would be committing a great injustice if, given adequate guarantees for
the future, they failed to help bury it.'[30]

All the while the review rolled on in a tide of forensic conscientiousness.
In mid-January, Lisco, the director of the imperial Department of Justice,
informed Bethmann that the regulation on military intervention was

illegal. It had never been published, never been introduced in Alsace-Lorraine, and never been understood as valid by the authors of the Prussian constitution who had consciously debated it as far back as 1850–1. On the other hand, Lisco conceded, the Cabinet order had not been superseded by the Prussian constitution either. It had been retained in subsequent revisions of the service regulations in 1851, 1861, 1863 and 1899. It thus remained valid for Prussian troops, irrespective of their location, like any other official order, by virtue of the emperor's authority as commander-in-chief.[31] Two days later, a follow-up memo confirmed official perplexity. The question of limits on the Prussian army's authority, Lisco concluded, was a matter for the courts.[32]

Falkenhayn objected almost immediately. The regulation had been law before 1848, he contended. Publication was irrelevant because those who were supposed to know about it did. The new legislation envisaged in the Prussian constitution had never been written. The regulation, he insisted, remained in force. Lisco and his colleague Beseler, the Prussian Minister of Justice, responded by return post with the cool superiority of law professors addressing the modestly gifted son of a rich alumnus. The regulation was not a law, Beseler wrote. Prussia had required publication of laws since 1810, and laws already on the books before the Prussian constitution was written anticipated all the eventualities the regulations were meant to cover. He was unpersuaded by Falkenhayn's effort to prove the validity of the regulation as a stopgap for contingencies unanticipated by past legislators. Lisco concurred. The existing regulations might be valid for Prussian troops, he wrote, but he found it hard to see how the regulation could be valid in Alsace-Lorraine where it had neither been published nor called to the attention of the civil authorities.[33] Falkenhayn manfully marched off to the library to study the Prussian parliamentary journal for 1849. He was still unconvinced, he replied the next day, but he was prepared to accept review and revision of the regulation as appropriate. It needed improvement anyway, he conceded.[34] On 30 January, representatives of the Ministry of War submitted a draft to an inter-agency committee. It provided for unilateral military intervention in the event (1) of war or proclamation of martial law, (2) of public disorder where public safety was in jeopardy and the civil authorities were incapacitated, (3) of interference with the performance of official duties, and (4) where danger to honour, life, limb or property justified reasonable self-defence.

A few days later, the matter was debated in the Prussian Cabinet. Falkenhayn stood alone. Bethmann was sceptical about the legality of the ancient Cabinet order and the existing regulation derived from it. 'The military's authority to decide must not be so wide that a commander can determine independently that the civil authorities have waited too long', he declared. He deferred the question of whether the army might have dealt more skilfully with the situation in Zabern. 'In any case, the possibility of repetition has to be eliminated', he said. Beseler was ordered to review the compatibility of the service regulation with the Prussian constitution.[35]

Within a week, Beseler submitted an extensive brief to his colleagues. It concluded that the police were responsible for maintaining domestic order and that the Cabinet order of 1820 had been superseded by the constitution, and noted that successive generations of Prussian ministers had questioned its constitutionality, most recently in 1899. He itemised the permissible use of military force: self-defence, prevention of escape, and so on, but also its limits in the event of civil disorder. This, he argued, was what article 36 of the Prussian constitution was about. The military could be used to put down civil disorder. But this was not a licence to act provocatively in order to intervene on their own authority against the disorder that ensued. Unsolicited intervention was allowed in the event of war or martial law, where the military was authorised to act when civil officials were incapacitated. But even here the incapacity had to be 'external', that is, have some objective reality independent of the local commander's interpretation. Beseler proposed that the military regulations be rewritten accordingly.[36]

A day later, Falkenhayn submitted a new draft on behalf of the committee for Beseler's consideration. It was met with tactful suggestions for amplification and clarification of its provisions. But what was most interesting was an omission. The text authorised unsolicited intervention to overcome attack or resistance, disarm attackers, prevent escape in case of arrests, and protect persons or objects in custody. It provided for unsolicited intervention in the event of war or a state of emergency, 'external' incapacity of civil authorities or disruption in the performance of their duties. 'The commanding officer is to give particular attention to determining the correct moment for intervention', the draft stated. 'But as soon as that moment arrives, responsibility for the restoration of public order will repose in him, and the civil authorities will proceed accordingly.' Behind figleaves of familiar language, much of it going back to Prussian laws of 1837, the Cabinet order of 1820 had disappeared.[37]

The problem now was both tactical and political. The possibilities included a Reichstag initiative for national legislation, an option the government deplored but could hardly dismiss out of hand; a negotiated settlement in the Bundesrat, where Prussia had little alternative but to acquiesce in the prevailing liberalism of the smaller states and the anomalous status of Alsace-Lorraine could only be an embarrassment; a Prussian law, which ultimately depended on the good-will of an Upper House that had only just declared Bethmann a dangerous liberal; or administrative action. None of the government favoured a Reichstag initiative. The question was whether they could pre-empt it. Delbrück, mindful of the

National Liberal resolution and its concomitant obligation on the government to keep the legislators informed, favoured 'occasional' memos on the government's progress. Falkenhayn conceded the dilemma but opposed direct representations. It was bad to allow attacks on the command structure, he said, but it was also bad to acknowledge them. Should the Chancellor none the less delegate someone to brief the Reichstag, he wanted to see the government's statement first. Lisco agreed that the Progressive draft might raise constitutional issues by impinging on the rights of the states. But it represented no threat to the emperor's authority as commander-in-chief as neither the definition of the civil jurisdiction nor of the prerogatives of the civil authorities were part of the supreme command. By now there were anxious rustlings in the Conservative press. As the Reichstag's Zabern committee convened, there was a representative of the imperial Department of Justice, though not from the Ministry of War, in attendance.[38]

The route through the Bundesrat was equally unpromising. There were reports that Bethmann had hoped to arrange a kind of treaty with Bavaria, Saxony and Württemberg, the empire's other military powers. But there was little likelihood of agreement. There was no German army, nor were the police a federal institution. The smaller states were reluctant to sacrifice further fragments of their autonomy merely to pull Prussian chestnuts out of the fire. In any case, the Bavarians were intransigent and the Alsatians were unlikely to co-operate.[39]

The failure of the Reichstag committee solved one problem. The Prussian Cabinet debated the others in mid-March. There was general satisfaction with the compromise draft. The Cabinet was informed that negotiations were still proceeding with the other governments. It was agreed that the legality of the existing regulation should be left to the courts. Anyway Bethmann thought it imprudent to deny its legality under the present circumstances. It sufficed to find a new arrangement acceptable to the interested Prussian ministries. Falkenhayn was unhappy, but also outvoted. Beseler found the new draft consonant with Prussian law. All that mattered, he thought, was that it be acceptable to Prussia and Alsace-Lorraine. To the bemusement of Admiral Tirpitz, Falkenhayn inquired about turning the old regulation into law. He still found it superior to the proposed alternative. His colleagues were unsympathetic. The new provision was clearer and narrower than the old one, Bethmann noted, agreeing that, in that sense, the old regulation went further. It was loss of precision, Falkenhayn replied, that he considered a real step backward. He anticipated the hypothetical case of a stubborn Alsatian police chief delaying a request for military help. But he was prepared to recommend the new version to the emperor if his colleagues felt otherwise. Beseler reassured him that he could tell the emperor how the new version did the job, while any alternative would require legislation with all the 'extremely inexpedient' circumstances this involved. He was sure the emperor would see the point. What had to be avoided at all costs, Bethmann emphasised, was any hint that the old Cabinet order was invalid. He thought judicial rulings were none of the Cabinet's business anyway, and that concession on this point was an obvious political danger. In Bethmann's opinion, the position of the Cabinet, and particularly the Minister of War, was best protected if reservations were limited to honest doubt.[40]

The outcome of the twenty-seven civil suits still pending in Zabern was eloquent evidence of his deeper fears and feelings. The first came up on 3 March. It was rescheduled for hearing with the others a week later. But none, in fact, ever got to court. The army, it was reported, had dispatched a 'prominent local figure' to the plaintiffs' lawyers, proposing an out-of-court settlement of 50 marks and expenses. Save for the few who claimed that the night in the palace cellar had permanently damaged their health, and wanted a bigger settlement, the group was amenable.[41] Wedel notified Bethmann that Deimling was passionately for settlement. Wedel favoured it too. He felt that a court hearing would be bad for public order and contrary to the interests of the army. There was also, as he hardly had to add, the real possibility that the army would lose in a civil court. Wedel thought the whole matter could be settled for 2,500 marks. He hoped the Chancellor would influence Falkenhayn accordingly. A few days later, the Chancellor informed him that Falkenhayn had made the necessary arrangements.[42] Libel charges against Wiebicke, the editor of the *Zaberner Anzeiger*, were dismissed on 28 March.[43]

In early April, Falkenhayn reported general agreement on the new regulation with the smaller states whose troops served under Prussian command, and with the other states that maintained contingents in Prussia, Baden and Alsace-Lorraine. The Strasbourg government also joined the arrangement with a proviso that military intervention require a signed, written request from the civil authorities as per the antecedent French law of 1791 which was still valid in the provinces.[44] An official spokesman released the new regulation a few days later. Wahnschaffe, concerned to pre-empt a leak and the expected indignation of the Conservative press,[45] cited the relevant paragraph last but without camouflage.[46]

Other loose ends were dispatched with pragmatic circumspection. One was the problem of the Zabern personae. On 31 January, the emperor finally authorised the transfer of Reuter and Forstner to another regiment. Bethmann notified Wedel the next day. Schad, 'a particularly well-hated figure', as Wedel described him, could stay, but was to be assigned to the battalion in the country if the regiment returned to town.[47] Mahl was to go too, but demoted to the sticks. Reuter was to leave with the Order of the Red Eagle, third class, a fact acknowledged with heavy irony in some quarters, despite claims that the decoration was specific to his rank and had been in the works since the previous August.[48] Forstner just went, transferred with presumably unintentional irony to Bromberg (Bydgoszcz), another border garrison, where he would be surrounded by Poles. He made a final appearance in Zabern at noon on 2 February. Teachers had warned their classes and the police had been prepared for the occasion. Though he was recognised, nothing very much happened. On a visiting card unceremoniously delivered to the prefect's office by his landlord, he none the less complained of harassment by schoolboys. Despite plans to spend the night, he was persuaded by a local police sergeant to catch a late afternoon train. Deimling confirmed the next day that the transfer had been satisfactorily effected and that the legal officer in Bromberg had instructions from the War Ministry to deal quickly and efficiently with any remaining charges.[49]

A second problem was the reconstruction of the provincial government. It had been an unavoidable preoccupation since at least the turn of the year. A dignified exit for the incumbents was problem enough. In late January even the hapless Zorn was so circumspect about impending resignation that it appeared the decision was reached only after the confrontation in the legislature. Wedel warned that he would soon feel compelled to announce his own previous offers of resignation – although 'the word Donaueschingen will naturally not be mentioned', he added delicately.[50] But there was no way for Zorn to go before he had a successor, or for Wedel to go before the departure of Zorn.

On 30 January, the top candidate, Fr. Wilhelm Loebell, a former Conservative deputy and under-secretary under Bülow, withdrew after extended conversations. His withdrawal left two more candidates, Michaelis, a senior civil servant, and Count Roedern, a patrician from the Saar. Michaelis, wartime chancellor by grace of General Ludendorff a few years later, dropped out too. This left Roedern, who was willing to take the job but firm about the conditions. He was going to need competent subordinates, he emphasised, particularly for justice and education. For the former he wanted a Catholic lawyer from Prussia, speculating that the Alsatian legislature would be more amenable to a Rhenish Catholic than an Alsatian Protestant.[51] What meanwhile interested Wedel was an honourable exit for the incumbent Petri. The governor proposed nominating him for the Alsatian Upper House. Referring demonstratively to Petri's recent 'anti-military' performance in the Lower House, Bethmann said 'no'. Wedel was indignant. 'To see what I consider criminal animosity towards the army in a speech motivated by self-defence and objective circumstance is absurd – or perfidious', he wrote to Valentini. Valentini none the less suggested withdrawal of the nomination.[52] 'I am hurt that our most gracious lord, notwithstanding his generally lofty sense of justice, has let himself be influenced by prejudice', Wedel replied resignedly a few weeks later.[53]

By now Roedern had replaced Zorn and was taking charge. Wedel was grateful he would soon be leaving, though concerned that a demonstration planned by local amateur choruses to honour him and his wife might be construed as a demonstration against Deimling. The Strasbourg City Council even wanted to name a street after Wedel in the Orangerie. But what really concerned him were demonstrations from the other direction. 'The attacks on me from my own party, the caricature of me, the distortions and falsifications, positively disgust me', he wrote to Valentini.[54]

Bethmann was willing to let Wedel's departure take its honorific course. The immediate problem was that of replacing him. The Chancellor still preferred Loebell. But Loebell was neither very eager nor in very good health. He was also believed to be more useful at his current job in the Ministry of Agriculture where, as it happened, he was holding out against much of the government on forthcoming trade negotiations that the Chancellor considered particularly important.

The alternative was Johann von Dallwitz, the Prussian Minister of the Interior, who was particularly close to the Conservatives.[55] Wedel was sceptical about Dallwitz for the same reasons the Chancellor found him an attractive candidate. He also doubted that Dallwitz could afford the incidental expenses of the Strasbourg job. Wedel anticipated the appointment of Klemens von Schorlemer, the Prussian Minister of Agriculture. But he preferred Count Hatzfeldt, a man who happened to be quite similar to himself. Hatzfeldt was a moderate man, an experienced administrator and parliamentarian, Wedel noted, a holder of the Order of the Black Eagle, Prussia's highest decoration. He was also rich and Catholic. It was just these qualifications that the emperor appeared to hold against him. Yet another *grand seigneur* in Strasbourg was more than he needed. What he wanted was a dependable bureaucrat who lived on his salary and held 'sound views' on Alsace-Lorraine.

Dallwitz certainly met those specifications. 'With all respect for the achievements of the Prussian state under monarchical direction, he considered popular participation inevitable, even necessary and desirable', he revealingly wrote of Bethmann. 'This, not pressure from the dominant, democratic press, is why he paralysed the influence of the German authorities by liberalising the Alsatian constitution, and opening the door to the agitation of nationalist (francophile) and other centrifugal forces in this heavily contested area while serving as Prussian Interior Minister, Secretary of State and Chancellor.[56]

'While he has been considered a resolute opponent of extensive democratisation of the Prussian suffrage, it would surely be wrong to classify him as a representative of "reaction", as sometimes happens', the *Illustrierte Zeitung* reported in April. 'On the contrary, it was he, for example, who introduced optional cremation in Anhalt and Prussia.' Dallwitz got Wedel's job.

The last problem was what to do about the 99th in its rustic exile. In February Falkenhayn and Bethmann wanted the regiment to return to town. Deimling was against it, but Falkenhayn found his arguments unconvincing. Relocation of the garrison would cost a million marks or more. The Reichstag was unlikely to appropriate money for the purpose, and even asking them for it was to compromise the emperor's authority. If anything, the possibility of new disorders was a reason for the regiment to return to town.[57] Bethmann agreed, at least to a point. The last thing he wanted to do was dissolve the Reichstag over the fight that was likely to follow relocation of the garrison. The question was tactical: making clear to Mahl's successor that he was responsible for public order, with all that implied.[58] The Chancellor preferred to take the initiative himself. Falkenhayn wanted to defer a decision until the Cabinet had settled the question of the new military regulation.[59]

Wedel, too, was opposed to the regiment's early return. If there were new disturbances, it would only mean trouble with the Alsatian Centre in Zabern where local elections were due in May, and in the Strasbourg legislature.[60] Bethmann agreed to defer his decision.[61] Falkenhayn was bitter that the government should be deterred by mere politics. 'If that party doesn't know that parliamentary actions won't influence administrative measures in the national interest, it's time they learned', he wrote. In any case, he doubted that there would be new incidents, or at least any provoked by the army. If so, Falkenhayn contended, it would be the first time in the history of the Prussian army that bad feeling had been allowed to supersede orders. Nor did he want the decision to be based on local feelings. Excessive caution in reaching a decision would only be read as a precedent, he argued.[62] Bethmann replied that Wedel wanted guarantees. He doubted that Deimling would comply, but was willing to change his views if the army assured him that civilian offenders would be turned over to the police.[63]

In mid-March Roedern again recommended postponement to avoid possible conflict with hearings still pending against individual soldiers. But he hoped to get things moving as soon as possible and also to cool the army's 'victorious euphoria', He wanted NCOs officially ordered to stay out of trouble, and officers not only to avoid friction on the street but to desist from protests against French speakers that had been occurring in the area. He reported that he had spoken firmly with the mayor and seen to changes of personnel in the prefect's office and the state police contingent.[64] Bethmann proposed that he approach Deimling with his wishes. 'You know how uncomprehending military circles are here about the problems of the provinces', he reminded Roedern.[65]

On 25 March, it was agreed that the regiment would return after Easter.[66] Roedern asked the Chancellor to defer publication of the decision, to notify the new prefect, and to brief the troops twenty-four hours before their return. The army agreed in principle to appropriate discretion. On 13 April, the regiment returned uneventfully to Zabern.[67]

At least in northern Germany, Zabern had only discredited the radicals and the Reichstag, Bethmann informed Eisendecher. What worried him now was foreign policy. He was anxious about Russia, Romania, the Austrian relationship with Serbia. He regretted letting the military get away with the Liman von Sanders mission to Turkey in the aftermath of the Second Balkan War. But the big problem, as he saw it, was re-assuring the French. It would not, he acknowledged, be easy to do.[68]

References

1   *The Times*, 6 January 1914.
2   Militär-Wochenblatt, Nr. 8, 1914.
3   See *Kölnische Zeitung*, 6–8 January 1914; *The Times*, 6–8 January 1914. The verdict is included in RK 172, Els.-Lothr. 6, 'Die Unruhen in Zabern [RK 170–73], ZStA Potsdam. For editorial comment see *Deutsche Zeitung*, *Kölnische Zeitung*, and *The Times*, 10 January 1914.
4   '... and every real German will join in the congratulations', a contemporary pamphleteer added. 'No!' says an anonymous marginal note in the copy in the Freiburg University Library. Herman Ays, *Die Wahrheit über Zabern* (Strasbourg and Kehl, n.d.), op. cit., ZStA Potsdam.
5   Reuter and Wedel letters of 11 January 1914, RK 171; see minutes of Prussian Cabinet, 30 January 1914, Hist. Abt. II, Rep. 90a, Abt. B, III, 2b, Nr. 6, Bd. 163, 1914, ZStA–II Merseburg.
6   RK 172, op. cit., ZStA Potsdam.
7   Wilhelm Höflich, *Affaire Zabern* (Berlin, 1931), pp. 196ff.
8   Bethmann to Wedel, 1 February 1914, RK 172, op. cit., ZStA Potsdam.
9   Session of 10 January 1914, *Verhandlungen des Preussischen Herrenhauses* (Berlin, 1914).
10   Session of 13 January 1914, *Kammer der Abg. des Bayerischen Landtages* (Munich, 1914).
11   Sessions of 13–15 January, *Preussisches Haus der Abgeordneten* (Berlin, 1911).
12   Lerchenfeld to Hertling, 24 January 1914, Abt. II, Geheimes Staatsarchiv 78163, 'Die Vorgänge in Zabern', BHStA Munich.
13   Sessions of 13–15 January, *Verhandlungen der II. Kammer, Elsass-Lothringscher Landtag* (Strasbourg, 1914).
14   Session of 19 January 1914, *Verhandlungen der I. Kammer, Elsass-Lothringscher Landtag* (Strasbourg, 1914).
15   Wedel to Valentini, 21 January 1914, Rep. 89H, 1 Els.-Lothr. 6, Bd. 2, ZStA–II Merseburg.
16   23 January, ibid.
17   Eisendecher report of 15 January 1914, I–A Els.-Lothr., Nr. 4, Bd. 16–17, AA Bonn.
18   Entry of 18 January 1914, Abschriften aus dem Tagebuch aus dem Nachlass W. v. Oettingen, Kl. Erw. 517/5, BA Koblenz.
19   Bethmann to Eisendecher, 19 February 1914, I–A Els.-Lothr., Nr. 4 (Geheim), Bd. 1–2, AA Bonn.

20   Drucksachen Nrs. 1281, 1296, 1302–4, 1309, I. Session, 1912–14, *Verhandlungen des Reichstages* (Berlin, 1914).
21   Lerchenfeld to Hertling, 24 January 1914, op. cit., BHStA Munich.
22   Session of 23 January 1914, *Verhandlungen des Reichstages*, op. cit.
23   Bethmann to William, 23 January 1914, RK 172, op. cit., ZStA Potsdam; Rep. 89H, Bd. 2, op. cit., ZStA–II Merseburg.
24   Bethmann to William, Hist. Abt. II, 2.2.1, Nr. 3577, ZStA–II Merseburg.
25   Eisendecher report, 26 January 1914, I–A Els.-Lothr., Nr. 4, Bd. 16–17, AA Bonn.
26   See *Berliner Lokal-Anzeiger*, 26 February 1914.
27   *Vorwärts*, 27 February 1914.
28   Bethmann to Falkenhayn, 24 January 1914, RK 1271, 'Belagerungszustand', ZStA Potsdam.
29   Prof. M. Höpfner, *Vossische Zeitung*, 31 January 1914.
30   Dernburg to Wahnschaffe, 21 January 1914, RK 1271, op. cit., ZStA Potsdam.
31   Lisco to Bethmann, 16 January 1914, ibid.
32   Lisco to Bethmann, 18 January 1914, ibid.
33   Falkenhayn, 20 January 1914; Lisco and Beseler, 20 January 1914, 'Betr. die zivilrechtliche Verfolgung von Personen des Soldaten-standes wegen Diensthandlungen', Rep. 84a, M12/9020, GStA West Berlin.
34   21 January 1914, ibid.
35   ibid.
36   ibid.
37   Draft of 7 February 1914, ibid.
38   Delbrück memo of 12 February, Falkenhayn memo of 14 February, Lisco memo of 15 February 1914, RK 1271, op. cit., ZStA Potsdam.
39   See *Magdeburger Zeitung*, 20 February 1914; *Hannoversche Courier*, 21 February 1914.
40   Minutes of the Prussian Cabinet, 18 March 1914, op. cit., GStA West Berlin.
41   *Zaberner Anzeiger*, 3 March 1914, *Zaberner Tageblatt*, 5 March 1914.
42   Wedel to Bethmann, 13 March 1914, Bethmann to Wedel, 15 March 1914, RK 173, op. cit., ZStA Potsdam; see Brissaud, *L'Affaire du lieutenant de Saverne* (1929), p. 116; Schenk, op. cit., p. 62.
43   See Brissaud, op. cit., p. 164.
44   Falkenhayn to Bethmann, 1 April 1914, RK 1271, op. cit., ZStA Potsdam.
45   Memo of 4 April 1914, ibid.
46   See Vorschrift über den Waffengebrauch des Militärs und, seiner Mitwirkung zur Unterdrückung innerer Unruhen vom 19. März 1914 (Berlin, 1914).
47   Telegram to Valentini of 31 January, Rep. 89H, Bd. 2, op. cit., ZStA–II Merseburg; Bethmann to Wedel, 1 February, Wedel to Bethmann, 13 February 1914, RK 172, op. cit., ZStA Potsdam.
48   See Erwin Schenck, *Der Fall Zabern* (Stuttgart, 1927), p. 97.
49   Knöpffler report of 4 February, Grossmann report of 7 February 1914, and Forstner complaint, D247/23, AdBR Strasbourg; Deimling report of 5 February 1914, RK 172, op. cit., ZStA Potsdam.
50   Wedel to Valentini, 29 January 1914, Rep. 89H, Bd. 2, op. cit., ZStA–II Merseburg.
51   Wahnschaffe to Valentini, 30 January, Roedern to Valentini, 5 February 1914, ibid.; see Valentini diary, op. cit.
52   Wedel to Valentini, 15 February and Valentini to Wedel, 18 February 1914, Rep. 89H, Bd. 2, op. cit., ZStA–II Merseburg.
53   Wedel to Valentini, 12 March 1914, ibid.
54   ibid.

55   Bethmann to Valentini, 30 March 1914, ibid.
56   Aus den Erinnerungen des verstorbenen Statthalters von Dallwitz, Nachlass Thimme, 16, BA Koblenz.
57   Falkenhayn to Bethmann, 7 February 1914, RK 172, op. cit., ZStA Potsdam.
58   Bethmann to Falkenhayn, 8 February, ibid.
59   Falkenhayn to Bethmann, 9 February, ibid.
60   Wedel to Bethmann, 12 February, ibid.
61   Bethmann to Falkenhayn, 16 February, ibid.
62   Falkenhayn to Bethmann, 17 February, ibid.
63   Bethmann to Falkenhayn, 24 February, ibid.
64   Roedern to Bethmann, 15 March, RK 173, op. cit., ZStA Potsdam.
65   Bethmann memo, 24 March, ibid.
66   Falkenhayn to Bethmann, 25 March, ibid.
67   Brissaud, op. cit., p. 160.
68   Bethmann to Eisendecher, 17 April 1914, I–A Els.-Lothr., Nr. 4 (Geheim), Bd. 1–2, AA Bonn.

8 *And So It Goes*

Is it possible to touch more delicately and happily both the
weakness and the strength of Germany; pedantic, simple,
enslaved, free, ridiculous, admirable Germany?
(Matthew Arnold)

The Reichstag addressed Zabern once more in early May in the course
of its scheduled debate on the military budget. At least on the left,
there was an unmistakably elegiac tone. Heinrich Schulz of the Social
Democrats recalled the darling buds of December when, as he said, the
House had shown 'courage and even some energy'. The time had come
again to show whether the House represented the German people, he
declared, whether it knew what it wanted, whether it was prepared to let
Falkenhayn march triumphantly into the summer recess. Was the House
prepared, in short, to accept the new regulation on military intervention
in civil disturbances?

The answer was obvious, but not simple. One of a very rare parliamentary speecies, the Bavarian Progressive Ernst Müller-Meiningen seemed to
echo Schulz. He assured his colleagues that he did not intend to say
another word about the incidents of the previous winter. He did not even
intend to recall the 'virtually inexplicable mass psychosis that had, with
the help of skilful political management, plunged tens of thousands of
nominally educated people into such a rage that they no longer noticed
that their own rights were being trampled underfoot'. The Reichstag
had only tried to defend the rights of the German middle class, Müller
declared to cheers from the left, and 'this failure of civic awareness in
broad circles of the German middle class is among the most regrettable
aspects of the entire Zabern affair'.

Yet even Müller conceded that the new regulation had not only ended
the affair, but that it represented a slight gain over its predecessor. The
structural problems none the less remained. There was, for an obvious
example, the situation of the Prussian Minister of War. Operating *de facto*
as War Minister of the entire German Empire, he was responsible only to
the Prussian Parliament, while the Chancellor, the one minister officially
accessible to the Reichstag, enjoyed only a fictitious responsibility for
the military. 'Only in such a constitutional chaos as now exists could such

an institution as the military Cabinet achieve such importance', Müller reminded his colleagues.

This was true enough in ways that became appallingly clear by the end of summer. But the May debate was hardly the time or place for a moment of truth. The House may have been unclear about what it wanted. At least it knew what it wanted to avoid. A self-assured Minister of War answered for the government. Falkenhayn had no fault to find with the old regulation. A single case in ninety-three years hardly impressed him as a burning emergency. But he acknowledged that the world had become more critical. It was necessary to meet hypothetical contingencies as well as practical needs. Therefore, he said, the emperor had rewritten the regulation. It was a royal prerogative. Truthfully, if a bit disingenuously, he added that the appearance of the new version had been delayed by differences between the states. But it had been accommodated to existing law and delimited the respective prerogatives of the civil and military authorities. The primary motive, he contended, was that the 'right and duty of the civil authorities to act independently and autonomously to keep order should not be compromised while they were still able to perform their jobs'.

Even Haegy of the Alsatian Centre acknowledged that the solution was probably the best attainable. He found the left excessively anxious. There had been no problems with the Zabern regiment under its new management, the new text was adequately clear and unsolicited military intervention was now conceivable only in the event of open revolution where it was bound to occur anyway, irrespective of the new regulation. 'But we can say one thing', he added. 'The appearance of the new regulation is an indirect condemnation of the incident in Zabern.'

This was true, but also a debating point. So was the Social Democrat Daniel Stücklen's reminder that the revised regulation, like the empire's revised law on freedom of assembly, was a product of administrative fiat, and therefore no liberalisation at all. Putative self-defence, the grounds for Forstner's acquittal, was like kleptomania, Stücklen added for good measure. Just as only the rich suffered from kleptomania, the poor presumably being given to mere theft, only officers practised putative self-defence.[1] Again, this was true.

So what was the point about Zabern? The answer was an elaborate calculus of greater and lesser evils, historical memories and personal experience. Almost inevitably the answers came easiest to foreigners, secure and even righteous in a world remote from the fragmented fears, hopes and realities of German life. Frederic William Wile, gleefully hauled in as a witness by the crown prince, was the qualified exception. Wile appreciated that Germany was not Indiana and that what 'would appear ridiculous and inappropriate in La Porte' might be a necessity in Zabern. A longtime resident of Berlin who wrote for the *Daily Mail*, the *New York*

Times and the *Chicago Tribune*, he called attention to the facts of German life: that the army was a popular institution, that 18,000 men had turned up for a regimental centenary in Wiesbaden and 4,000 for a regimental reunion in Berlin, that even Social Democrats ordinarily recalled their military experience with some pleasure. It was the army that had made Germany, Wile reminded his readers. For a country in Germany's political and geographical situation it was crucially important. To punish Reuter for doing what he believed to be his duty seemed to Wile like hearing an executive of US Steel publicly announce that he had reconsidered his position on free enterprise.[2] Among foreign observers, Wile's was an extreme position but a refreshingly unconventional one.

In general, foreigners saw in the affair what they wanted to see. 'There are "incidents" in public life that somehow illuminate the inner nature of a certain order of things by the flash that emerges from a comparatively trivial event with unusual force and clarity', Lenin noted.[3] It was really the same point as Wile's: that behind Germany's civil and constitutional façade the army was in charge. The proposition hardly raised an eyebrow in France. 'Germany can't get along without its army', the later ambassador and high commissioner André François-Poncet informed his readers. 'It can get along without the Reichstag.'

'You may pretend that the Prussian military is a fossil that will soon take its place in a museum', he continued. 'I find it in singularly good health, lively, vigorous and ready to act.'[4]

Compelled to live as best they could alongside the cage, Frenchmen responded in different ways. But there were few who denied the common premiss. Rightwing Frenchmen, ambivalent in their undeniable admiration for the monarchical purposefulness of German life, none the less strained to contrast German barbarism with French civilisation and cursed a cowardly republic for its neglect of the lost provinces. Leftwing Frenchmen speculated on an 'other' Germany, largely represented by the Social Democrats. They thought wishfully with the teutonophile Jaurès, as he strove to help the 'good' Germans on their way to peaceful revolution. Middle-of-the-road Frenchmen fudged. Justice without reconquest — logically dubious but politically realistic, as Gilbert Ziebura has noted — was their party line on Alsace.[5]

Scepticism and dry powder was the party line on Germany in general. Reaching resourcefully into the inventory of historical analogy, they compared Germany with France before 1848 or the Britain of 1830–50 and speculated with good reason on their neighbours' limited tolerance for domestic conflict.[6] Zabern unsurprisingly confirmed innumerable suspicions. But attention tended to focus on domestic reaction rather than the events themselves. Fearful that Germans might be looking for a violent reaction on their part that would justify a new war, and convinced that their Teutonic neighbour was at a crossroads, Frenchmen gave top priority to even-tempered inconspicuousness. There was to be no provocation.[7]

British diplomats read the papers, filed their dispatches, and nodded. Like the Austrian ambassador Szögyény, who did the same, Vincent Corbett, HM Consul in Munich, made much — too much — of the breach between north and south.[8] 'Possibly the two great forces of German public opinion which have clashed at Zabern will clash again and again, and Germany may go through a period similar to that through which England went in the time of Charles the First', J. Ellis Barker told readers of the *Nineteenth Century*. But he doubted it. 'It seems more likely that the powers of feudalism and absolutism, which, under the cloak of parliamentarism at present govern the country, will try to avoid a domestic conflict by provoking a foreign one', he concluded.[9] Robert Crozier Long, incomparably more sophisticated, tooted the same horn. 'Und der König absolut/Wenn er unseren Willen tut', he quoted the poet Chamisso ('And the monarch without peer/When he says what we want to hear'). The point about Prussian Germany's Conservatives was that they were, at heart, a revolutionary lot whose 'subversive zeal' for the army and the monarchy were ultimately a threat to both.

Paradoxically, Crozier Long observed, it was they who were *de facto* champions of a parliamentary executive since they, like the real parliamentarians, believed in no-confidence votes only as the outward and visible evidence of real power, of which there had been none in December. By comparison with the Conservatives, Germany's democratic parliamentarians were anglophile tabby cats who confused gestures with reality. His prognosis was hardly one to make Whig hearts sing. 'It is a British principle that honest and fit administration and general prosperity are impossible without free citizens exercising severe control', Crozier Long wrote. 'But Germany, against British doctrines, shows that free citizens exercising severe control are not essential to efficiency and prosperity; for in efficiency and prosperity Germany is not behind us, and in freedom and control she is close to Russia.' The gap, he argued, was actually increasing since 'general national fitness' grew while political development stood still 'where, indeed, under Prusso-militarist pressure, it is not moving back'.[10]

It was a view most Germans shared, be they for it or against it. The consensus extended from the hawkish right, demonstratively aggressive in its conviction of victory, to the Social Democrats, momentarily bound in the solidarity of seemingly permanent opposition.[11] Liberals shared it, too, reflecting an embarrassment that could be regarded as the resignation of habitual losers.

'One thing I hope we might never again experience is that a chancellor declares: "Illegalities have taken place and will be expiated", and that a military court is vindicated by his failure to appeal when it answers "Illegalities have not taken place and will not be expiated"', Conrad

Haussmann wrote to his colleague Groeber in a birthday message. 'The Reichstag should find a way to free itself of any responsibility', he added revealingly.

'Only the extreme right can find any satisfaction in the Zabern business, and possibly the extreme left, who can see it as wind in their sails', Groeber answered. 'The middle class did not look good and generally left its deputies in the lurch', he acknowledged. 'And so absolutism triumphs again by knowing how to play off the parties against one another and prevent the people's representatives from achieving any significance of their own.'[12]

What seemed a kind of high-minded wistfulness on the left-end of the German liberal spectrum was that much more acute on the right, where the National Liberals seemed intent on confirming single-handedly what Groeber said. Riven like the Social Democrats, their rifts seemed, in fact, to increase as their numbers dwindled.[13] A personification of that perennial oscillation between principle and panic that had nipped the heels of German liberalism since the 1870s, Gustav Stresemann managed in day to go the full route from civil libertarian indignation to calculated opportunism.

'No colonel has the right to set himself above the law as Reuter did, and I regret the decision of the military court that, for the first time in Germany, elevates illegality to a principle', Stresemann wrote to a hawkish Saxon constituent. Stresemann saw no difference between an officer's honour and that of any other public official. 'If, for example, the members of the supreme court in Leipzig are threatened by a popular demonstration, they have no alternative but to request aid from the civil authorities, despite being some of the most prestigious men in Germany.' And even if aid failed to materialise, Stresemann continued, this was no excuse to reach for a revolver and blast away at anyone who happened by.

He was again dismayed that Reuter had ordered up machine-guns because thirty or forty feckless civilians had called people names. 'In my opinion, it has never before happened since the empire's creation that a bumptious lieutenant presumes to arrest judges and public prosecutors as they go peacefully about their business, although no one gave him the right to do anything of the kind', Stresemann declared. 'These gentlemen obviously have no idea of the principle that all citizens are equal under German law, for when one of the arrested gentlemen introduced himself as a public prosecutor, he was immediately released while the others were kept in custody.'

The obvious prejudice of the military court only confirmed his worst suspicions. Ignorance of the law was no excuse for ordinary people. Yet it sufficed for acquittal of a colonel. 'Somebody can steal according to the same law, and declare in his defence that he had no idea stealing was illegal in Germany', Stresemann protested. 'To show how little idea

Colonel von Reuter actually has of the law, he wanted to exclude the public prosecutor from a house search, and announced that it would be just fine with him if there were bloodshed.'

'Please forgive my opinion, but this is contempt for the law, not recognition of it, and testifies to the military spirit of earlier centuries', he concluded.[14] It was a long and eloquent letter. His letter to Bassermann a few weeks later was a contrast in every sense.

Dear Bassermann,
The situation of the German military mission in Turkey represents a regrettable blow to our prestige.
Wouldn't it be desirable in this connection if we undertook an initiative that might, given the present fluid state of things, regain the sympathies of those groups that turned on us as a result of the Zabern business? Best wishes.[15]

Yet even if things fell apart, it was not self-evident that they might not fall back together and still less inevitable that the centre – in this case the Catholic Centre – could not hold. Erzberger's end-of-session report to the party's constituents is full of plausible self-assurance. A kind of British MP or US Congressman manqué, Erzberger tended to see the government neither as St George nor the dragon but as a normal constitutional adversary. He was unintimidated by the executive branch, this 'system without a system' as he referred to it, that looked to the Reichstag to pull its legislative chestnuts out of the fire. He regretted nothing in the preceding months, save, perhaps, the ineptitude of the government, the obstructionism of the Bundesrat, and the spinelessness of the National Liberals. Their performance in February had torpedoed a perfectly satisfactory solution of the military regulation problem, Erzberger declared. He was still satisfied with the way things turned out. There was now a common statute for all troops in Alsace-Lorraine, 'considerable' progress from the standpoint of civil authority and civil liberties in Prussia, and no need for any compromise by the non-Prussian German south. Erzberger considered the December censure vote evidence of parliamentary progress. The Reichstag had made its point.

Budgetary blockade, the SPD tactic, struck Erzberger as melodramatic and silly under the circumstances. It was the gesture of a permanent minority with no responsibility or capacity for damage. Rejection of the budget was a last resort and only credible as such. He considered it pointless where the government had, in fact, done what the Reichstag wanted. In the aftermath of Zabern, Erzberger was ready as ever to take on the army, to challenge the authority of the War Minister, and to assert parliamentary authority in the appointment and promotion of officers and the liberalisation of military justice. Like Stresemann's retreat to the shelter of the grass roots, this was parliamentarism German-style. But it was parliamentarism none the less, different in degree perhaps but not in kind from what might be practised by a Radical from Lyons or a Republican from Iowa. Erzberger was proud that he had carried his party and the Reichstag majority with him in rejecting a new public relations department at the War Ministry. He had also caught the military Cabinet in an elaborate real-estate manipulation designed to get itself a new building without a Reichstag appropriation. The officers and civil servants behind the deal had been ordered to assume responsibility for the resulting 6 million marks in costs, he reported briskly.[16]

Erzberger's purposeful optimism was shared by Hans Delbrück, a pillar of the academic establishment, who graciously passed on his own modestly heterodox thoughts for the Chancellor's perusal. The parties performed a useful, if problematic, role in Germany's political life, Delbrück argued. The army might be the foundation of Germany's political system but it was not the only element in its equilibrium, he continued. The army had provoked the confrontation between civil and military, party and party, officers and civil servants, even Germans and Prussians. Taken literally, the appellate ruling on Forstner could threaten the life of any citizen luckless enough to collide with an officer. If the Reichstag was in the ascendancy as a result, the equilibrium could be restored Delbrück contended. He was confident that the empire would survive the current situation and that national feeling would suffice to contain Prussian particularism. The system worked, he argued. The Reichstag majority avoided interference with the command structure, the military realised that a conscript army was dependent on the support of the Reichstag and the Chancellor had made it clear to the commander-in-chief that the military regulations needed revision. The parties exaggerated conflicts by their nature, Delbrück concluded. But he actually saw the conflicts receding. 'In Britain, France and no less the United States, politicians and patriots have much tougher problems to deal with', he claimed.[17] Considering the débâcle half a year ahead, his optimism was, to say the least, premature. But it was not *prima facie* foolish.

A little less than five years and one world war later, Bernhard Schwertfeger, an establishmentarian like Delbrück and a respected military commentator of mildly conservative disposition, found Zabern the root of all evil. With the war and Alsace-Lorraine lost beyond imaginable recovery, he saw the episode not as the vindication but the essence of the imperial system. Forstner's follies would have created an uproar anywhere, Schwertfeger mused. Anywhere else German public opinion would have condemned him unambiguously. But it had to happen in Alsace where the military could be presumed to be grateful for an opportunity to dump Wedel's administration, and suspicion followed suspicion in circular self-fulfilment.

The consequences had been felt around the world. The Germans concluded that Alsatians were enemies. Alsatians concluded that Germans were militarists and barbarians. A wartime administration treated them accordingly, Schwertfeger added. Now, as Van Calker had wailed in that memorable Reichstag debate, 'it's all kaput'.[18]

In May 1919 Zabern echoed again in the first volume of Bethmann's memoirs. The merits of the case were, revealingly, left undiscussed. Still the master of the common denominator, the ex-Chancellor instead deplored the protests of the democratic parties that led foreigners to believe the government was in the hands of the ultra-right. A second shot was aimed at the presumptions of Prussian particularism that allowed the French to believe that German unity might not survive a war. A third was directed at the arms lobby that had implied that Germany was keen to come out swinging. A fourth addressed the general malaise and dissatisfaction of the immediate prewar years that seemed to prove that Germans were anxious for adventure.[19]

In time, the echoes congealed in conventional wisdom. A reflection of the affairs itself, there was even a conventional wisdom of the right and one of the left. Erwin Schenk's monograph, written from interviews and public sources, appeared in 1927 with an introduction by Fritz Kern of the University of Bonn, neither then nor since a notably activist institution. The book was a contribution to domestic revisionism. It was also a story without a hero, Kern explained, since Forstner had been a *provocateur*, the civil administration had been incompetent, the Chancellor had been unimpressive, and the un-Prussian Deimling had been a most untypical ass for protecting Forstner as Hindenburg presumably would not have done. The fact that Deimling had experienced his own wartime epiphany and emerged a thoroughly untypical defender of the postwar republican order[20] was only another irony.

Kern recalled Deimling's early days with evident relish: how he had ignited his troops in Southwest Africa with visions of Prussia's highest decoration hanging from the mountainsides; how he had antagonised the Reichstag and unforgivably pushed the Centre to the left; how he had referred to pacifists as people 'in pants with nothing in them'.[21] Consistently censorious, Schenk's text seemed dedicated to the proposition that the truth lay somewhere in the middle, as in 'middle class'. He acknowledged the insensitivity of the army, the reality of the provocation, and the irresponsibility of the press. He regretted the loss of Alsace-Lorraine, firm in the conviction that the new French administration there was no improvement. Provincial autonomy was no solution either, he added. Clearly written for domestic consumption, the book contained no hint that anything about the affair had been systemic.

Three years later, Karl Bachem, the doyen of the Centre, displayed a Centrist even-handedness, neatly dispatching the incompetence of the

German administration, the subversiveness of French propaganda, the fatuous and inappropriate references of Forstner, and the anti-militarism of the left in a single sentence. He also recalled Fehrenbach's Reichstag speech with admiration. It was, in fact, the only one he cited. In Bachem's view, Zabern had advanced the cause of parliamentarism and reconciled the German and Alsatian Centre. It had also undermined German morale and had a catalytic effect on French combativeness.[22]

Nothing quite like this was seen again for nearly two generations. It then appeared in the more congenial climate of a new republic, with overtones of democratic black, red and gold. Although Zabern was un-questionably an issue of military authority, both Chancellor and War Minister had acknowledged the obligation to defend the decisions of the commander-in-chief, Ernst Rudolf Huber argued in his voluminous post-war history of German constitutionality. Since neither the civil nor the military authorities could any longer dodge parliamentary criticism by invoking the autonomy of the commander-in-chief, the episode, in Huber's view, reflected a fundamental constitutional transformation.[23] Conditionally useful as a guide to the transformation of German constitu-tionality, Huber's version in any case illuminated the transformation of German conservatism.[24]

The left continued to regard Zabern as the very essence of the imperial system, if not of Germany itself. Foreigners have understandably found it easy to make this perspective their own. The almost aphoristic dismissal of the affair in standard foreign treatments of the era is symptomatic, virtually a suggestion that there were no questions left to be asked.[25] Writing in 1928 Arthur Rosenberg, a leftwing historian of idiosyncratic originality, saw Zabern as nothing less than the characteristic mani-festation of a pre-revolutionary era.[26] The most useful of all Zabern documentations, Arnold Heydt's *Der Fall Zabern*, published in Strasbourg in 1934, suggests a tactical leak in a tactical place at a tactical moment by French officials in possesssion of German documents still hopelessly inaccessible on the other side of the Rhine. A reporter on the *Dernières Nouvelles*, née *Neueste Nachrichten*, Heydt had distinguished himself the year before with an acidly anti-German novel on the Alsatian experience in the First World War. Zabern, he informed his readers, was what German rule was like – in case they might have forgotten.

The liberating revisionism of postwar German historians, beginning with the calamity of the Third Reich and progressing relentlessly backwards through the Weimar period and the First World War to the flawed creation of a German superpower in the nineteenth century, inexorably led again to Zabern. Successive scholarly sub-generations advanced from the discon-tinuities to the continuities of German diplomacy, from German diplomatic to political, and then to social, history. As the pivot of Bismarckian orthodoxy, 'the primacy of foreign policy', yielded to a new orthodoxy, 'the primacy of domestic politics', attention shifted incrementally to the dynamics of business and trade, the institutional interests of bureaucracies, and the politics of organised interests. Hans-Günter Zmarzlik, the first researcher to see the government documents in the East German archives, found Zabern corroborative evidence for the explosive stalemate in German politics on the eve of the First World War.[27]

The historical discussion had come full circle. Gerhard Ritter, the maverick conservative and dean of postwar German historiography, who remembered from personal experience how his contemporaries' hearts had leapt to the call of 'global foreign policy' and 'seapower',[28] subsumed Zmarzlik's views in his magisterial study of the militarisation of German politics.[29] In principle, Ritter's view had once been Lenin's. Unsurprisingly, the Lenin—Ritter view met little resistance in East Germany.[30] Hans-Ulrich Wehler, a founding father of the new West German social history, rediscovered Zabern a few years later finding significance even in the voluminous non-references to the affair in the memoir literature of the preceding half-century.[31] He considered Zabern a great constitutional defeat like those in the 1860s.[32]

But was it? The complexities of the answer appropriately reflect the complexities and idiosyncrasies of the system, its often underestimated strengths as well as its endlessly familiar shortcomings. Nations may, or may not, deserve the governments they get. But from Dreyfus to Watergate they show a startling propensity for the crises they deserve, those unanticipated flashes, of which Lenin wrote, that illuminate the stresses and workings of whole societies.

A test of nerve, constitutionality and civic culture, Zabern was, above all, very German. In a matter of weeks the affair recapitulated virtually everything that has perplexed and fascinated foreigners then and since about that curious house that Bismarck built, where Steif animals, the Lorelei and *Hänsel and Gretel* apparently coexisted with Bayreuth and Beethoven, idealist philosophers and industrial chemists, with Krupp, reserve officers and whole armies of Herr Doktors.

But the affair was as remarkable for its coincidences as its apparent inevitability. Forstners were arguably a standard model in the Prussian — or any other contemporary — army, not to mention university. In a pre-Wilsonian Europe, there was no shortage of Alsaces either, where military occupation merged pragmatically with national defence in ways Europeans declared unacceptable only a few years later. On the other hand, Zabern happened only once. At least to some degree, the vehemence of the reaction was a response to its very uniqueness. It was as though a *Simplicissimus* cartoon had suddenly come alive, nature imitating art. Nor was there anything self-evidently typical about Reuter or Deimling. Their immediate deputies behaved with consistent, unobtrusive and documented good sense. Had either been in command in late 1913 there might not have been an affair.

The same can be said *a fortiori* of the emperor and the crown prince. William may have been an impetuous man and his son a foolish one, for reasons that continue to preoccupy their biographers. But neither impetuousness nor foolishness was inevitable in the job description, a natural consequence of constitutional monarchy, or even a self-evident family failing. In any case, while conspicuous and noisy, William's role, let alone his son's, was ultimately of secondary importance. Since at least the *Daily Telegraph* affair, the emperor had been a symbol and a public entertainer. On occasion he was an infernal nuisance. But only in the most abstract sense was he his country's chief executive.

If Zabern tested the domestic consensus, it also affirmed it in all its complicated imperfections. Seditious grandees might fantasise about turning back the clock to 1847. Social Democrats continued to recite their revolutionary litanies. But neither revolution nor counter-revolution, Spartakus nor the Kapp Putsch, was more realistic in 1914 than it actually proved to be in 1919–20 after the century's first great war had swept away most of the traditional norms and restraints that stood in their way, and when revolution did come, it was neither the heirs of Liebknecht and Luxemburg nor disgruntled Prussian bluebloods who made it. If only out of an unwillingness to pay the price of alternatives or trust their fellow citizens, the vast majority of prewar Germans was willing to accept, and even defend, the status quo. If it was inextricably connected to a sclerotic constitution and high risk foreign policy, it also assured them a generally honest and efficient administration, legal security and the highest standard of living they had known.

What Zabern did not prove was that imperial Germany was particularly violent or autocratic, though there was not much evidence that it was easily reformable let alone a closet democracy, either. It was the USA where they assassinated presidents, Russia where they assassinated grand dukes and emperors. It was Homestead, Haymarket and Pullman that set the going standards for industrial violence, Paris's 'mur des fédérés' or St Petersburg's 'bloody Sunday' that set them for the continuation of politics by bloody means. There were places in 1913 where troops shot workers and unarmed civilians. Germany was hardly one of them. Blanck's head and people's feelings aside, no one got hurt over Zabern. Friedrich Stampfer's characterisation of Germany as 'the best administered, worst governed country in Europe' was only a bit of a caricature. It still implied a meaningful distinction between imperial Germany and other places, before and since, whose administration was worse and governments no better.

In many ways, the affair proved the empire to be what contemporaries, foreign and domestic, always claimed it was. If Zabern showed it to be timorous, indecisive, authoritarian and belligerent, the affair could as credibly be read as evidence for its stability, flexibility, even legitimacy in the eyes of its citizens. The emperor's windy truculence, the crown prince's telegrams, the smug bloody-mindedness of the military courts and the high-handedness of provincial schoolmasters, Wedel's tenacious but self-defeating guerilla campaign, the repudiation of Petri and the demotion of Mahl, the flounderings of Bethmann and the whimpering disintegration of an unprecedented Reichstag majority: all of them are part of the story. It was an odd system where the Chancellor's very strength derived from his near-isolation.

On the other hand, both contemporary and later observers failed to see, or hesitated to acknowledge, that the civilians got what they wanted, or at least a lot of it. Reuter, Forstner and Schad were transferred. Forstner was punished, at least to a point. In direct response to a spasm of public outrage. Prussian officials faced down a Prussian Minister of War and a Hohenzollern monarch tacitly sacrificed a symbolic piece of his pre-constitutional patrimony. Victims of arbitrary arrest by the state's most prestigious representatives were rather speedily compensated by an army liable, unlike the Ohio National Guard, to civil courts[33] and demonstrably unwilling to take its chances before civil judges. A smalltown editor of no pedigree and little distinction was acquitted of libel charges brought against him by a Prussian colonel. The warrantless search of his office was duly prosecuted. Zabern regained its garrison.

In a sense, there was no defeat or victory save as thinking made it so. Social Democrats and their Progressive associates, concerned with a radical transformation of the game where most of their fellow citizens were concerned instead with the integrity of the prevailing rules, were beaten because they said they were. The younger officers, sunning themselves in the acquittals of Forstner, Schad and Reuter, were winners for the same reason.

The aftermath was as Janus-faced as the epilogue. The army ordered that Alsatian recruits would henceforth have to serve away from home, though in Italy or France this had always been the normal case.[34] Breitkopf & Härtel, the Leipzig music publishers, notified the Strasbourg police of an order for a student songbook called the 'Chansonnier de l'Etudiant Alsacien-Lorrain' that included a song of dubious loyalty. Breitkopf cancelled the contract.[35] In Strasbourg there was a ban on lectures by French-speaking foreigners on political, economic or cultural subjects.[36]

There was also a round of vindictive litigation, some harmless, some less so. In June 1914 the *Zaberner Anzeiger* reported the trial of two adolescent proletarians on charges brought by the assiduous 10-year-old son of a railway official responding to solicitations from his teacher. But both boys were acquitted on the evidence of 12- and 13-year-old witnesses.[37]

Practitioners of *lèse-majesté* had a harder time. The proceedings against them read like something out of *Simplicissimus*, imperial Germany at its punitive and pedantic silliest. In mid-January 1914 the public prosecutor's office in Berlin, after a judicious inquiry of the Prussian Ministry of Justice, brought charges against Hans Leuss, aged 53, the editor of a small leftish journal, for an editorial headlined 'Wilhelm the Last?' With the now-famous telegrams in mind, Leuss had declared the crown prince Germany's most effective republican agitator. 'If he had actually tried to persuade us of the absurdity of monarchism, he could hardly have done better than in this, his preferred way', he wrote.

Since Leuss had neither proposed action nor incited to violence, there was, in fact, a question of what charges to bring. It was March before the prosecution settled on libel. But conviction was speedy once Leuss was finally tried *in camera*, though his superior was acquitted on the grounds of not having seen the article before its appearance. The crown prince, who only learned of the case from the newspapers, was evidently surprised but not averse to the proceedings. The court admitted its incapacity to compel reverence for the royal family. It none the less censured the defendant's tactlessness, particularly considering his apparent intelligence and education. Formally guilty of intentional insult, Leuss, in effect, was declared guilty of aggravated bad manners. Since he had already been twice convicted of libel he was denied the more honorific fortress arrest and sentenced to six months in jail, though the prosecution had asked for nine.

Pending an appeal, Leuss fired off a short piece pointing out that the official verdict had taken six weeks to reach him. At least the verdict was in acceptable German, he added, though otherwise counter-productive. An embarrassed letter from the prosecutors blamed the delay on an associate judge. A disciplinary action followed, as did rejection of Leuss's appeal by the supreme court in Leipzig. He was jailed in June.

In May, Karl Liebknecht informed the Reichstag that Ernst Meyer, an editor of the party's flagship newspaper, the *Vorwärts*, had been sentenced to three months on the same charge as Leuss and that two more journalists, Carl Schneidt and Georg Zepler, had been sentenced to six weeks of fortress detention for a parodistic view of the crown prince's departure from Danzig that Zepler had written and Schneidt reprinted.

Meyer too was tried *in camera*. Schneidt and Zepler appeared in public, save for the moment of truth when the incriminating piece was read. Though it already had been published, the courtroom was then cleared. The prosecutors were ambivalent and acquittal was at least a possibility since there was a gnawing awareness that a proliferation of libel charges might actually create sympathy for the defendants. But consistency won out. With charges already filed against Leuss, the idea that Meyer *et al.* should get away with their irksome frolicsomeness was irritating to the guardians of the law. Despite an expert witness called in Zepler's defence who testified that parodies only rarely represented libelous intent, the court came through again. Zepler's piece, written in the persona of a schoolgirl leaving the alma mater, was offensive *per se* the prosecutor insisted. Nothing could be more humiliating to a grown man than being compared with a schoolgirl. Like Leuss, Meyer, Schneidt and Zepler appealed against their convictions. Like Leuss's, their appeals were rejected. In early August, nearly a month after an intervention by the crown prince, Meyer and Leuss were pardoned. Bethmann, consulted by Beseler in the matter, approved the pardon providing the public was informed that the crown prince had not initiated it.

Meanwhile the Justice Ministry opposed prosecuting a Social Democratic paper in Erfurt that hoped the crown prince's current African safari might go on indefinitely and that he pay his own expenses. In November the emperor himself dismissed charges pending since May against a Polish paper for a piece whose author reported waking from a dream in which the crown prince, now William III, had dismissed Parliament and dispatched the fleet to take over England, Scandinavia and North America.[38]

Like the abortive charges of the spring and summer, what failed to happen in the aftermath of Zabern was also a matter of some interest. One Diefenbach, a district court judge in Colmar with thirty years' residence in Alsace and presumably a representative of a vocal and militant minority of his compatriots, dreamed expansive dreams of a final solution to the Alsatian problem. The French-language press was to be banned, the clergy of both Christian denominations re-educated, advanced German secondary education for girls was to be promoted, French businesses germanised, Alsatian troops and civil servants assigned to posts and jobs east of the Rhine, and transport between Baden and Alsace improved.[39] Alexander von Hohenlohe-Schillingsfürst, the son of the old imperial governor and chancellor, even demanded liquidation of the provinces' *de facto* autonomy and their annexation to one or several of the German states, preferably Prussia.[40] In Germany itself, business and industry pressed for harassment of organised labour with renewed aggressiveness and there were speculations on a heavily polarised election campaign,[41] like the flag-waving *tour de force* Bülow had pulled off in 1907 and a Gaullist regime was to pull off under remotely similar circumstances sixty-one years later.[42]

But there was neither a parliamentary siege nor a rightwing coup. Neither was there an election campaign that was as likely to worsen the government's situation as to improve it. There was also no significant assault on existing freedoms of assembly or of speech, no invasion of editorial offices or confiscation of published editions, no coercion of the judiciary, no evidence of chill in a vigorous, diverse and outspoken public opinion. There was no assault on the constitution of Alsace-Lorraine, no

interference with its press or legislature, no real likelihood of a collabora-
tive counter-coup of army and Old Germans against the provinces' *de facto*
home rule like the curious episode in progress at almost the same time in
Ireland.[43]

In itself, Zabern showed imperial Germany to be neither significantly
more nor less repressive than other Western societies, only that it was
endowed, like others, with a fragile and complicated social and political
equilibrium and an accident-prone executive that again was neither the
first nor the last of its kind. There was reason to note and deplore the
easy brutality of a Prussian lieutenant. There were also grounds to admire
the spontaneous dismay of a Germany outraged by the relative incon-
venience caused a remote handful of provincials by their overnight arrest.
There were certainly reasons to regret the passing of this Germany in the
years that followed.

More and bigger accidents, of course, were just ahead.[44] They affected
the lives of Zabern's personae as they did the lives of countless millions
of others. In summer 1915 Forstner was killed in the Carpathians in a
campaign initiated, ironically, by Falkenhayn.[45] In 1926 Reuter, a colonel
in Frankfurt on the Oder in the summer of 1914, was listed as lieutenant-
general in a directory of retired officers.[46] By the late 1920s Deimling,
the fire-breather of Strasbourg, had become a pillar of the Reichsbanner,
the para-military republican guard organised to resist similar organisations
on the far left and right. By the end of the war Bethmann and Falkenhayn,
pursued by nemesis and one another, had retired in disgrace.[47] Falkenhayn
fell to Bethmann in late summer 1916, Bethmann to the combined pressures of the generals and a disoriented Reichstag a summer later. For the
nominal victors both were pyrrhic victories.

A little more than a year later, the imperial regime and its fragile
equilibrium had vanished too and Zabern had again become Saverne.
Henck, Blelly and Scheibel, the recruits of 1913, returned to the comfortable obscurity of Alsatian life. In 1933 Mahl was located as director
of the Strasbourg social security office, itself a surviving monument to
German rule in a France that, with the exception of Alsace and Lorraine,
still awaited the arrival of modern social legislation.[48]

If the First World War was the epilogue of the affair, it was also the
transition to a new era whose symbolic loci were neither the Curragh nor
Zabern, but the Gulag and Auschwitz. The new Germany was governed
neither by Prussian aristocrats nor Social Democrats. In 1918 the new
commander-in-chief had been an Austrian corporal in the service of the
King of Bavaria. In 1940 he turned Saverne back into Zabern. The Social
Democrats mercifully survived him. Prussia, its aristocrats and its army
did not and in 1944 Zabern once again became Saverne.

References

1   Sessions of 5–7 May 1914, *Verhandlungen des Reichstages* (Berlin, 1914).
2   Translation and memo of 2 February 1914, RK 172, Els.-Lothr. 6, 'Die Unruhen in Zabern' [RK 170–73], ZStA Potsdam.
3   H.-U. Wehler, 'Der Fall Zabern von 1913–14 als eine Verfassungskrise des Wilhelminischen Kaiserreichs', *Krisenherde des Kaiserreichs* (Göttingen, 1970), p. 66.
4   Quoted by Paul Bourson, 'Vingt ans après', *La Vie en Alsace* (1934), p. 64.
5   Gilbert Ziebura, *Die deutsche Frage in der öffentlichen Meinung Frankreichs von 1911–14* (Berlin, 1955), pp. 30ff.
6   ibid., pp. 81ff.
7   ibid., pp. 91ff.
8   See Corbett's dispatch of 8 December 1913, FO 371–1653/3676, PRO London; report of the Austrian ambassador in Berlin, 28 January 1914, HHStA and Kriegsarchiv Vienna.
9   J. Ellis Barker, 'Autocratic and democratic Germany: the lessons of Zabern'. *Nineteenth Century* (February 1914).
10   Robert Crozier Long, 'German lambs and Prussian wolves: a letter from Berlin', *Fortnightly Review* (March 1914).
11   See Dieter Groh, *Negative Integration und revolutionärer Attentismus* (Frankfurt, Berlin and Vienna, 1973), p. 521.
12   Haussmann to Groeber 10 February, Groeber to Haussmann, 16 February 1914, Nachlass Haussmann, HStA Stuttgart.
13   See Dan S. White, *The Splintered Party* (Cambridge, Mass. and London, 1976).
14   Stresemann to Rüger, 11 January 1914, Nachlass Stresemann, Vol. 138, AA Bonn.
15   Stresemann to Bassermann, 18 January 1914, ibid., Vol. 135.
16   Matthias Erzberger, *Die Zentrumspolitik im Reichstage* (Berlin, 1914).
17   Delbrück article, 'Zabern und kein Ende', *Politische Korrespondenz* (1 February 1914); offprint in RK 172, op. cit., ZStA Potsdam.
18   Ein Rückblick auf den "Fall Zabern"', unpublished ms., Nachlass Schwertfeger, BA Koblenz.
19   Theobald von Bethmann-Hollweg, *Betrachtungen zum Weltkrieg* (Berlin, 1919), pp. 103–4.
20   See Berthold von Deimling, *Aus der alten in die neue Zeit* (Berlin, 1930), *passim*.
21   Erwin Schenk, *Der Fall Zabern* (Stuttgart, 1927), pp. i–ix.
22   Karl Bachem, *Vorgeschichte, Geschichte und Politik der Deutschen Zentrumspartei* (Cologne, 1930), Vol. 7, pp. 404–11.
23   E. R. Huber, *Deutsche Verfassungsgeshichte* (Stuttgart, Berlin, Cologne and Mainz, 1969), Vol. 4, p. 347.
24   See Winfried Baumgart, *Deutschland im Zeitalter des Imperialismus* (Frankfurt, 1972), p. 122.
25   See Gordon Craig, *The Politics of the Prussian Army* (New York, 1964); Barbara Tuchman, *The Guns of August* (New York, 1963), p. 47 and *The Proud Tower* (New York, 1967), p. 405.
26   Arthur Rosenberg, *Die Entstehung der Weimarer Republik* (Frankfurt, 1961), p. 57.
27   Hans-Günter Zmarzlik, *Bethmann-Hollweg als Reichskanzler* (Düsseldorf, 1957), *passim*.
28   See Baumgart, op. cit., p. 47.
29   Gerhard Ritter, *Staatskunst und Kriegshandwerk* (Munich, 1960), Vol. 2 *passim*.

30   See Kurt Stenkewitz, *Gegen Bajonett und Dividende* (East Berlin, 1960).
31   Wehler, 'Der Fall Zabern', pp. 351–2.
32   ibid., p. 72.
33   See 'Tragic Kent State', editorial page, *New York Times*, 31 August 1975; 'Ohio approves $675,000 to settle suits in 1970 Kent State shootings', *New York Times*, 5 January 1979, p. A12.
34   Martin Kitchen, *The German Officer Corps 1890–1914* (Oxford, 1968), pp. 217ff.
35   Correspondence of 23 January and 5 February 1914, D247/677, AdBR. Strasbourg.
36   12 February 1914, ibid.
37   *Zaberner Anzeiger*, 25 June 1914, D388/677, AdBR. Strasbourg.
38   Hist. Abt. II, 2.5.1., Nr. 10109, ZStA–II Merseburg.
39   Undated memo, 1914, M10, Bd. 1087, HStA Stuttgart.
40   Undated ms., early 1914, Nachlass Hohenlohe, BA Koblenz.
41   See Groh, op. cit., pp. 522ff.
42   See D. B. Goldey, 'The events of May and the French general election of June 1968', *Parliamentary Affairs*, Vol. 21, no. 4 and Vol. 22, no. 2 (Autumn 1969).
43   See Sir James Fergusson. *The Curragh Incident* (London, 1964); A. J. Ryan, *Mutiny at the Curragh* (New York, 1956); Randolph S. Churchill, *Winston S. Churchill* (Boston, Mass., 1967), Vol. 2, pp. 470–93.
44   See A. J. P. Taylor, 'Fritz Fischer and his school', *Journal of Modern History* (March 1975), pp. 121–2.
45   Joseph Kaestlé, *Ein Sturmsignal aus dem Elsass* (Strasbourg, 1933), p. 143.
46   *Ehrenrangliste des ehemaligen deutschen Heeres* (Berlin, 1926), p. 145.
47   See Karl-Heinz Janssen, *Der Kanzler und der General* (Göttingen, 1967), *passim*.
48   Kaestlé, op. cit., p. 109.

Bibliography

(1) Archival sources

AA Bonn (Politisches Archiv des auswärtigen Amtes):
I—A Els.-Lothr., Nr. 4, Bd. 16—18; Nr. 4 (Geheim), Bd. 1—2; Nachlass Stresemann.
AdBR Strasbourg (Archives du Bas-Rhin):
A. L. 132, Paq. 13, Nr. 25; D247/23; D388/677.
BA Koblenz (Bundesarchiv):
Papers of Alexander Hohenlohe, Schwertfeger, Südekum, Thimme; letters of Bethmann-Hollweg, Kl. Erw. 517/2.
BHStA Munich (Bavarian Hauptstaatsarchiv):
Abt. II, Geheimes Staatsarchiv 78163, 'Die Vorgänge in Zabern'.
GStA West Berlin (Geheimes Staatsarchiv):
Rep. 84a, 6342.
HHStA (Haus-, Hof- und Staatsarchiv) and Kriegsarchiv Vienna:
Reports of ambassador and military attaché for 1913—14.
HStA Stuttgart (Hauptstaatsarchiv incl. Heeresarchiv):
Papers of Conrad Haussmann; M10, Bd. 41, 'Aufzeichnungen der Vertrauenskommission des Reichstags über die militärische und politische Lage Deutschlands im 24. April 1913; M10, Bd. 1087.
PRO London (Public Record Office):
Reports of ambassador, consuls, military attaché for 1913—14 (Foreign Office).
StA Dresden (Staatsarchiv):
Berichte des Militärbevollmächtigten 1913, 1434; Berichte des Gesandten von Salza und Lichtenau, Neue Serie 1975, Bd. 3.
ZStA Potsdam (Zentrales Staatsarchiv):
Reichsjustizamt 3612, 'Das Verhalten des Militärs in Zabern'; RK 170—73, Els.-Lothr. 6, 'Die Unruhen in Zabern'; RK 1271, 'Belagerungszustand'; RK 158/1.
ZStA—II Merseburg (Zentrales Staatsarchiv, Historische Abteilung II):
Hist. Abt. II, 2.2.1, Nr. 3577, Rep. 89H, Bd. 3; Hist. Abt. II, 2.5.1, Nr. 10109; Kgl. Hausarchiv Rep. 53J, Lit P, Nr. 16; Rep. 89H, 1 Els.-Lothr. 6, Bd. 2; Rep. 90a, Abt. B, III, 2b, Nr. 6, Bd. 163, 1914; Abt. D, 1,1, Nr. 2, 1913; RK 158/1.

(2) Documentary Collections

Preussisches Haus der Abgeordneten (Berlin, 1914).

Verhandlungen der I. Kammer des Landtags (Strasbourg, 1914).
Verhandlungen der II. Kammer des Landtags (Strasbourg, 1914).
Verhandlungen des Preussischen Herrenhauses (Berlin, 1914).
Verhandlungen des Reichstages, XIII. Legislaturperiode, I. Session, Vol. 291 (Berlin, 1914).

(3) Books and Pamphlets

Arnold, Ernst, *Mars regiert die Stunde* (Basle, 1914).

Ays, Hermann, *Die Wahrheit über Zabern* (Strasbourg and Kehl, n.d.).

Bachem, Karl, *Vorgeschichte, Geschichte und Politik der deutschen Zentrumspartei*, Vol. 7 (Cologne, 1930).

Bald, Detlef, *Der deutsche Generalstab 1859–1939* (Munich, 1977).

Bald, Detlef *et al.*, *Zur sozialen Herkunft des Offiziers* (Munich, 1977).

Balfour, Michael, *The Kaiser and his Times* (Boston, Mass., 1964).

Barnett, Corelli, *Britain and her Army 1509–1970* (Harmondsworth, 1974).

Berghahn, Volker, *Rüstung und Machtpolitik* (Düsseldorf, 1973).

Beyens, Napoléon Eugène, *Deux Années à Berlin 1912–14*, Vol. 2 (Paris, 1931).

Brissaud, *L'Affaire du lieutenant de Saverne* (1929) (no initials, no place of publication).

Buchheim, Karl, *Das deutsche Kaiserreich* (Munich, 1969).

Busch, Eckart, *Der Oberbefehl, seine rechtliche Struktur in Preussen und Deutschland seit 1848* (Boppard, 1967).

Churchill, Randolph S., *Winston S. Churchill: Young Statesman* (Boston, Mass., 1967).

Craig, Gordon, *The Politics of the Prussian Army* (New York, 1964).

Craig, John Eldon, "'A mission for German learning': the University of Strasbourg and Alsatian society 1870–1918" (unpublished dissertation, Stanford, Calif., 1973).

Cunliffe, Marcus, *Soldiers and Civilians* (Boston, Mass. and Toronto, 1968).

Czempiel, Ernst-Otto, *Das deutsche Dreyfus-Geheimnis* (Munich, Berne and Vienna, 1966).

Deimling, Berthold von, *Aus der alten in die neue Zeit* (Berlin, 1930).

Epstein, Klaus, *Matthias Erzberger* (Princeton, NJ, 1959).

Erzberger, Matthias, *Die Zentrumspolitik im Reichstage* (Berlin, 1914).

Eschenburg, Theodor, *Das Kaiserreich am Scheideweg* (Berlin, 1929).

Fergusson, Sir James, *The Curragh Incident* (London, 1964).

Fischer, Fritz, *Krieg der Illusionen* (Düsseldorf, 1969).

Gerard, James W., *My Four Years in Germany* (New York, 1917).

Gerlach, Helmut von, *Das Parlament* (Frankfurt, 1907).

Groener, Wilhelm, *Lebenserinnerungen* (Göttingen, 1957).

Groh, Dieter, *Negative Integration und revolutionärer Attentismus* (Frankfurt, Berlin and Vienna, 1973).

Grosser, Dieter, *Vom monarchischen Konstitutionalismus zur parlamentarischen Demokratie* (The Hague, 1970).

Haller, Johannes, *Aus dem Leben des Fürsten Philipp zu Eulenburg* (Berlin and Leipzig, 1926).

Hamerow, Theodore S., *The Social Foundations of German Unification* (Princeton, NJ, 1969).

Harries-Jenkins, Gwynne, *The Army in Victorian Society* (London, 1977).

Hasenbein, Heinrich, 'Die parlamentarische Kontrolle des militärischen Oberbefehls im deutschen Reich vom 1871 bis 1918', (unpublished dissertation, Göttingen, 1968).

Heckart, Beverly, *From Bassermann to Bebel* (New Haven, Conn. and London, 1974).

Henkin, Louis, *Foreign Affairs and the Constitution* (Mineola, NY, 1972).

Herre, Paul, *Kronprinz Wilhelm* (Munich, 1954).

Herwig, Holger, *The German Naval Officer Corps* (Oxford, 1973).

Herzfeld, Hans, *Die deutsche Rüstungspolitik vor dem Weltkriege* (Bonn and Leipzig, 1923).

Heydt, Arnold, *Der Fall Zabern* (Strasbourg, 1934).

Höflich, Wilhelm, *Affaire Zabern, mitgeteilt von einem der beiden 'Missetäter'* (Berlin, 1931).

Hohenlohe-Schillingsfürst, Chlodwig von, *Denkwürdigkeiten* (Stuttgart and Leipzig, 1907).

Howard, Michael, *Studies in War and Peace* (New York, 1972).

Howard, Michael (ed.), *The Theory and Practice of War* (New York, 1965).

Huber, Ernst Rudolf, *Deutsche Verfassungsgeschichte* (Stuttgart, Berlin, Cologne and Mainz, 1969), Vol. 4.

Hutten-Czapski, Bogdan Graf von, *Sechzig Jahre Politik und Gesellschaft* (Berlin, 1936).

Jaffé, Fritz, *Zwischen Deutschland und Frankreich* (Stuttgart and Berlin, 1931).

Jarausch, Konrad H., *The Enigmatic Chancellor* (New Haven, Conn. and London, 1973).

Jellinek, Walter, *Zabern: Uber das Verhaftungsrecht des Militärs* (Tübingen, 1914).

Kaestlé, Joseph, *Ein Sturmsignal aus dem Elsass* (Strasbourg, 1933).

Kitchen, Martin, *The German Officer Corps 1890–1914* (Oxford, 1968).

Kleber, Emile Jacques Daniel, *Wir verleumdeten Elsässer* (Munich, 1914).

Leberecht, Gerd Fritz (pseud.), *Zabern und des Königs Rock* (Berlin, 1913).

Mackey, Richard William, 'The Zabern affair' (unpublished dissertation, UCLA, 1968).

Manchester, William, *The Arms of Krupp* (Boston, Mass., 1968).

Mayeur, Jean-Marie, *Autonomie et politique en Alsace: la constitution de 1911* (Paris, 1970).

Morrison, Jack G., 'The intransigents: Alsace-Lorrainers against the annexation 1900–1914' (unpublished dissertation, Iowa, 1970).

Pogge von Strandmann, Hartmut and Geiss, Immanuel, *Die Erforderlichkeit des Unmöglichen* (Frankfurt, 1965).

Poidevin, Raymond, *Les Rélations économiques et financières entre la France et l'Allemagne de 1898 à 1914* (Paris, 1969).

Prill, Felician, *Ireland, Britain and Germany* (Dublin and New York, 1975).

Puhle, Hans-Jürgen, *Agrarische Interessenpolitik und preussischer Konservatismus im wilhelminischen Reich 1893–1914* (Hanover, 1966).

Quidde, Ludwig, *Caligula* (Leipzig, 1896).

Ralston, David B., *The Army of the Republic* (Cambridge and London, 1967).

Ritter, Gerhard, *Staatskunst und Kriegshandwerk* (Munich, 1960), Vol. 2.

Rossé, Joseph *et al.*, *Das Elsass von 1870–1932* (Colmar, 1936–8).

Rovère, Julien, *L'affaire de Saverne* (Paris, 1919).

Rüdt von Collenberg, Ludwig, *Die deutsche Armee von 1871 bis 1914* (Berlin, 1922).

Ryan, A. J., *Mutiny at the Curragh* (New York, 1956).

Sampson, Anthony, *The Arms Bazaar* (New York, 1977).

Sarason, D. (ed.), *Das Jahr 1913: Ein Gesamtbild der Kulturentwicklung* (Berlin and Leipzig, 1914).

Scheer, C., *Zum Verständnis der elsässischen Seele* (Marburg, 1914).

Schenk, Erwin, *Der Fall Zabern* (Stuttgart, 1927).

Schlesinger, Arthur M., *The Imperial Presidency* (Boston, Mass., 1973).

Silverman, Dan P., *Reluctant Union* (University Park, PA, 1972).

Spitzemberg, Hildegard Baronin von, *Tagebuch* (Göttingen, 1961).

Stein, Lorenz von, *Die Lehre vom Heerwesen* (Stuttgart, 1872).

Stern, Fritz, *The Failure of Illiberalism* (New York, 1972).

Stieve, Richard, *Zabern im Elsass* (Zabern, 1900).

Stolberg-Wernigerode, Otto Graf zu, *Die unentschiedene Generation* (Munich, 1968).

Stoskopf, Gustave, *Zabern* (no place or date).

Vietsch, Eberhard von, *Bethmann-Hollweg* (Boppard, 1969).

Vorschrift über den Waffengebrauch des Militars und seine Mitwirkung zur Underdrückung innerer Unruhen vom 23. März 1899 (Berlin, 1913).

Weber, Max, *Gesammelte politische Schriften* (Tübingen, 1958).

Wehler, Hans-Ulrich, *Krisenherde des Kaiserreichs* (Göttingen, 1970).

Wehler, Hans-Ulrich, *Das deutsche Kaiserreich* (Göttingen, 1973).

White, Dan S., *The Splintered Party* (Cambridge, Mass. and London, 1976).

Witt, Peter Christian, *Die Finanzpolitik des deutschen Reiches* (Hamburg, 1970).

Wolff, Theodore, *The Eve of 1914* (New York, 1936).

Zapf, Wolfgang, *Wandlungen der deutschen Elite* (Munich, 1965).

Zeydel, Edwin H., *Constitution of the German Empire and German States* (Washington, DC, 1919).

Ziebura, Gilbert, *Die deutsche Frage in der öffentlichen Meinung Frankreichs von 1911–14* (Berlin, 1955).

Zmarzlik, Hans-Günter, *Bethmann-Hollweg als Reichskanzler* (Düsseldorf, 1957).

Zorn von Bulach, Weihbischof Freiherr von, *Eine ernst-friedliche Stimme zu den Vorgängen in Zabern* (Strasbourg, 1914).

(4) Articles

Angress, Werner, 'Prussia's army and the Jewish reserve officer controversy', *Year Book XVII* (London: Leo Baeck Institute, 1972).

Barker, J. Ellis, 'Autocratic and democratic Germany: the lessons of Zabern', *Nineteenth Century* (February 1914).

Bourson, Paul, 'Vingt ans après', *La Vie en Alsace* (1934).

Crampton, R. J., 'August Bebel and the British Foreign Office', *History* (June 1973).

Crozier Long, Robert, 'German lambs and Prussian wolves: a letter from Berlin', *Fortnightly Review* (March 1914).

Deist, Wilhelm, 'Die Armee in Staat und Gesellschaft', in Michael Stürmer (ed.), *Das kaiserliche Deutschland* (Düsseldorf, 1970).

D., H. J., 'Die Zaberner Affäre', *Dernières Nouvelles*, nos. 259—62 (édit. franc. et edit. bilingue) (Strasbourg, 1963). (only initials given).

Draude, Marie, *Almanach Saint-Odile 1964* (Saint-Odile, 1964).

Epstein, Fritz T., 'Germany and the United States', in George L. Anderson (ed.), *Issues and Conflicts* (Lawrence, Kans. 1959).

Frauendienst, Werner, 'Demokratisierung des deutschen Konstitutionalismus', *Zeitschrift für gesamte Staatswissenschaft* (1957).

Gasser, Adolf, 'Deutschlands Entschluss zum Präventivkrieg 1913/14', in Marc Sieber (ed.), *Discordia Concors, Festgabe für Edgar Bonjour* (Basle, 1968).

Gilliot, P., 'Ephemeriden zur Zaberner Affäre', *Journal de Saverne*, no. 133 (1923)—no. 6 (1924).

Heil, C. P., 'Die Revolution in Zabern', *Frankfurter Allgemeine Zeitung* (2 November 1963).

Hunt, James C., 'Peasants, grain tariffs and meat quotas', *Central European History* (December 1974).

Lüthy, Herbert, 'Schicksalstragödie', *Der Monat* (August 1964).

Messerschmidt, Manfred, 'Die Armee in Staat und Gesellschaft — die Bismarckzeit', in Michael Stürmer (ed.), *Das kaiserliche Deutschland* (Düsseldorf, 1970).

Mommsen, Wolfgang, 'Domestic factors in German foreign policy', *Central European History* (March 1973).

Mommsen, Wolfgang, 'Die latente Krise des Wilhelminischen Reiches', *Militärgeschichtliche Mitteilungen*, vol. 1 (1974).

Pikart, Eberhard, 'Die Rolle der Parteien im deutschen konstitutionellen System', *Zeitschrift für Politik* (1962).

Sauer, Wolfgang, 'Das Problem des deutschen Nationalstaates', in Hans-Ulrich Wehler (ed.), *Moderne deutsche Sozialgeschichte* (Cologne, 1966).

Sheehan, James J., 'Leadership in the German Reichstag 1871–1918', *American Historical Review* (December 1968)

Taylor, A. J. P., 'Fritz Fischer and his school', *Journal of Modern History* (March 1975).

Vierhaus, Rudolf, 'Kaiser und Reichstag zur Zeit Wilhelms II', *Festschrift für Hermann Heimpel* (Göttingen, 1971).

'Zabern', *Deutsche Juristen Zeitung* (15 December 1913).

Zechlin, Egmont, 'Bethmann-Hollweg und die SPD', *Der Monat* (January 1966).

Index